Myth in the
Modern World

Myth in the Modern World

Essays on Intersections with Ideology and Culture

Edited by DAVID WHITT
and JOHN PERLICH

McFarland & Company, Inc., Publishers
Jefferson, North Carolina

ALSO OF INTEREST

Millennial Mythmaking, edited by
John Perlich and David Whitt (McFarland, 2010)

LIBRARY OF CONGRESS CATALOGUING-IN-PUBLICATION DATA

Myth in the modern world : essays on intersections with ideology and culture / edited by David Whitt and John Perlich.
    p.   cm.
Includes bibliographical references and index.

ISBN 978-0-7864-7840-8 (softcover : acid free paper) ∞
ISBN 978-1-4766-1449-6 (ebook)

1. Myth.   2. Myth in literature.   3. Myth in mass media.
4. Myth in motion pictures.   I. Whitt, David, editor of compilation.   II. Perlich, John R., editor of compilation.
BL304.M865 2014
201'.3—dc23   2014011329

BRITISH LIBRARY CATALOGUING DATA ARE AVAILABLE

© 2014 David Whitt and John Perlich. All rights reserved

No part of this book may be reproduced or transmitted in any form or by any means, electronic or mechanical, including photocopying or recording, or by any information storage and retrieval system, without permission in writing from the publisher.

Cover images © 2014 Photodisc

Printed in the United States of America

*McFarland & Company, Inc., Publishers
Box 611, Jefferson, North Carolina 28640
www.mcfarlandpub.com*

For our families

Acknowledgments

Dave would like to thank Adam Richman for being such an entertaining subject of study and inspiring him to someday take a food challenge. He would also like to thank his mom who reluctantly allowed her DVR memory to hover dangerously close to 100 percent, recording numerous episodes of *Man v. Food* for transcription. Lastly, he would like to thank Johnny P. for being a co-editor. Doing a book on mythology was always your idea from the start, and there is no way I could have done one book, certainly not three, which we now have done together, on my own. You are my hero.

John would point out the muse for this project (and the previous two books) came from the dissertation research of David Whitt and so all credit for this collection should fall squarely on his shoulders. It has been an honor working with the world's best collaborative writer. Thanks are also given to John's wife and two amazing daughters (Caiden and Kelyn) for their love and support during a very busy year! Admonishments are given to the drought we experienced last year, which prevented John from pursuing a project exploring the intersections between myth, rhetoric, and storm chasing.

We would also like to thank all the authors who contributed to this volume. Your enthusiasm, dedication and insights made this process an incredibly rewarding one. We appreciate all your hard work writing, revising, and revising some more.

Finally, special thanks to our families and friends for their encouragement and support, even when they were not exactly sure what it was we were doing.

Table of Contents

Acknowledgments vi

Introduction 1

Part 1: Envisioning Heroes and Evolving Frontiers

Breaking Bad and Blending Boundaries:
  Revisioning the Myths of Masculinity and the Superhero
    LISA WECKERLE 7

20th Century Boys:
  Blending Eastern and Western Storytelling
    MICHAEL W. MAREK *and* PIN-HSIANG NATALIE WU 33

A Change of Scenery: The Southern, the Western and the
  Evolution of the Frontier Myth in *Justified*
    AARON DUNCAN 61

Part 2: Right or Left of Center

The Mythology of Suffering and Redemption
  in the Discourse of Al Qaeda
    JASON A. EDWARDS 83

Mothers and Monsters: The Return of the Great Goddess in
  George R. R. Martin's *A Song of Ice and Fire*
    SHARON DEE GOERTZ 102

Myth and Meaning-Making in Showtime's *The L Word*
    JUDY BATTAGLIA 123

The Day Environmentalism Stood Still: Film, Myth
 and the Ecological Jeremiad
  RICHARD D. BESEL   148

Part 3: Reality Bites

Fields of Dreams and Gods of the Gridiron:
 The Trinity of Myth, Sport and the Hero
  KAREN L. HARTMAN   165
Reclaiming the Wolf Myth in the Shadow of the *Twilight* Films:
 The Quileute People's Exhibit
  LINDSAY R. CALHOUN *and* KEATON MADDOX   185
The Ultimate Hunger Games:
 Adam Richman as Comic Hercules in *Man v. Food*
  DAVID WHITT   207

About the Contributors   227
Index   229

Introduction

The opening ceremony for the 2012 Summer Olympic games in London was a colorful, eclectic and often humorous mix of British history, royalty, politics, and popular culture. Entitled "Isles of Wonder," the ceremony attempted to condense 2,000 years of British history into a three-hour and 45-minute spectacle—giant smokestacks emerged from beneath the Olympic stadium signifying the Industrial Revolution, hundreds of children bounced on large hospital beds celebrating the country's National Health Service, Sir Paul McCartney led the athletes and spectators in a chorus of the Beatles' "Hey Jude"—each moment simultaneously compressed and emblemized an epoch.

The ceremony's visual centerpiece was a 40-foot-tall steel-and-fiberglass oak tree (*The Independent*, 2012) set on top of a large grass-covered hill, representing Glastonbury Tor located near Somerset. According to the U.K. National Trust, Glastonbury Tor is "known as being one of the most spiritual sites in the country. Its pagan beliefs are still very much celebrated" with legend having it that King Arthur and his knights visited this hill in search of the Holy Grail (*National Trust*, 2012). The fact that the British featured Glastonbury Tor so prominently during the Olympic opening ceremony not only spoke to the significance of myth in their cultural heritage, but also to the power of myth to connect with a larger global audience. In this way the artificial Glastonbury Tor in London's Olympic Stadium provided a timely and meaningful example of mythology in contemporary life.

Mythic scholar Joseph Campbell defined myth as "stories of our search through the ages for truth, for meaning, for significance.... Myths are clues to the spiritual potentialities of human life" (1988, p. 5). To use Campbell's words, myth has a thousand faces; each countenance has similarity and nuance when compared with another. The myths of gods, goddesses, heroes and their adventures can be traced back centuries to not only the ancient Greeks and Romans, but also to tribes in Africa, Australia, and the Americas. Their stories of creation, rituals, and the afterlife "speak to our deep longing to understand the human condition: to know where we came from, why we are here, what will become of us" (Stock, 1993, p. 240). While myth is certainly a link to the past, it can also provide a unique perspective on the present, as well as the future. The final scene of the Academy Award–winning David Fincher film *The Social Network* (2010) incorporates a mythic allusion in relation to Facebook founder Mark Zuckerberg. After a deposition in which Zuckerberg (Jesse Eisenberg) is being sued by his former business partner Eduardo Saverin (Andrew Garfield), defense lawyer Marylin Delpy (Rashida Jones) tells Zuckerberg, who has acted arrogantly and condescendingly toward almost everyone in the room, "Creation myths need a devil." In this instance, Zuckerberg, the creator of this financially lucrative billion-user service, is the "devil," corrupted by fame and fortune at the expense of his friends. The devil, a figure in Christianity and Islam dating back thousands of years, thus becomes the mythic metaphor for Zuckerberg, and, consequently, a cautionary tale for the twenty-first century.

Myth, Ideology and Culture

Our previous two volumes on comparative mythology, *Sith, Slayers, Stargates and Cyborgs: Modern Mythology in the New Millennium* (Peter Lang, 2008) and *Millennial Mythmaking: Essays on the Power of Science Fiction and Fantasy Literature, Films and Games* (McFarland, 2010), examined myth as it related primarily to the worlds of science fiction/fantasy television and film. However, the second to last essay of *Millennial Mythmaking* was something of a precursor to this book, moving away from television and film to examine other texts that incorporate mythic themes into narrative, in this case, the online virtual world of *Second Life*. This was a conscious decision on our part as the analysis of mythology is certainly not limited to female vampire slayers, boy wizards, and galaxies far, far away. Consequently, our goal with this volume is one of diversity, as we continue to explore how myth is an important element in science fiction/fantasy, but also how these stories are evident in other contexts such as sport, terrorist rhetoric and even exhibits. In this way the power of myth extends beyond ancient stories of gods and heroes to express the hopes, fears and reality of everyday life.

Because of their ubiquity and longevity, myths have been, and always will be, an inherent part of culture. According to Brukner (2000) "myths integrate human history—even without chronological continuity—from Paleolithic matrilineal relations in prehistory to contemporary primal societies, to industrial and postindustrial cultures of the present century. The complex significance of myth is contained in its morphology, regardless of the location and time of its inception" (p. 23). In other words, long before recorded history, and for millennia after, one constant in civilization's development has been its stories, its myths. Kittelson (1998) explains, "myths change with the demands of the times, in response to new requirements" (p. 7). For example, the novel *Frankenstein* (1818) by Mary Shelley was more than just a story about an artificial creature tormenting its creator; it was a nineteenth-century commentary about science, ethics, and progress. Today, the Frankenstein myth is reflected in questions over what impact our continuing human/machine merger may have on individual identity reflected in television programs like *Battlestar Galactica* (2004–2009) and the films *Avatar* (2009) and the *Iron Man* trilogy (2008, 2010, 2013). Leeming (1997) perhaps best summarizes the interplay between myth and culture, stating "myths spring from the particular problems and concerns of a given race or tribe, but on a deeper level their source is the universal soul of the human race itself" (p. 5). This collection of essays explores the intersection of myth, ideology, and culture to better understand how these narratives define, explain, and, in some instances, oppose cultural attitudes and beliefs.

Overview

The ten essays in this volume represent a small slice, or "handful of mirrors"; these selections reflect the workings of myth in the modern world. The essays have been organized into three parts. The first, "Envisioning Heroes and Evolving Frontiers," considers the changing face of the hero and how scene, or location, is an important part of mythic narratives. The first essay, by Lisa Weckerle, examines the AMC television series *Breaking Bad* and how its main character, Walter White, reflects the myths of masculinity and the superhero. Next, Michael W. Marek and Pin-hsiang Natalie Wu provide an analysis of the Japanese film trilogy *20th Century Boys*, applying Joseph Campbell's concept of the monomyth to its heroes and their journey, while also discussing additional themes that relate to myth. Finally, Aaron Duncan explores how the FX television program *Justified* shifted the Frontier Myth from the Old West to the South, or, more specifically, the backwoods of modern-day Kentucky. The next part, "Right or Left of Center," is a reference to ideology, those philosophical, political or religious ideas, both moderate and extreme, that influence and frame our worldview. Jason A. Edwards begins this part by exploring the religious rhetoric of the terrorist group Al

Qaeda and their use of the mythic themes of suffering and redemption to inspire followers and justify their violent actions. Next, Sharon Dee Goertz uses various theories of the mother goddess to deconstruct the major female characters in George R.R. Martin's *A Song of Ice and Fire* novels and the HBO television series. Judy Battaglia then offers a feminist perspective of another television series, Showtime's *The L Word,* analyzing its characters through myths of the Amazon, Medusa, Sorceress and Vampire. In the last essay of this part Richard D. Besel compares and contrasts the science fiction film classic *The Day the Earth Stood Still* (1951) with its 2008 remake in relation to the jeremiad, arguing that the original film, set during the Cold War, empowered the audience with hope for the future, while the more modern version, with its environmental message, failed to do so.

The final part, "Reality Bites," is something of a double entendre, suggesting myths are more than just a part of everyday life; they are also stories that can be a battleground of cultural meaning, and in the case of the final essay, can literally and figuratively offer food for thought. Karen L. Hartman leads off this part by critiquing the current state of sports in the United States, contending that despite controversies like steroids and sexual abuse scandals the myth of the moral hero prevails. Next, Lindsay R. Calhoun and Keaton Maddox tour a museum exhibit created by the Quileute, describing how this American Indian tribe attempted to reclaim their cultural identity by redefining the wolf myth featured in the popular *Twilight* books and films. In the last essay David Whitt argues that Adam Richman, host of the Travel Channel reality television series *Man v. Food*, embodies the comic persona of the mythic hero Hercules, and discusses what this program says about the importance of food in contemporary culture. The analysis and conclusions of the authors support the contention of Storey (1993) that myths "attempt to put us at peace with ourselves and our existence" (pp. 73–74).

Conclusion

Back in 2004, after we participated in a panel discussion on modern myth at a national convention, John had the idea that we should perhaps look into doing a book on this subject. Ten years later we could not have envisioned completing a "trilogy" on comparative mythology, with copies of our books sitting on library shelves in academic institutions and homes around the world. Perhaps in the future, like George Lucas returning to *Star Wars* to create another film trilogy, we will create another book trilogy, examining exciting new mythic texts. Until then, we hope our books encourage others to study myth and appreciate the relevance of these stories in contemporary culture. We end with a quote from Joseph Campbell, who was an inspiration for us both throughout our publishing adventures. In *The Power of Myth* (1988) Campbell tells Bill Moyers, "Myth helps you to put your mind in touch with this experience of being alive" (p. 5). For us, Campbell's words could not ring more true.

References

Brukner, B. (2000). An archaeomythological reflection of the labyrinth. *Revision.* 23(1), 23.
Brunetti, D. (Producer), and Fincher, D. (Director) (2010). *The social network* [Motion picture]. United States: Columbia Pictures.
Campbell, J., and Moyers, B. (1988). *The power of myth.* New York: Doubleday.
The Independent (August 14, 2012). 2012 things to remember the London Olympics by. Retrieved August 20, 2012, from http://www.independent.co.uk/sport/olympics/news/2012-things-to-remember-the-london-olympics-by—part-1-1-to-1108-8045941.html.
Kittelson, M.L. (1998). *The soul of popular culture: Looking at contemporary heroes, myths, and monsters.* Chicago: Open Court.
Leeming, D.A. (1998). Mythology: The voyage of the hero (3d ed.). New York: Oxford University Press.
National Trust (2012). Glastonbury Tor. Retrieved August 20, 2012, from http://www.nationaltrust.org.uk/glastonbury-tor/history/.
Stock, G. (1993). *Metaman: The merging of humans and machines into a global superorganism.* New York: Simon & Schuster.
Storey, J. (1993). *An introductory guide to cultural theory and popular culture.* Athens: University of Georgia Press.

PART 1
Envisioning Heroes and Evolving Frontiers

Breaking Bad and Blending Boundaries
Revisioning the Myths of Masculinity and the Superhero

Lisa Weckerle

> Chemistry is well ... technically, chemistry is the study of matter but I prefer to see it as the study of change ... just think about this—electrons they change their energy levels, molecules change their bonds, elements they combine ... and change into compounds, that's all of life right, it's the constant, it's the cycle, it's solution, dissolution. It is growth then decay then transformation. It is fascinating really.
> —Walter White (Gilligan, 2008, "Pilot")

In the above quote from the pilot of AMC's *Breaking Bad* (2008–2013),[1] high school teacher Walter White is excitedly talking about chemistry, but he could just as easily be talking about mythology. Like chemistry, mythology traces themes of individual and collective transformation through cycles of growth and decay. Spirits are revitalized (energy levels), alliances are made and broken (bonds), and individual characters, conflicts, and contexts combine to create something new (compounds). *Breaking Bad* is infused with allusions to both classical and contemporary myths. Walter White's frequent use of fire parallels the Prometheus story; his struggles with father figures like drug kingpin Gus Fring echo the Oedipal complex. His inability to support his family as a teacher critiques the American Dream while his subsequent success as a methamphetamine cook who speaks the language of capitalism can be read as a parody of the American Dream. The myth of the frontier is also evoked by the western tropes like black and white hats, wide sweeping vistas of wilderness, and gun slinging duels.

The series opens with Walter White, a suburban high school chemistry teacher, receiving a diagnosis that he has inoperable lung cancer. Walt was already working a second job to support his pregnant wife, Skyler, and his teenage son, Walter Jr., who has cerebral palsy. Now with expensive medical bills looming, Walt knows that his family will descend into poverty without his salary after he dies. After seeing a drug bust of a crystal meth lab on television in which authorities collected thousands of dollars, Walt accompanies his DEA agent brother-in-law Hank on a ride along to another meth drug bust. At the bust, he sees a former student, Jesse Pinkman, escaping out of a neighbor's window. Rather than turn him in, Walt lets him get away and later makes Jesse an unusual proposition of becoming partners in crime: "I know the chemistry, you know the business" (Gilligan, 2008, "Pilot"). Jesse and Walt form an unlikely alliance and Walter White's transformation into a drug kingpin begins.

Although *Breaking Bad* is a realistic television program set in contemporary times, it echoes the structure of the classical monomyth as defined by Joseph Campbell (2008):

> a hero ventures forth from the world of the common day into a region of supernatural wonder: fabulous forces are there encountered and a decisive victory is won: the hero comes back from this mysterious adventure with the power to bestow boons on his fellow man [p. 23].

Walt ventures out of his tightly scripted suburban life and enters into an "other" world, the underworld of the illegal drug trade. Once he has crossed the threshold of this world with his former student Jesse as his guide, he must undergo the initiation phase which includes a series of trials: stealing supplies, cooking meth, evading the police, and killing his enemies before they kill him. These trials allow Walt to bring back the boon of the drug money that he then stows away for his family to inherit after he dies. While the money is material and not spiritual, it represents to Walt the salvation of his family's future as underscored by his act of hiding it within his future daughter's nursery.

In this essay I will trace how Walter White embodies two related mythologies: the myth of masculinity and the myth of the superhero. As Walter White transforms from an emasculated character to an aggressive, sexualized subject, he demonstrates many of the ideals of masculinity. The myth of the superhero is evoked by Walt's creation of the Heisenberg persona, a shadow self that moves through the drug underworld becoming more powerful and destructive. While both of these myths are enacted by the character of Walter White, his character also complicates and questions these myths by exposing the constructed nature of both the masculine ideal and the metaphors of identity construction and segmentation present within the superhero myth.

Myth of Masculinity

When I refer to masculinity, I do not mean a universalized masculine essence common to all men. Rather, I refer to the concept of what sociologist R.W. Connell calls hegemonic masculinity (1990). As Morrell (1998) states:

> it [hegemonic masculinity] presents its own version of masculinity, of how men should behave and how putative "real men" do behave, as the cultural ideal. The concept of hegemonic masculinity provides a way of explaining that through a number of masculinities coexist, a particular version of masculinity hold sway, bestowing power and privilege on men who espouse it and claim it as their own [p. 608].

What exactly hegemonic masculinity entails is difficult to define, as it is constantly changing and culturally contingent. Nevertheless there have been some attempts to define it. In Gilmore's *Manhood in the Making* (1990) he argues:

> Although there may be no "universal male," we may perhaps speak of a "ubiquitous male" based on these criteria of performance: ... to be a man ... one must impregnate women, protect dependents [sic] from danger and provision kith and kin.... We might call this quasi-global personage something like "Man-the-Impregnator-Protector-Provider" [p. 223].

In the book *The Forty-Nine Percent Majority* (1976), David and Brannon define four models of masculinity that still resonate today: (1) No Sissy Stuff: the rejection of anything vaguely feminine; (2) The Big Wheel: ambition, success, breadwinning, fame, status, competition; (3) The Sturdy Oak: toughness, confidence, physical strength, stands his ground, self-reliance; and, (4) Give 'Em Hell: adventure, daring, aggression, violence. More recently, Trujillo (1991) traced how former major league baseball player Nolan Ryan embodies similar features of hegemonic masculinity: (1) physical force and control, (2) occupational achievement, (3) patriarchal role in family, (4) the archetype of the adventurous, outdoorsy cowboy, and (5) heterosexuality. Drawing on these constellations of qualities of the mythic masculine, I will concentrate on the following six aspects of masculinity in my analysis: man as a provider, protector/possessor, active subject, sexual subject, competitor, and wielder of violence. Before I analyze Walt's performance of masculinity, I will briefly summarize these masculine ideals and illustrate how they permeate mythology and popular culture.

HEGEMONIC MASCULINE IDEALS IN MYTH

One of the enduring mythic images of masculinity is man as provider. Ancient myths and cultural stories depict gods and men as providing for their progeny. In Christianity, God gives Adam and Eve the Garden of Eden. Television portrayals of fathers as the financial providers for their families include *Leave it to Beaver* (1957–1963), *The Flintstones* (1960–1966), *Home Improvement* (1991–1999) and even the criminal breadwinners in *The Sopranos* (1999–2007). Just as femininity has been traditionally associated with the private sphere and domestic work, masculinity has been traditionally associated with the public sphere and wage-earning work. The reality is that men do not always provide for their families: some men are unable or unwilling to financially support families, some women earn more than their male counterparts, and some families are entirely supported by one or more women. However, culturally we still tend to measure masculinity by earning power, especially how that earning power enables one to support one's spouse and children. In his analysis of masculinity, Kimmel (1996) found that "the American male, by definition, must provide for his family. He is responsible for his support of his wife and children" (p. 248). Likewise, Hunter defines the traditional masculine role as "breadwinner, nine to fiver, and father, at the helm of both the economic and the social order of the family" (2011, p. 96).

Another enduring myth is that of man as protector of his property. While masculinity is associated with the pride of providing, it is an anxious pride because once property is claimed it must be constantly policed and protected. The archetypal masculine embodied in the father figure is a protector, benefactor, or owner (Greenfield, 1983). The Trojan War demonstrates the lengths that a man will go to in order to reclaim his stolen property; in this case, declaring war in order to reclaim his wife. Men also are seen snatching back their daughters and wives in contemporary films like *Die Hard* (1988), *Taken* (2008), and *Taken 2* (2012). Territorialism also finds its expression in actual wars and military simulation board games like *Risk* and *Monopoly*, in which players win by accumulating the most territory. The division of territory was also essential to the hierarchy of the gods in ancient Greece: Zeus wins the draw by gaining the heavens, Poseidon gets the seas, and Hades loses by getting the underworld. The territorialist aspect of masculinity is incorporated into a variety of new iterations of myth: from the Western, in which a man defends his homestead from outlaws, to the alien invasion film, in which a hero leads the fight to reclaim earth.

While femininity has been associated with passivity and objectification, masculinity has been linked to active agency. Men are valued and rewarded when they become "men of action" who know what they want and go get it themselves. This "man of action" ideal can take many forms including warrior, brave knight, pioneer, and decisive CEO. The ideal of man as active subject is sometimes represented by extreme mobility, as in fleet footed Mercury

(Greenfield, 1983), or superheroes like Flash or Superman. Sometimes this ideal takes the form of anti-establishment: a man rejecting the confining scripts of society to assert his own will and do what he knows is best (Cantano, 2004). Men are often stigmatized for being passive objects and rewarded for being active subjects. A man who cannot enforce his volition on the world around him risks being labeled ineffectual, homosexual, or feminized. Even language attests to the association of masculine with action and the emasculating penalties of failing to fit this ideal: "man up" means to be brave and take action, while "pussy out" means to be afraid and do nothing.

Masculinity has long been equated with virility, potency, and sexual dominance. Greenfield (1983) states:

> The active mode of functioning of the animus results in behaviors which have an intrusive and generative character. This is, of course most obvious in sexuality; in its positive form the masculine is that which impregnates and creates, and in its negative form that which rapes and destroys [p. 35].

"The Father of Gods," Zeus exemplifies the masculine ideal of active sexual subject; he rapes and impregnates frequently and daringly, propelled by his own desire and unencumbered by laws or need for consent. Masculinity is often portrayed as engaging in sex that is risky, daring, and adventurous. Figures like Don Juan, Casanova, and James Bond attest to the valorization of male heterosexual conquest. Sex is portrayed as a way to compete with other men, inflict one's will on others, and mark one's territory. In his analysis of the image of the sexual athlete, Sabo (2003) states that manliness in sports and sex has traditionally been associated with being "competitive, successful, dominating, aggressive, stoical, goal-directed, and physically strong" (p. 264).

Another aspect of the masculine ideal is man as a fierce competitor, especially with other men. The Olympics encapsulate the idea of men in competition with each other to win glory for themselves and their homeland. In his analysis of ancient Greek masculinity, Van Nortwick (2008) suggests, "To grow up, a man must stand apart not only from his mother but from his fellows. Human achievement ... is always to be measured in difference, who is fastest, the most handsome, the richest" (p. 13). Fairy tales like "The Glass Mountain" and "Sleeping Beauty" feature men competing for the prize of a princess by attempting dangerous tasks. Boxing-themed movies like the *Rocky* series (1976–2006) and *Cinderella Man* (2005) reinforce the linkage between public displays of strength and assertions of manhood. The hero proves his worth by literally bringing his opponent to the ground. However, rivalry need not be about who is strongest, but can also be about who is the smartest, the most powerful, or even who is the best Ice Road Trucker. According to Edwards (2006), "From the boardroom to the bedroom and from the bar counter to the bar bell, masculinity would seem to be all about performing, showing off or, more particularly, to be about being competitive" (p. 114).

Masculinity is also inextricably connected to an ideal of man as inherently violent. Violence is venerated in myth as both an expression of idealized masculinity and a method of recuperating a lost masculine primitive essence. Weltzein (2005) states, "Manliness is defined by the virtues of the warrior, at the same time tested and confirmed by violence" (p. 243). Hero-warriors use violence to eliminate their enemies, win competitions, and gain glory. Connell (1987) points out, "It is no accident that the classic hero is usually a specialist in violence ... Aeneas, Achilles, Siegfried, Tristan and Lancelot hack their respective ways through quite a tonnage of flesh and bones" (p. 249). Films like *Fight Club* (1999) extol violence as a means of reconnecting alienated men with their "true masculinity." The Western film genre also presents violence as a regenerating force (Slotkin, 1992, p. 12). The ability to inflict and endure violence is depicted as an integral characteristic, almost synonymous with masculinity itself: "Manliness, understood ... also as the capacity to fight and to exercise violence (especially in acts of revenge), is first and foremost a *duty*" (Bourdieu, 2001, p. 51). Indeed the idea of violent revenge on behalf of one's family is a prevalent theme of ancient and modern myth, such as Boon (2005) suggests, "There is little difference between Odysseus slaughtering suitors in The *Odyssey* to regain his wife and Bruce Willis in *Die Hard* slaughtering terrorists to regain his wife" (p. 308). Another dimension of masculinity and violence is the validity of using pre-emptive violence. For example, the Greek titan Cronus kills his own father and—fearing the same will happen to him—he eats all of his children to avoid being killed by them. Similarly, war movies and actual wars are often rationalized as pre-emptive strikes necessary for self-preservation: we must get "them" before "they" get us.

WALT'S MASCULINE EVOLUTION

The pilot episode of *Breaking Bad* includes numerous references to Walt's problematic performance of masculinity. When Walt holds a gun for the first time and comments that it is heavy, Hank, his DEA agent brother-in-law, says, "Yeah, that's why we only let *men* hold it" (Gilligan, 2008, "Pilot"). Jesse also questions Walt's manhood by calling him a "faggot" when Walt wears an apron while cooking meth (Gilligan, 2008, "Pilot") and later accusing him of letting his wife "wear the pants in the family" (Gilligan, 2008, "Cat Is in the Bag..."). As Walt strips down to his underwear to avoid getting fumes in his clothes, Jesse teases: "You're maybe the world's only second biggest homo" (Gilligan, 2008, "Pilot"). The fact that other men are calling Walt a non-man, a homosexual, or a woman shows that while he may be biologically male, he is misperforming his masculinity at the beginning of the series. In this section I will trace how Walt evolves in his performance of significant ideals of masculinity: man as provider, property owner, active subject, sexual dominator, competitor, and inflictor of violence.

Evidence of Walt's failure as provider pervades the opening episodes: he works two jobs, his wife is selling off possessions on eBay, the water heater is breaking, and bill collectors are calling. In a scene that demonstrates both Walt's money problems and his wife's domination, Skyler interrogates him about a charge on their credit card. When Walt confesses that he charged printer paper, she chastises him: "Walt, that's the card we *don't* use" (Gilligan, 2008, "Pilot"). Clearly she is juggling debt back and forth among various cards and even Walt's meager purchase has the potential to disrupt the precarious system of staving off debt.

Related to the ideal of man as provider is the taboo against men accepting charity. When Walt's former business partner offers to pay for his cancer treatment, Walt refuses. Rather than accept charity and be perceived as less than a man, Walt opts to earn his own money by using his chemistry skills to cook crystal meth. Lured by the promise of piles of drug bust money seen on a news report, Walt accompanies his DEA brother-in-law Hank on a drug bust. Walt is using the ride-along to explore how he might leverage his chemistry knowledge to enter the drug trade and thereby solve his money problems. Given the choice between entering a dangerous and illegal business or accepting charity from a sexual and intellectual rival, Walt chooses the former. This choice demonstrates the power that the myth of man as provider holds: the threat of death and imprisonment are no match for the humiliation and social death that failing to provide would bring.

Walt's distaste for charity resurfaces during "Phoenix" (Shiban, 2009). His son Walter Jr. sets up a website to honor his dad, but when Walt discovers the website's purpose is to collect donations for Walt's impending operation, he tells him disapprovingly that they cannot ask for money. Skyler takes Walt aside and tries to convince him to let the website go forward:

SKYLER: You can't ask him to take it down ... it will crush him.
WALT: It's *charity*, Skyler.
SKYLER: Why do you say that like it's some sort of dirty word?

Because of societal expectations that a "real man" provides for his family, charity is indeed a dirty word that connotes weakness, failure, and impotence. Furthermore, Walt does not just want the family to be provided for, he wants the credit for being the provider. When Walt's lawyer later suggests that Walt use his son's charity website as a vehicle for laundering money, Walt balks: "I am not going to have my family think that some mystery benefactor saved us." He wants the glory and admiration and he wants it for himself; he asserts *"I earned that money, me."*

Perhaps the clearest articulation of the myth of the provider within the series is during "Mas" (Gilligan and Walley-Beckett, 2010). In an attempt to convince Walt to reenter the meth trade, drug kingpin Gus appeals to Walt's duty as a provider:

> WALT: I have made a series of very bad decisions and I cannot make another one.
> GUS: Why did you make these decisions?
> WALT: For the good of my family.
> GUS: Then they weren't bad decisions. What does a man do, Walter? A man provides for his family.
> WALT: This cost me my family.
> GUS: When you have children, you always have family, they will always be your priority, your responsibility. And a man? A man provides, and he does it even when he's not appreciated, respected, or even loved. He simply bears up, and he does it, because he's a man.

An important aspect of the provider myth that Gus articulates is that because the act of providing is for the sake of the family, the evils committed can be excused—the ends justify the means. Because providing is a moral duty of masculinity, the immoral means of providing becomes sanitized. In another scene, Walt argues that the only thing that makes his "sacrifices" worth it, is knowing that his family will benefit from the crimes he has committed.

> I've done a terrible thing, but I did it for a good reason ... I did it for us ... Skyler, that money is for this roof over your head, the mortgage that you are not going to be able to afford on a part time bookkeeper's salary when I'm gone.... Please, this money, I didn't steal it, it doesn't belong to anyone else, I earned it. The things I've done to earn it -things I've had to do—I've got to live with them, Skyler. All that I've done, all the sacrifices that I have made for this family, all of it will be for nothing if you don't accept what I've earned [Gould, 2010, "Caballo Sin Nombre"].

Walt goes so far as to say that the money has no intrinsic value to him; if it is not used to support the family the money means nothing to him. The myth of the provider is both his motivation for committing the crime and the means of redeeming the criminal actions. As Walt becomes more successful as a provider, he also becomes more possessive about his family, his money, and his business. In "Over" (Gilligan and Walley-Beckett, 2009), Walt's increased possessiveness becomes evident during his celebration party. Skyler announces that Walt accepted charity to pay for his cancer treatment, leading Walt to feel humiliated and start drinking to excess. When Walt realizes that his own son is idolizing his uncle rather than his dad, he decides to get his son drunk too. Hank urges Walt to go easy on the liquor, but Walt refuses to listen, even pouring tequila on Hank's hand when Hank attempts to block Walt from pouring. Finally, Hank takes the tequila bottle away, and Walt stands up and yells, "Bring the bottle back ... this is *my* house, *my* son, *my* bottle." In a later episode, Walt demonstrates his territoriality by intimidating encroaching competitors. After spotting a meth cook at the local hardware store, he follows him into the parking lot, stares down the cook's much larger partner and warns them to stay out of his territory (Catlin, 2010, "Green Light"). Not only is he territorial, he is also proprietary. When Walt finds out Jesse is cooking product on his own, he forbids him to sell it and screams at him: "This is *my* product, *my* formula, *mine!*" (Walley-Beckett, 2010, "Mas").

When we first meet Walt, he is a passive character who suppresses his own desires for the sake of others. He is dominated by a wife who usurps his decisions: she tells him what to eat, which credit card to use, and when to be home. Walt's boss at his car wash job takes advantage of him by reassigning him from his designated job at the register to wash cars and forcing him to stay late for no extra pay. While washing cars, Walt is spotted by his chemistry students who mock him and all Walt can do is endure their disrespect. His domination by others is especially emasculating because he is dominated by populations that are usually depicted as subordinate to white male masculinity—women, minorities, and children. In all three of these cases, Walt suppresses his own desires in deference to social pressures: pressure to keep his wife happy, pressure to do what his boss tells him, pressure to avoid fighting with his students. Walt is so entrapped in social scripts that his own volition is completely suppressed; he is performing a role rather than enacting his own choices.

One instance of Walt breaking out of the social script and appearing self-actualized is when he demonstrates chemistry for his class. Walt's inner fire is paralleled by the spectacle of fiery chemical reactions he creates, but his students' lack of enthusiasm causes him to end his attempt at inspiration, turn off the burner, and return to the script of the textbook. Later as his family tries to convince him to undergo chemotherapy, he articulates how he feels about his lack of choice in his own life (Gilligan, 2008, "…And the Bag's in the River"):

> What I want—what I need—is a choice.... I feel like I never actually make any of my own choices, I mean my entire life, it just seems I never had a real say about any of it, but this last one, cancer, all I have left is how I choose to approach this.... What good is it to survive if I am too sick to work, to enjoy a meal, to make love? For what time I have left, I wanna live in my own house, I wanna sleep in my own bed, I don't wanna swallow down 40 pills…. I choose not to do it.

As the series progresses, Walt rejects the dominating force of others and regains his individual subjectivity and volition. One of the methods he uses to do this is employing obscenity. Easthope (1990) characterizes the use of anal and genital swearing as a transgressive exercise of the male ego against the rules of politeness and good behavior. When Skyler interrogates him at the ultrasound appointment about his whereabouts, he tells her through gritted teeth: "I would really appreciate it if you would climb out of my ass" (Gilligan, 2008, "The Cat's in the Bag"). His use of anal obscenity accuses her of being a dominating penetrator, while also demanding that she relinquish that role. Walt also uses obscene gestures with his boss; he screams: "Wipe this down" (Gilligan, 2008, "Pilot") and then grabs his crotch and knocks the merchandise to the floor. By referring to his boss servicing Walt sexually, Walt casts the boss as feminine and subservient and himself as masculine and dominating. His use of obscenity also enacts a transgression of boundaries from acceptable to taboo language, just as his cooking of meth enacts a transgression from law-abiding to criminal behavior. Through using obscenity, Walt breaks his social script of polite subservience to both wife and boss and reasserts his own authority as masculine not feminine, subject not object.

The cancer diagnosis seems to give Walt the impetus he needs to act on his own volition and regain his status as an empowered subject. He remains interconnected with his family, but becomes less dominated by them. For example, he chooses to do the chemo because he smells his wife's moisturizer, looking dreamily nostalgic about his sensory connection with her, not because she demands it. His choice to cook meth to make money for his family simultaneously reinforces and deviates from social scripts. Walt is following the script of masculinity which dictates that men should provide for their families, but he is also subverting the script by his illegal means of achieving breadwinner status. He starts out with small legal transgressions such as lying to the police and stealing equipment, but quickly progresses to selling drugs and committing murder. At first Walt's character seems to reify the breadwinner ideal, but the fact that he can only achieve it through illegal means shows that society's prescriptions for masculinity are unrealistic. In order to be a "real man" by society's standards, Walt must break the laws of that same society.

Another area in which Walt transforms from passive object to active subject is his expression of sexuality. Walter begins as sexually passive, an object that does not express demands. His sex life is domesticated and depressing. His wife starts to manually stimulate him, and then becomes distracted by her eBay auction and forgets about him (Gilligan, 2008, "Pilot"). In contrast, after his first foray into the drug trade, he approaches his wife with a sexual dominance and vigor that is so out of character that she asks, "Walt, is that you?"

(Gilligan, 2008, "Pilot"). The linkage between Walt's criminal activity and increased libido is demonstrated during a school meeting in which administrators are discussing the theft of lab equipment. As the administrators detail the crime that Walt himself committed, Walt becomes aroused and starts to feel his wife up under the table. While at first she protests, he persists and Skyler eventually allows his hand to wander up her skirt. Later, they have sex in the car in the parking lot and Skyler asks, "Where did that come from and why was it so good?" Walt replies, "Because it was illegal" (Gilligan, 2008, "...And the Bag's in the River"). Walt's illegal activity coincides with an increased libido and a more adventurous approach to sex. However, his sexual domination sometimes reaches excess and causes problems in his marriage. When he sees a drug dealer commit murder and fears that he might be the next victim, he has the odd reaction of trying to force himself on his wife, attempting to use sex and dominance as a way to anesthetize his pain. While Walt's increase in sexual expression is an invigorating force, it also has the potential to be destructive. Walt's sexuality evolves from passive, to assertive, to excessively aggressive.

Walt transforms from a conflict avoidant victim to a man of violent action, someone who punishes those who disrespect him or trespass on his territory. His embracing of violence is demonstrated by his blowing up of a car belonging to a guy who stole his parking space. As the car burns in the background, Walt walks away with a satisfied smirk on his face. Walt earns money and respect by using violence in the drug business. After blowing up a drug dealer's office with fulminated mercury and threatening to blow it up again, the dealer gives in: "You got balls, I give you that, alright I give you your money" (Mastras, 2008, "Crazy Handful of Nothin'"). The language of manhood is associated with violence, and violence is portrayed as the way to inhabit and perform masculinity. After successfully winning back his money, Walt struts to his car, sets the money down, and lets out a primal ape-like grunt. His act of violence gives him a rush of adrenaline and self-satisfaction.

As Walt becomes more physically violent, his violence is often associated with either self-protection or protection of his family. On a shopping trip, a group of teenagers makes fun of Walter Jr., and Walt and his family overhear. His son is upset and his wife tries to get Walt to do something. Walt seems to be abandoning his family when he leaves through the back door, but in a moment he comes blazing through the front door and takes the teenagers by surprise, knocking one down onto the floor. He pins his leg to the floor and says: "What's up chief? Having a little trouble walking?" (Gilligan, 2008, "Cat's in the Bag"). When the kid threatens to punch him, Walt puffs his chest out and stands his ground: "You've got one shot, you better make it good ...

what, you waiting for your girlfriends?" Not only does Walt use violence to assert his role as protector of his family, he also questions the ringleader's masculinity and heterosexuality by referring to his male friends as girlfriends.

Walt goes up against a series of drug dealing enemies who want to exterminate him—Crazy 8, Tuco, and Gus. In all three of these cases Walt uses violence preemptively; he feels he must kill his enemy before his enemy kills him. As Walt considers his first premeditated murder of Crazy 8, he makes a list of pros and cons. There is only one con, but it is persuasive: "He will kill you and your entire family" (Gilligan, 2008, "...And the Bag's in the River"). Walt justifies his own use of violence as necessary for the protection of his family (as in Crazy 8), the protection of his partner (as in assassinating Gus's two goons), or self-protection (as in Emilio and Gus).

The acts of violence that are most troubling are those that Walt commits against "innocent" people, or at least people who are not trying to kill him. In a last ditch effort to save his own life, Walt orders Jesse to kill his lab assistant Gale. While Gale is a criminal, he is non-violent and has never been anything but admiring of Walt. Gale has no idea that Gus is planning to kill Walt and use Gale to replace him. Instead, Gale thinks he is learning Walt's recipe so that he can replace Walt when he dies of cancer. Yet, Walt justifies Gale's execution by saying that if it is going to come down to him or Gale, he chooses himself. Even more troubling are those deaths that Walt causes or risks in violation of his own rule of loyalty to his partner, Jesse. Jesse is situated as part of Walt's family—he calls him son, pretends to be his father as a cover, and even refers to him as a hypothetical "troubled nephew" in seeking advice about how to save him from heroin addiction. However, Jesse's girlfriend Jane becomes a problem for Walt when she threatens to turn him in to the police. After Jesse and Jane have taken heroin and fallen asleep, Walt breaks in and accidentally knocks Jane onto her back. She begins to vomit and choke. Realizing that Jane's death would solve all his problems, he lets her choke to death. Jane's father is devastated by the news of her death. He returns to his job as an air traffic controller while still in the midst of grief and shock. In his distracted state, he allows two planes to crash, killing over a hundred people. For the sake of protecting his position within his own family, Walt destroys Jane, her family, and the families of all the plane crash victims.

Deconstructing Masculinity

Walter White is propelled onto his heroic journey specifically because of expectations regarding gender roles. Just as a Cinderella story transforms a deserving girl into a married princess endowed with all the ideals of femininity,

Walt seems to be rewarded for fitting into the traditional masculine role. As the series progresses, Walt regains his status as provider-protector of the family, moves from passive object to dominating subject, becomes sexually aggressive, and is regenerated through competition and violence. His initiation into the drug world transforms him into a symbol of hegemonic masculinity, much as an initiation rite transforms a boy into a man.

While the show may reify gender norms by celebrating Walt as a fantasy of hyper-masculinity, Walt's performance of masculinity actually deconstructs these norms by revealing them as unreachable, mythic ideals. As the series progresses, it becomes evident that while Walt is better able to inhabit some areas of masculine identity, he is unable to inhabit all of them simultaneously. As Walt begins to excel in certain areas of masculinity, he starts to fail in others. For example, as Walt is better able to provide for his family, he ends up placing them in greater danger, failing as a protector. In addition, Walt's secretive means of providing for his family so enrages Skyler that she kicks him out of the house—segregating him from his family. The birth of Walt's daughter Holly demonstrates the tensions that exist between competing images of masculinity. Walt needs to deliver meth to a new buyer, a secretive one who is particularly hard to enter into business with. Unfortunately the meeting falls on the same day that his wife goes into labor. Walt chooses to finish the business deal (thereby providing for his family), but then he misses his daughter's birth. To underscore his inability to fulfill his father and provider roles simultaneously, his wife's love interest Ted is the one that drives her to the hospital and shares in the birth, usurping Walt's position as father and husband.

In another scene, Walt's competitive nature jeopardizes his ability to provide for and protect his family. After Walt's lab assistant Gale is found dead by the DEA, Hank tells Walt that he believes Gale was actually the mastermind meth cook Heisenberg, when in actuality Heisenberg is Walt's alter ego. Although letting Hank believe that Heisenberg is dead would throw suspicion off of Walt, Walt's competitive nature prevents him from allowing Gale to be credited with the Heisenberg empire. After a few glasses of wine, Walt makes a point of convincing Hank that Gale was not capable of being a mastermind and urges Hank to keep pursuing Heisenberg because he is still out there. While this act is self-destructive, it is also completely compatible with Walt's proprietary pride in his meth cooking. Walt's competitive pride puts his ability to provide at risk, just as providing interfered with his fulfillment of his father/husband role. It is as if Walt is trying to plug up the holes in his masculine identity, but as he plugs one hole, new ones spring forth. Rather than reify masculinity, Walt's evolution reveals that masculinity is a contradictory and artificial construct.

Myth of the Superhero

While *Breaking Bad* explores the masculine ideal and its deconstruction, it also draws deeply on one particular incarnation of the masculine ideal: that of the superhero. Benton (1989) delineates several distinguishing characteristics of the superhero: (1) a distinctive costume or mask, (2) a type of superpower, (3) an alter ego, (4) the presence of a younger sidekick and (5) the motivation to perform good works in order to promote the common good (pp. 174–5). Walt displays most of these characteristics: he wears a gas mask and black hat as a drug dealer, his chemistry knowledge enables him to work what looks like miracles, in the drug world he goes by the name "Heisenberg" to protect his true identity, and Jesse is his sidekick. However, in the earlier seasons, Walt deviates from the superhero myth because instead of performing good works to promote the common good, he is performing criminal activity in order to promote his family's wealth and security. As the series progresses, Walt transforms into an egomaniacal super villain who commits violent criminal acts in order to promote his own wealth, fame and power. I will now shift to a discussion of how Walt's embodiment of the superhero myth further explores the themes of masculinity through its exploration of mask and costume, duality, and good/evil dichotomies.

Mask and Costume

Like a superhero, Walt wears a mask, both literal and metaphorical. As Walt takes on the persona of a drug dealer, he must wear a gas mask for cooking meth. The choice of a gas mask is both practical (it allows him to work around harmful chemicals) and symbolic (it conveys his effort to remain pure as he delves into criminality). The gas mask is an imperfect mask because it is transparent—it distorts but does not hide the identity of the wearer. Frustrated by his first experience as a meth cook, Walt chucks the gas mask into the desert where it is later found by the DEA. Because Walt stole the mask from his high school chemistry lab, his mask ironically becomes a clue to Walt's secret identity rather than a means of hiding it.

As Heisenberg, Walt chooses to wear a black pork pie hat, which features a wide brim and a flat top. The hat symbolizes the role of villain and also differentiates himself from his usual appearance. The Heisenberg hat is displayed only at strategic times, either as a signal that he intends to commit violence or that he needs to ward off violence. As Walt's violence reaches a peak in season five, the hat appears in almost every episode. Weltzein (2005) argues that changing clothes "signifies a step outside of the realm of normality" and claims that mask in particular "displays heroic masculinity as a sacred violence in the name of a higher order" (p. 245). The higher order that Walt is trying to protect being the financial and physical well being of his family and himself. Walt engages in violence to protect himself and his family, but ultimately his aims are selfish rather than altruistic. He is in fact betraying society in order to save himself, rather than risking his life to save society as conventional superhero formulas dictate. Weltzein (2005) states, "The male masked hero protects not only the walls of the community but moreover intrinsic ethical qualities and values" (p. 243). In Walt's case, he is not only protecting his family, but also the ideals of family values, capitalism, and masculinity.

In "Seven-Thirty Seven" (Roberts, 2009), Skyler and Walt appear to each other, both masked in different ways. After applying an avocado mask to her face, Skyler hears the front door slam. She calls for Walt, but when she gets no response she leans out of the bathroom; this shot mimics the way many superheroes are depicted—a close up on the mask at a jaunty angle that appears suddenly around a corner. Even the bright green of her mask evokes the faces of superheroes like the Green Lantern and the Hulk. Skyler finds Walt wearing a black hat, turned away from her, flipping aimlessly through the television channels. Walt has just returned from witnessing a murder, and is traumatized, in fear for his life. As the camera shifts to Walt's face, there is a moment of what Kawin (1984) calls "subjective camera," when we are projected into Walt's consciousness. We hear a high-pitched sound and underneath this, the muted sound of Skyler's voice calling him from far away. Walt does not appear to notice Skyler until she puts her hand on him, simultaneously startling him and returning the sound to normal. Walt looks at Skyler clad in a surreal green mask as if he does not recognize her. Skyler is annoyed that he does not answer her and then asks if his hat is new. Walt removes the hat and follows Skyler into the kitchen. He cries into her shoulder and then begins to forcefully initiate sex. Although she tells him to wait until she can remove her mask, he escalates and finally she yells at him to stop and pushes him off. In the scuffle, she falls into the refrigerator, smearing it with her avocado mask.

The scene is significant in how it uses masks to evoke themes of isolation and estrangement. The two characters start out physically isolated from each other in different rooms of the house, and then as Skyler moves closer to Walt, the mask and Walt's inner turmoil keep him psychologically isolated. While the physical touch of Skyler seems to improve communication by returning Walt's hearing to normal, Walt's subsequent sexual aggression shows that physical touch cannot overcome the extensive alienation that the masking of identities has caused. Even though Walt has removed his Heisenberg hat, the violence he has witnessed still persists in his consciousness and poisons his behavior toward his wife. The mask leaves traces even when it is removed: Skyler's avocado smear, Walt's trauma, and even the clue of the gas mask left behind in the desert.

Along with masking, Walt's use of clothing draws several parallels with superhero costumes, especially that of Superman. Superman is often pictured ripping off his Clark Kent suit to reveal a muscle hard chest covered with his iconic initial *S*. Like Superman, Walt engages in shedding clothes as he transforms. During the first contact with the drug world, Walt waits patiently in the back seat of the police car, covered in a bulletproof vest. Like Superman's suit constructed from special materials, Walt is wearing armor, but the armor is put on over his regular clothes and is labeled with the DEA logo rather than his own initial. Later, as Walt asks Jesse to be his partner, he wears his everyday suburban clothes, devoid of armor or the authority that the armor bestows. Finally, when Walt starts cooking meth, he removes most of his clothes in order to avoid absorbing the smell of the chemical fumes.

Like many superheroes, Walt must change costumes in order to change identities. The shedding of clothes represents a shedding of former identity. While most traditional superheroes wear tights and a brief covering their privates, Walt appears completely naked and wearing only a pair of underwear. Whereas Superman's costume is indestructible, perfect, and brightly colored, Walt's is soft, flawed, and naked. As Walt drives the Winnebago, his clothes flap in the wind like capes until they are eventually blown away. While Superman is able to fly into the heavens and use X-ray vision, Walt's inability to see through his gas mask results in him crashing into a ravine. After the crash, he attempts to reclothe himself, but half of his clothes are missing. Just as Walt cannot go back to the man he used to be, he cannot put on the clothes of his former identity. He is forever changed by what happened in the desert that day. Walt is in effect the anti–Superman, vulnerable and earthbound, whereas Superman is invincible and transcendent.

Superhero costumes and uniforms imbue the wearer with a license to do things ordinary citizens are not allowed to do, like question, arrest, and even shoot at people (Weltzein, 2005). Bryan Cranston, who plays Walter White, notes:

> The other thing Walt's done, which I think is interesting, is that even though he's told his hair is going to start growing back, he shaves his head. I think it's a subliminal feeling from Walt, like "I don't recognize that guy in the mirror." He's dropped a considerable amount of weight; he's gotten a lot older in the past four

or five months. And as long as he's looking in the mirror and seeing someone he doesn't recognize he can justify what he's doing: "That's not me; that's Heisenberg" [Cranston interview, *Breaking Bad* webpage].

Walt's change in appearance—shaved head, age, weight loss—is what allows him to disassociate from his former self and give himself license to transgress legally and morally.

Another way *Breaking Bad* incorporates the superhero myth is the theme of dual identities. Part of the superhero formula is having a self and alter ego—the ordinary person and the extraordinary superhero. For example, Peter Parker becomes Spider-Man and Clark Kent becomes Superman. *Breaking Bad* alters this formula by depicting the ordinary person and the extraordinary criminal. The law-abiding family man Walter White becomes Heisenberg when conducting drug deals, the kid Jesse Pinkman becomes Cap'n Cook when cooking meth, and Gus the businessman is secretly international kingpin Gustavo. In Walt's case, the Walter White identity is the law-abiding family man, while the Heisenberg identity is an increasingly violent and powerful criminal. The Walter White/Heisenberg duality corresponds to several sets of opposites: real/ideal, self/shadow self, emasculated/masculine, and good/evil.

The alter ego symbolizes a psychic split, an inner conflict manifested in two distinct personalities. One source of inner conflict is the tension between what Walt wants to do and what he is expected to do, a conflict between id and superego. Because so much of his life is scripted, he suppresses his own desires for the sake of others. However, as Heisenberg, he becomes reinvigorated by finally doing what he wants to do instead of what he should do. The dual identities can also be conceptualized as a splintering of self resulting from the trauma of Walt's cancer diagnosis. In the face of death, the things that Walt lacks in his own life become projected onto the idealized persona of Heisenberg. For example, Walt has squandered his scientific acumen in order to support his family, but as Heisenberg he is proclaimed a "god damned artist" by Jesse, and the best in the business by many others. As a meth cook, Walt finally gets the admiration for his scientific prowess that he failed to achieve as a teacher.

The choice of the name Heisenberg is significant, not just because it is the name of a successful scientist chosen by an unsuccessful chemistry teacher, but also because of the nature of Heisenberg's uncertainty principle. The uncertainty principle states that it is impossible to measure the present position while also determining the future motion of a particle (*Encyclopedia Britannica Online*). The inability to determine present position parallels Walt's identity crisis; he has two conflicting selves, Mr. White and Heisenberg. Not being able to determine the future motion parallels the unpredictability and volatility of the Heisenberg persona. Unlike Walter White who is trapped in a stagnant position that follows a steady and scripted trajectory, Heisenberg is extremely unpredictable and his rise to power is astronomic and exponential. Although Walt creates the Heisenberg persona, the identity takes on a life of its own that spins out of Walt's control. As in *Dr. Jekyll and Mr. Hyde*, the shadow self threatens to take over and displace the "true" self.

As I outlined in the previous section, Walter White is associated with emasculation, while Heisenberg is associated with the masculine ideal. Easthope (1990) notes a similar divide:

> Superman, however, has his other side, Clark Kent, and together they form a pair of opposites.... Clark Kent has many of the social attributes of traditional femininity.... Superman understands little else but mastery and legitimated aggression.... So this version of the dominant myth wants boys to identify with Superman as a supermasculine ideal by rejecting the Clark Kent side of themselves [p. 29].

Walter White represents the feminized male that must be rejected, and Heisenberg represents the masculine ideal that should be embraced. Walter White is an emasculated suburban dad and creates the Heisenberg persona that allows him to play out all the things that his own life is lacking. Walt becomes especially synonymous with his Heisenberg persona in season five, which features an increased presence of the black hat. During one episode, Walt's pride in his Heisenberg persona is emphasized when he insists that rival drug dealers say his name (Heisenberg) and then says, "Damn right I am" (Schnauz, 2012, "Say My Name").

The theme of dual identity is underscored through the incorporation of mirror imagery. Palindromic numbers appear frequently: the plane that Jane's father allows to crash is a 737, Jesse's townhouse is number 323, and Walt stands up to his son's bullies in a store numbered 919. Walter White's initials are also mirror images of each other, even the "W" is a mirror image of itself. Actual reflections are incorporated at key moments throughout the series. When Walt gets his cancer diagnosis we see his face reflected in the doctor's shiny desk and then the camera pans up to his actual face, implying that his life has been turned upside down by what he has just heard. When Walt goes to Gus' house for dinner and Gus instructs him to chop garlic, Walt sees his own face reflected in the blade of a kitchen knife. Because the knife is a potential weapon, Walt's seeing of his reflection in it links him with danger, either as victim or perpetrator. Later, as Walt surveys his new lab equipment, feeling guilty about becoming a criminal, he sees a spot on his own reflection and wipes it off. In another scene, after Walt finds out that his cancer is in remission, he sees his reflection in the mirrored paper towel dispenser. Enraged by what he sees, Walt punches his own reflection repeatedly, thereby bruising his knuckles, damaging the mirror, and distorting the image into a fun-house version of his own face. It is possible that Walt is disgusted with the Heisenberg persona he has created, and tries to expel it or suppress it through attacking his own reflection. It is equally possible that he is disgusted with being "Mr. White" and is refusing to return to being ordinary after tasting what it is like to be extraordinary. Ironically as he attacks the reflection which is both him and not-him, he does real physical damage to his hands. But the reflection persists—it stares back at him, distorted and fuzzy but unquestionably present, an apt metaphor for the shadow self he has created.

The concept of linked opposites is directly articulated by Walt in his lecture to his chemistry class (Gillian, 2008, "Cat's in the Bag"):

> Just as your left hand and your right hand are mirror images of one another, identical and yet opposite, so too, organic compounds can exist as mirror image forms of one another.... But although they may look the same, they don't always behave the same way ... for instance, Thalidomide: the right handed isomer is a perfectly fine good medicine you can give to a pregnant woman to prevent morning sickness ... but make the mistake of giving that same woman the left handed isomer of the drug Thalidomide, and her child will be born with horrible birth defects. So: chiral, chirality: active/inactive, good/bad.

Throughout this lecture Walt appears to lose his train of thought, perhaps distracted by the similarities between chiral elements and his double life. Immediately following this speech about good and bad existing in mirrored form of each other, Walt imagines that a student asks, "Is this going to be on the murder?" (Gillian, 2008, "Cat's in the Bag"). In actuality the student said midterm, not murder. Walt is flustered by his auditory hallucination; sinister music starts to play as he struggles to answer the student's question. What this shows is that Walt's shadow self—the drug dealing meth killer—is starting to erupt into his everyday life. He cannot keep the two sides of himself completely separate because like chiral elements they are identical but opposite; they are both a part of him.

The problem with the dual identity of a superhero is that while the protagonist tries to keep the identities separate, the two identities inevitably end up bleeding into each other. Walt strives to maintain a clear difference between his meth cook persona and his family man persona. He wants to keep his true identity secret from police and criminals in order to remain untraceable. However, invariably the criminals discover his true identity. In one instance, Walt disguises himself with a ski mask in order to threaten a lawyer, but when he starts to cough, the lawyer recognizes his cough from an earlier meeting and his cover is blown. Walt also tries to keep his meth cook identity hidden from his family to protect his image as a "good person." He takes great lengths to keep his secret from Skyler: he uses a second cell phone to conduct business and he invents cover stories for his long disappearances. However, as in any superhero story, the secret identity can only be kept secret for so long. Just as Lois Lane discovers that Superman is really Clark Kent, Skyler eventually figures out that Walt is a drug dealer. While Walt would like to keep the two identities discrete and imagine they have nothing to do with each other, the two identities are inextricably linked and the boundaries between them are ineffectual and largely imaginary. Heisenberg is both a masquerade and a transformation. As Walt takes on the persona of Heisenberg, he is transformed through the inhabitation of the imaginary identity.

Another aspect of the superhero myth is the way that good and evil are portrayed. In traditional superhero stories, there is a polarized relationship between good and evil. However, *Breaking Bad* depicts good and evil as more complex, showing characters that are morally ambiguous. While Walt's manufacturing of crystal meth contributes to the societal problems of addiction, poverty, and violence, he does it for what he thinks is a good reason. As the series progresses, Walt constantly does bad things for "good reasons." The violence Walt commits escalates throughout the series: he kills several drug dealers out of self defense, then orders a hit on a fellow meth cook, and later poisons an innocent child in order to frame a kingpin that is threatening his own family. Series creator Vince Gilligan explains:

> I rationalize all kinds of things I do. And that's one of the most human conditions there is. Nobody thinks of themselves as a bad guy—Walt certainly doesn't. I believe in the fundamental goodness of human beings, but I think that the universal thing we all have in common is that given the right set of circumstances, for a day or an hour or five minutes we could be bad guys; we could be very bad guys. And I think if folks watching can realize that about themselves, then they can always find a way to sympathize with Walt, or at least understand why he's making the choices he makes [Gilligan interview, *Breaking Bad* webpage].

Breaking Bad uses several techniques to get the audience to identify and sympathize with Walt. First, the series emphasizes psychological realism, so that the audience understands Walt's motivations. Second, the series integrates a subjective camera perspective, which propels the audience into the sensory experience of Walt. For example, when Walt hears the news about his cancer diagnosis, the doctor's voice becomes muted and his lips move in slow motion, conveying Walt's inner disorientation. Third, the series initially portrays Walt as "the good guy" by associating him with superhero motifs. Even his last name White implies that he is a good guy, because white is associated with the hero in many Western cultural stories (e.g., the Lone Ranger's white hat and horse). However, these heroic cues are mixed with villain imagery. Walt's black hat and dark sunglasses evoke images of Western outlaws and mafia gangsters. When Walt shaves his head, Jesse tells him he looks like Superman's archenemy Lex Luthor. In season two, Walt repeatedly claims that he is not a bad guy or a criminal. However, in season four, he warns Skyler that he is not afraid of danger, he *is* the danger (Hutchinson, 2011, "Cornered"). While most characters in superhero stories are easy to define as good or evil, the conflicting cues make it difficult for the audience to neatly define Walt as hero or villain, especially in the early seasons of the series.

Breaking Bad depicts good and evil not as absolute static characteristics, but rather as contingent upon context and perspective. For example, there is a scene in which the hitman Mike entertains his granddaughter with balloons. He gives her one to take home and keeps the rest for himself, saying "You're never too old for balloons" (Caitlin and Gould, 2010, "Half Measure"). At first this seems to be a charming character quirk—a tough guy with a child's heart—but in the next scene we see how Mike uses the balloons to short out electrical wires, causing a black-out which enables him to eliminate a rival operation. The juxtaposition of balloon as child's toy and balloon as weapon demonstrates how items are not wholly good or evil in and of themselves; it depends on how they are used. In short, context is everything, and context is necessary for evaluating the goodness or evil of any object, act, or person.

A similar shift in context occurs at the end of season four. Walt needs Jesse to help him kill Gus. However, Jesse is now ingratiated to Gus, a trusted employee in the fold and Walt is the one on the outs. Walt asks Jesse to poison Gus using a ricin cigarette, but Jesse refuses to go through with it. When Jesse's surrogate son Brock suffers from ricin symptoms and the cigarette turns up missing, Jesse thinks that Gus poisoned Brock. This heinous act is the catalyst for Jesse luring Gus to his enemy Salamanca's hospital room. In this room, Gus prepares to kill Salamanca. Salamanca cannot scream for help because he is mute, with only a bell for communication. As Gus is about to inject him with poison, Salamanca starts frantically ringing his bell which activates a bomb that Walt has placed under Salamanca's wheelchair. The entire room blows up, but we see Gus in profile rising from the ashes, seemingly unharmed. He straightens his tie, steps forward, and then falls to the floor revealing that the other side of his face is completely blown off, much like the villain Two-Face from Batman. The switch in the visual angle changes Gus from a survivor to a dead man. Similarly at the end of the episode it is revealed that it was not Gus who poisoned Brock; it was Walt. Although Brock recovers, the lines between Gus and Walt become blurred as we realize that Walt is also able to risk the life of a child for his own purposes.

Over the course of the series, Walt transforms from a sympathetic character whose evil acts are somewhat understandable into a violent egotistical criminal who is largely unsympathetic. Series creator Vince Gilligan states: "We want to make Walt White a truly bad guy. He's going from being a protagonist to an antagonist. We want to make people question who they're pulling for, and why" (Bowles, 2011). Walt shifts from killing violent drug dealers to murdering relatively innocent bystanders who get in the way of his master plan. He lets Jesse's girlfriend Jane choke on her own vomit in order to prevent her from blackmailing him. He orders his co-worker Gale to be murdered so that he himself will remain too precious to his boss's operation to be killed. He poisons Brock, the son of his partner's new girlfriend, in order to throw suspicion onto Gus and prompt Jesse into helping him kill Gus. Every act of violence has a rationalization or a motive. However, the deaths of Crazy 8, Gus's goons, and Gus himself are easier to sympathize with because they have threatened to kill Walter or his partner. Jane, Gale, and Brock are all in their own way innocent bystanders. In the case of Brock, he is a complete innocent, a child who is neither a direct nor indirect threat to Walter.

In the fifth season of *Breaking Bad*, Walt's transformation into super villain is almost complete. His violence escalates in quantity over the course of eight episodes, culminating in the assassination of ten witnesses in two minutes. Walt's attitude toward violence appears increasingly cavalier. When new business partner Todd executes a young boy who witnessed them robbing a train, Jesse is devastated and wants Todd to be kicked off the team. Walt decides to keep Todd and assures Jesse that this kind of violence will not happen again. Although Walt tells Jesse he is losing sleep over the boy's death, Walt whistles as he works, a sign to Jesse and the audience that he is not so horribly haunted by what happened. Walt's reaction to the murder of the young boy situates him as a callous and calculating businessman who pretends empathy only to keep Jesse placated. While previously Walt killed as a last resort to protect himself and his family from danger, in season five he is killing to cover up his secrets, prevent his exposure, and even to retaliate for disrespect.

As Walt becomes more violent, he also becomes more egomaniacal, another trait associated with villains. After he kills Gus, Walt acts as if he has usurped Gus's position. However, Mike warns him, "Just because you killed Jesse James, that doesn't make you Jesse James" (Gilligan, 2012, "Live Free or Die"). Walt becomes increasingly annoyed with Mike's disrespect. Walt's antagonism toward Mike reaches a crisis when Mike refuses to give him the names of the nine former business partners that can tie Walt to Gus Fring's operation. These nine partners have been arrested, so Walt wants to assassinate them before they reveal his identity. Instead, Mike admonishes Walt: "We had a good thing ... but no, you just had to blow it up. You and your pride and your ego. You just had to be the man. If you'd done your job, known your place, we'd all be alright now" (Schnauz, 2012, "Say My Name"). Enraged by Mike's words, Walt storms off, retrieves a gun, and impulsively shoots Mike. While Walt has killed before, this is the first time that the kill was not strategic but rather motivated by anger. Mike questioned Walt's masculinity and authority, and his ego could not withstand the attack, so he struck Mike down.

In season five, Walt's use of family as justification for committing evil acts becomes increasingly difficult to believe. Walt embraces and kisses Skyler saying "family is the best reason," as she is clearly terrified of him and repulsed by his touch (Gilligan, 2012, "Live Free or Die"). Later, he threatens to institutionalize Skyler if she prevents him from seeing his kids. Although Walt wants to protect his family from other people, he sees no problem with terrorizing his own wife. The deterioration of Walt's family is evident when Skyler states, "I'm not your wife, I'm your hostage ... but since you insist on keeping me imprisoned, I'll make you a deal ... I will launder your money, keep your secrets, but the kids will stay at Hank and Marie's" (Mastras, 2012, "Dead Freight"). Clearly his role in the meth empire is not helping his family, but destroying it. Yet, even through his estrangement of his family and the resignation of his partners, Walt refuses to sell his part of the business. While he previously used family to justify his illegal activities, he now uses the lack of family to rationalize the same behavior. When Jesse asks Walt why he will not quit the meth business, Walt replies, "You know my kids are gone ... my wife told me she is counting the days until my cancer comes back.... This business is all I have left now. It's all I have left and you want to take it away from me" (Hutchinson, 2012, "Buyout").

Walt moves from being an everyman character to a morally ambiguous superhero that embodies good and evil simultaneously to an unsympathetic super villain. His increase in violence, egomania, threatening of his own family, and lack of justification for his actions situate him as evil, fulfilling Vince Gilligan's original plan of transforming Walt into a truly bad guy. Walt's transformation also situates evil and good as indiscrete, overlapping, and fluid categories with porous boundaries.

Conclusion

If myths are a major way of passing on the values of society, then new versions of old myths have the potential to either reify or transform the way we think about gender. *Breaking Bad* employs mythic elements to universalize Walt's quest and situate him as a hero, while simultaneously deconstructing that heroic narrative. Walt's progression from emasculated victim to hypermasculine victor seems at first to celebrate masculinity, but actually evolves into a critique of masculinity as uninhabitable and artificial. Walt embodies the masquerading and dualistic aspects of the superhero, but inverts the superhero's altruistic motivations. Instead of saving society at the expense of himself, he saves himself and his family at the expense of society. Good and evil are also portrayed as contingent and fluid, rather than as absolute and fixed. The superhero figure is both a powerful mechanism for reifying ideal masculinity, but also for revealing masculinity as a masquerade, a struggle with duality, and a false dichotomy. In both of these manifestations of myth, *Breaking Bad* takes traditional binaries and questions their boundaries—masculine and feminine, self and other, good and evil. Like the difficulty Walt experiences in trying to keep his Heisenberg/Walter White identities separate, *Breaking Bad* reveals how binaries are indiscreet and fluid. The series' mythic structure and allusions shape our expectations, while its departure from the formula violates our expectations, making the series deeply satisfying, infinitely troubling, and, like chemistry and mythology, fascinating.

Notes

1. Because of the publication deadline, this essay does not include the final eight episodes of *Breaking Bad* in the analysis. The final draft of the chapter was completed before the final eight episodes of *Breaking Bad* aired August–September 2013.

References

Abraham, P. (Writer), and Walley-Beckett, M. (Director). (2009). Over. [Television series episode]. In V. Gilligan (Creator), *Breaking Bad*.
AMCtv.com. (2009). Q & A with Bryan Cranston (Walter White). Retrieved from http://blogs.amctv.com/breaking-bad/2009/06/bryan-cranston-interview.php.
AMCtv.com. (2009). Q & A with Vince Gilligan (Creator). Retrieved from http://blogs.amctv.com/breaking-bad/2009/06/vince-gilligan-interview.php.
Benton, M. (1989). *The comic book in America: An illustrated history*. Dallas: Taylor.
Boon, K. A. (2005). Heroes, metanarratives, and the paradox of masculinity in contemporary western culture. *The Journal of Men's Studies, 13*(3), 301–312.
Bowles, S. (2011, July 13). "Breaking Bad" shows man at his worst in Season 4. *USA Today*. Retrieved from http://www.usatoday.com.
Brown, J. A. (1999). Comic book masculinity and the new black superhero. *African American Review, 33*(1), 25–42.
Campbell, J. (2008). *The hero with a thousand faces*. Bollingen Series IVII (3d ed.). Novato, CA: New World Library.
Catano, J.V. (2000). Entrepreneurial masculinity: re-tooling the self-made man. *Journal of American and Comparative Cultures, 23*(2), 1–8.
Catlin, S., and Gould, P. (Writers), and Bernstein, A. (Director). (2010). Half Measures. [Television series episode]. In V. Gilligan (Creator), *Breaking Bad*.
Connell, R. W. (2005). *Masculinities* (2d ed.). Berkeley: University of California Press.

David, D. S., and Brannon, R. (Editors). (1996). *The forty-nine percent majority: The male sex role*. Reading, MA: Addison Wesley.
Easthope, A. (1990). *What a man's gotta do: The masculine myth in popular culture*. Boston: Unwin Hyman.
Edwards, T. (2006). *Cultures of masculinity*. New York: Routledge.
Gilligan, V. (Writer and Director). (2008). Pilot. [Television series episode]. In V. Gilligan (Creator), *Breaking Bad*.
Gilligan, V. (Writer), and Bernstein, A. (Director). (2008). Cat's in the Bag. [Television series episode]. In V. Gilligan (Creator,) *Breaking Bad*.
Gillian, V. (Writer), and Bernstein, A. (Director). (2008). And the Bag's in the River. [Television series episode]. In V. Gilligan (Creator), *Breaking Bad*.
Gilligan, V. (Writer), and McKay, J. (Director). (2008). Cancer Man. [Television series episode]. In V. Gilligan (Creator), *Breaking Bad*.
Gilligan, V., and Walley-Beckett, M. (Writers), and McKay, J. (Director). (2010). Mas. [Television series episode]. In V. Gilligan (Creator), *Breaking Bad*.
Gilligan, V. (Writer and Director). (2010). Full Measure. [Television series episode]. In V. Gilligan (Creator), *Breaking Bad*.
Gilligan, V. (Writer), and Slovis, M. (Director). (2012). Live Free or Die [Television series episode]. In V. Gilligan (Creator), *Breaking Bad*.
Gould, P. (Writer), and Bernstein, A. (Director). (2008). Caballo Sin Nombre. [Television series episode]. In V. Gilligan (Creator), *Breaking Bad*.
Hutchinson, G. (Writer), and Slovis, M. (Director). (2011). Cornered. [Television series episode]. In V. Gilligan (Creator), *Breaking Bad*.
Hutchinson, G. (Writer), and Buckley, C. (Director). (2012). Buyout. [Television series episode]. In V. Gilligan (Creator), *Breaking Bad*.
Gilmore, D. D. (1980) *Manhood in the making: Cultural concepts of masculinity*. New Haven: Yale University Press.
Greenfield, B. (1983). The archetypal masculine: its manifestation in myth and its significance for women. *Journal of Analytical Psychology, 28*, 33–50.
Heisenberg Uncertainty Principle. (n.d.). *Encyclopedia Britannica Online*. Retrieved from http://www.britannica.com/EBchecked/topic/614029/uncertainty-principle.
Hunter, L. (2011). Fathers, sons, and business in the hollywood "office movie." In E. Watson and M.E. Shaw (Eds.), *Performing American masculinities: The 21st-centry man in popular culture*. (pp. 76–104). Bloomington: Indiana University Press.
Kawin, B. (1984-5). An outline of film voices. *Film Quarterly*, 38–46.
Kimmel, M. (1996). *Manhood in America*. New York: Free Press.
Lawrence, J. S., and Jewett, R. (2002). *The myth of the American superhero*. Grand Rapids: William B. Eerdman.
Mastras, G. (Writer), and Hughes, B. (Director). (2008). Crazy Handful of Nothin'. [Television series episode]. In V. Gilligan (Creator), *Breaking Bad*.
Mastras, G. (Writer and Director). (2012). Dead Freight. [Television series episode]. In V. Gilligan (Creator), *Breaking Bad*.
Pleck, J. H. (1981). *The myth of masculinity*. Cambridge: MIT Press.
Roberts, J. (Writer), and Cranston, B. (Director). (2009). Seven Thirty-Seven. [Television series episode]. In V. Gilligan (Creator), *Breaking Bad*.
Schnauz, T. (Writer and Director). (2012). Say My Name. [Television series episode]. In V. Gilligan (Creator), *Breaking Bad*.
Slotkin, R. (1992). *Gunfighter nation: The myth of the frontier in twentieth-century America*. New York: Atheneum.
Trujillo, N. (1991). Hegemonic masculinity on the mount: media representations of Nolan Ryan and American sports culture. *Critical Studies in Mass Communication, 8*, 290–308.

Weltzien, F. (2005). Masque-*ulinities*: Changing dress as a display of masculinity in the superhero genre. *Fashion Theory, 9*(2), 229–250.

Williams, K. D. (2011). (R)Evolution of the television superhero: comparing *Superfriends* and *Justice League* in terms of foreign relations. *The Journal of Popular Culture, 44*(6), 1333–1350.

Winant, S. (Writer), and Caitlin, S. (Director). (2010). Green Light. [Television series episode]. In V. Gilligan (Creator), *Breaking Bad*.

20th Century Boys
Blending Eastern and Western Storytelling

MICHAEL W. MAREK *and*
PIN-HSIANG NATALIE WU

Few endeavors in the twenty-first century lack international implications. Local businesses (even those without international partners) often sell products made in other countries. Cultural symbols and artifacts flow with increasing ease across international boundaries. Interest in literature, music, films, and sporting events quickly transcends national borders and "foreign" markets are often a primary consideration in the development of these events.

In years past, the American movie industry made movies specifically for the domestic market. Any international revenue was considered to be "gravy." Today, however, international revenue is vital to Hollywood, in 2011 accounting for 58.4 percent of the total revenue produced by the top 100 grossing films in the United States, up from 57.3 percent in 2010 (Hancock, 2012). In 2012, American studios started releasing some of their movies in other countries first, in part in order to gain positive fan reaction abroad that would spur domestic attendance (Herships, 2012; Kaufman, 2012; Zeitchik, 2012). But although business decisions depend on the international marketplace, movie storylines and artistic values usually remain narrower. Often, these film narratives make use of familiar situations and images from the culture of the storyteller, usually America, with characters and situations drawing on narrative structures used in ancient myths and legends (Campbell, 1986). Although "myth" is sometimes used in common language to refer to an illusion or false story, in literary criticism it is a story which may or may not be actually true but which is often retold, reflecting ideas or beliefs that define or offer a lesson to a culture or society (Bulfinch, 1978; Douglas, 1953; Tofighian, 2010).

This essay considers a Japanese three-film creation, *20th Century Boys* (2008, 2009 and 2009), based on a manga graphic novel series (1999–2007). The name of the series is inspired by the 1973 song *20th Century Boy* by the British rock group T-Rex, which appears on the movie soundtrack. The story depicts the establishment of an international cultural empire lead by a mysterious, masked figure who the audience knows is actually evil, calling forth everyday heroes to defeat the villain. The ambitious three-movie series reflects the growing international culture by drawing on storytelling conventions in both Western and Eastern myths and legends, blended into a compelling epic that appeals to international audiences. In Japan, *20th Century Boys* was a financially lucrative trilogy, with the first movie finishing tenth in gross revenue in 2008 and movies two and three placing twenty-first and ninth, respectively in 2009 (BoxOfficeMoJo, N.D.).

20th Century Boys is set in Japan, spanning the years 1969 to 2017, often switching back and forth among the intervening years in nonlinear storytelling. It is about a group of eight boys and one girl who form a secret club as young children. As part of their game, they develop a story about an "evil organization" that is intent on destroying the world. They create a *Book of Prophesies* story, in which the members of the club are nine heroes who must save the world. But years later, living prosaic and unexciting adult lives, the members of the club realize that the story they created as children is coming true. They discover that a religious cult is growing, centered on a masked figure known as "Friend" and that many of the specific details of their original story are happening in real life, including acts of terrorism. Realizing that Friend must be one of their childhood friends, the classmates begin trying to solve the mystery. Friend eventually takes over the government of Japan and brands his former classmates as terrorists. The group then proceeds to function as an underground movement, opposing Friend.

The first movie is told from Kenji's perspective, a childhood leader of the club circa 1970, who believed that rock music would save the world. At the end of the millennium, when the classmates confront a giant robot spewing a deadly virus sent into the streets of Tokyo by Friend, Kenji disappears. The second film centers largely on his niece, Kanna, who becomes the leader of the resistance movement against Friend. Ultimately, Kenji returns in the third movie, now set in 2017. Friend is unveiled and defeated, and rock music does, indeed, save the world. The final plot twist happens when we learn that Kenji, himself, wronged Friend as a child, which triggered the entire campaign for world destruction. For viewers, the evil Friend becomes somewhat of a tragic figure, due to the actions of the hero.

Mythic scholar Joseph Campbell (1986) observed that creative artists are truly creative only to the extent that they are innovative. This represents a dichotomy in his work, given that his scholarly focus when studying ancient myths was the similarities among them, not differences. In today's media environment, however, it is the differences compared to what has come before, i.e., the creativity, which produces popular stories. This happens because they are at the same time familiar and accessible to audiences as a result of drawing on time-tested character archetypes and situations, yet feel fresh as the result of new approaches or unexpected deviations from the expectations held by the audience. It is these innovative and creative stories that give rise to pop culture metaphors and idioms, thus playing the role of modern myths (Marek, 2008) and go on to serve as "mythology engines" in modern culture (Irvine and Beattie, 1998), providing stories that are watched and quoted again and again.

The story arc of the three films draws on common mythic structures of Western culture, as embodied in Joseph Campbell's Hero's Journey, combined in innovative ways that feel creative and therefore appealing to audiences. *20th Century Boys*, however, goes beyond the template of mythic storytelling outlined by Campbell and also superimposes other literary themes and devices. In addition to exploring the intersection with Campbell, including the overarching theme of ordinary people called upon to do extraordinary things, and the supporting theme that "rock music saves the world," we will delve into Game Theory as a creative motif for the story. We will show that each of these ways of storytelling has its roots in ancient or contemporary myth and that it is the innovative combination of these myths that leads to the creativity embodied in *20th Century Boys*.

The Hero's Journey

Joseph Campbell (1904–1987) is well known for his analysis of mythic storytelling and his conclusion that that there are common storytelling structures that underlie narratives from many times and cultures. According to Campbell (1949), the formula is that "a hero ventures forth from the world of common day into a region of supernatural wonder; fabulous forces are there encountered and a decisive victory is won; the hero comes back from this mysterious adventure with the power to bestow boons on his fellow man" (p. 23). Campbell lists a series of common steps in mythic stories, some of which are optional or highly symbolic, but they group into three main phases:

- Departure: in which a young, reluctant hero is called to adventure and takes the first steps, with companions, usually including a wise or powerful mentor
- Initiation: the tests and trials by which the hero moves from innocence and reluctance to facing the adversary forthrightly
- Return: during which the hero returns to the prosaic world from whence he came, bringing benefits and understanding of both the normal and extraordinary worlds

Table 1 lists selected more detailed steps in the journey of the hero, which Campbell called the monomyth, because he considered it to be a single structure that spans many cultures. Although Campbell was writing about similarities in ancient myths and legends, this fundamental structure has been used time and again by modern storytellers. In the visual media alone, the essence of Campbell's monomyth can be seen in *Star Wars* (1977), *The Terminator* (1984), *The X-Men* (2000), and *Harry Potter* (2001), among many other stories. A reluctant hero comes into contact with an unseen world, resists becoming involved but eventually proceeds with a group of friends, and is assisted by a mentor who is eventually removed from the stage, causing the hero to take the primary role in defeating evil.

Table 1. Key Steps in Campbell's Monomyth.

	Step	Description
Departure	Call to Adventure	A young hero, usually male, is called to an adventure in the unknown, often in some miraculous or amazing context that is hidden from the normal world. Examples: Luke Skywalker, Harry Potter and Bilbo Baggins.
	The Refusal	The hero may initially decline to become engaged in the adventure, favoring self-interest or reluctance to leave his comfort zone. But often, circumstances make his involvement inevitable.
	Supernatural Aid	The hero who gives in to the call encounters a protective support figure, such as a fairy, hermit, or wizard. It is usually this figure who provides the initial call, symbolic of destiny, such as Obi Wan Kenobi, Dumbledore, or Gandalf. Other "hero helpers" also join in, each with unique skills.
	Crossing the First Threshold	Some barrier is encountered at the point of crossing into the zone of magnified power to challenge the hero, who moves from a passive to more active role in the adventure.

	Step	Description
The Initiation	The Road of Trials	The hero is tested several times and/or endures ordeals, covertly assisted by the advice, amulets, or secret agents of the supernatural helper.
	Meeting with the Goddess	The hero encounters a powerful knowledge and makes a connection. This knowledge is often embodied in a female figure, symbolic of the totality of what can be known.
	Atonement with the Father	The hero faces an actual or symbolic power figure and completes his initiation by taking on the role of initiator or guide for others, thus completing his initiation.
	Apotheosis	The hero achieves great understanding or insight, or transcends to a higher place, reborn at least figuratively.
	The Ultimate Boon	After his many trials, the hero uses his newfound power and insight to achieve final victory.
Return	The Return	The hero returns home, carrying the benefits or trophies of his victory, sometimes with further adventures, eventually crossing a return threshold.
	Master of Both Worlds	The hero becomes free to move back and forth between his normal and marvelous worlds without the worlds contaminating each other.

It is necessary to note here that Campbell performed his first comparative analysis of ancient myths in *The Hero with a Thousand Faces* (1949), well before the American gender equality movement that began in the 1960s. Even his final work, *The Masks of God*, a series of four books published from 1959 to 1968, was published before the fruition of the feminist movement of the mid and late twentieth century. Campbell's writing, therefore, almost always uses male pronouns, except for an occasional reference to a fairy tale with a female lead character, leading to the implication that the hero is always male. Campbell has sometimes been criticized for this, even though in his era, writing "he" was assumed to include both genders.

THE CALL TO ADVENTURE

The *20th Century Boys* movies are psychological works that explore the nature of evil and of personal responsibility. The primary theme of the three-part story is ordinary people finding themselves in extraordinary circumstances and rising to the occasion to become heroes, paralleling Campbell's framework, at least in general terms. As the classmates begin to recognize elements of their childhood story coming true, they, in effect, experience the Call to Adventure. At first, they are only intrigued, pursuing their curiosity about the rise of Friend's cult. As the events unwind, however, they are repeatedly tested and achieve the conviction that they must act.

At the time of their call, the childhood dreams of each one of them have given way to prosaic lives, such as Kenji working in a convenience store, Yoshitsune selling copy machines, and Yukiji caring for an airport drug dog that has never found any drugs. Their call to adventure is not straightforward, such as Bilbo's visit from Gandalf and the dwarves. Indeed, it is the villain, the adult Friend, who subtly extends a call, using the same "come out and play" language typical of children. Although they feel like anything but heroes, they are drawn, step-by-step, into the world they, themselves, had created as children, as transformed into reality by Friend.

Kenji

In the first film, the main protagonist, Kenji, is under pressure from the management of his chain convenience store and burdened with caring for his infant niece, Kanna. He sees himself as a failure because he did not succeed at his youthful dream of becoming a guitarist in a rock band. He is also secretly in love with the lone female children's club member, Yukiji, who all his friends imagine to be a glamorous narcotics agent or professional wrestler. He receives his first glimpses of Friend's cult during his regular deliveries to customers, and a dimly-remembered logo of a fist with index finger pointing upward that he and his young friends themselves created, now being used to represent the cult.

Kenji's first step on the hero's journey is an invitation to his class reunion, which he debates attending, an initial refusal of the call to adventure. However Kenji decides to go to the reunion and meets his friends again after years apart. As they begin comparing notes about the cult, the audience can relate to their insecurities, their lack of feelings of success, and their hesitation at becoming involved in the important events going on outside the view of the general public. This allows the audience to be swept along with the Kenji and his fellows as the mystery of Friend's identity unfolds and they become more and more involved. Kenji's underlying psychology is revealed in a scene from his youth, when he defends a friend from bullies. "A man's got to do what a man's got to do, against all odds," he says as he dashes into the fight.

There is no overt mystical mentor to guide Kenji in the early stages of his journey, along the lines of Gandalf or Obi Wan (we do meet a homeless man who appears to be able to see the future, and whose hat is embroidered with the name "God"—he assists Kenji briefly a couple of times, at least superficially fulfilling the role identified by Campbell). Overall, however, Kenji and his friends, who Campbell calls the "hero partners," begin their journey slowly, not as a major event of departure. Their concerns about Friend elevate slowly to the point where they feel the need to take action. Instead, the partners tend to support each other such that one might consider "the team" to be the mentor and it is only in the climax of the first film that Kenji is ultimately on his own as hero, to climb into the giant robot and confront the villain. Each member of the team has skills that contribute to the whole, such as the warrior Otcho, who has worked for hire under the professional name "Shogan," but who returns to Japan when Kenji calls for help.

Kenji's first major test comes when he "crashes" a music event staged by Friend. The music appears to be a kind of religious rock, glorifying Friend, but Kenji senses a profound wrongness. After he interrupts the music, Friend confronts Kenji verbally, leading Kenji to finally understand the hidden world in which he has been called to play. His figurative "meeting with the goddess" to obtain knowledge comes when Kenji and the hero friends locate their hidden original *Book of Prophesies* and come to comprehend the full story Friend intends to play out. Ultimately, when Friend sends the giant robot into the streets of Tokyo, spraying a deadly virus, Kenji and his hero partners' act of atonement for creating the original story of the virus is to enter the stage alone to try to stop the robot. Kenji climbs high into the robot where he again confronts Friend. Kenji blows up the robot, ending the threat, but Kenji disappears, not returning to the story for years. Friend also survives to begin plotting anew.

In terms of the alignment of *20th Century Boys* with Campbell, we might therefore say "so far, so good." The films seem to reflect the spirit, if not every single step-by-step detail of Campbell's formula. But when Kenji disappears at the end of the first film, something happens that is not expected under Campbell's mythic paradigm. When the hero, Kenji disappears, a new young hero arises, and she is a strong, dynamic female.

KANNA

In the second movie, set circa 2015, Kenji has been gone for fifteen years and his niece, Kanna, now a young adult, leads the resistance against Friend, not because she feels heroic but because she feels she owes it to the missing Kenji to carry on his quest. It is clear that she often feels she and her own hero partners face insurmountable odds, yet she overcomes her reluctance out of loyalty to Kenji. Although she last saw him when she was no more than a child in grade school, Kenji represents a spiritual older mentor who has departed the stage. As is typical of Campbell's young male heroes, Kanna feels inadequate and not in control of her own life, as do many of her associates who see little hope but remain faithful to their cause.

Kanna's personal journey closely parallels that of Campbell's young male hero. She has doubts about the possibility of victory, yet she perseveres for Kenji, who was her personal protective figure from her infancy into her grade school years and who fulfills the role of Kanna's wizard. Yet Kanna also possesses some of the characteristics of an Eastern hero because she enters the story with extraordinary powers already in place. For example, she has ESP and is able to bend a spoon with her mind. Rival gangs in Tokyo come to believe that bullets cannot touch her because she runs into the middle of gunfire to stop violence. Furthermore, Kanna is charismatic and gathers loyal followers, both her hero helpers and Kenji's classmates, who care for Kanna and respect her, making her the focal point of the resistance against Friend. Kanna's mentor, Kenji, is gone when she discovers her secret connection to Friend. Just as in *Star Wars: Episode V: The Empire Strikes Back*, where it is revealed that Darth Vader is Luke Skywalker's father, Friend informs Kanna that he is her father (her mother, Kenji's sister, had disappeared into Friend's organization, leaving Kanna in Kenji's care). There are even hints, not stated explicitly, that Friend somehow caused his daughter to be born with ESP, paralleling the ancient heroes who were the offspring of a human parent and a god.

Examples of female heroism have been available for millennia, but in popular culture and fiction, male heroes have long been the rule and female heroes the exception. Female heroes, i.e., strong female lead characters, have become increasingly common, such as in *Charlie's Angels* (the 1976–1981 television series and the 2000 and 2003 films), *Buffy the Vampire Slayer* (1997–2003), and a host of others. Indeed, many dramatic television series today either have stand-alone female lead characters, or female leads who are co-equal with their male counterparts, such as in *Bones* (2005-), *Castle* (2009-), and all of the police procedural television shows. Joss Whedon, creator of *Buffy* (1997–2003), *Firefly* (2002), and *The Avengers* (2012), is reported to have answered an interviewer who asked why he keeps writing strong female characters by saying, "Because you keep asking me that question" (Alexander, 2012). This trend clearly influenced the creators of *20th Century Boys* because Kanna, as a character, was crafted to be strong, dynamic, and charismatic.

Friend as Hero?

In typical mythology, evil people are evil simply because they are. This is because the construction of characters normally draws on stereotypes about moral character, thus a bad or evil character is assumed to have certain behaviors and attitudes that need no further explanation (Wright, 2009). *Star Wars* Episodes I, II, and III did attempt to tell the story of how Anakin Skywalker left the path of the hero and embraced the evil dark side of the Force, but the psychology and motivations of villains are often not clearly explained. This is because the villain is often a cardboard character in the story, and it is the hero who is more important when it comes to character development. There was no need to justify why Sauron was evil in *The Lord of the Rings*. He just was. On the occasions that we do understand a villain's backstory, it often transforms the antagonist into a different sort of character.

In *20th Century Boys*, Friend is subject to this exploration of psychology and he is a finely crafted character. Both as a child and an adult, he isolated himself from others by wearing a mask. As his cult gains prominence, he wears a formal suit, but his face is covered by a cloth mask with the pointing finger logo over his face. He struggles, at the subconscious level at least, to see himself as a hero. From his perspective, *he* is the reluctant hero, accused wrongly of a crime by his classmates who become representatives of an evil society. Friend has a much more clear protector than Kenji, a magician, Manjome, who helps Friend create parlor tricks like levitation to impress his cult followers. Yet Friend is the leader and Manjome clearly the follower. Friend has the vision and the determination, distancing himself from others, often sitting alone in his office. He only engages in social relationships when it suits his purpose, such as seducing Kenji's sister in order to produce baby Kanna. Just as Campbell's hero has the ultimate goal of benefitting society, Friend's twisted goal is to create what he imagines is an ideal society, but it is a goal which requires killing billions of people in order that the few can survive. Ultimately, Friend stages a death-and-resurrection mimicking that of Jesus in Christian tradition to elevate his status to that of an immortal.[1] He does this to make himself even more appealing and charismatic in the eyes of the public, yet it directly parallels Campbell's Apotheosis, or rebirth of the hero Friend believes himself to be.

As a child in school, Friend is ostracized after being wrongly accused of theft of a trivial item. This parallels many realities of school life, in which bullying is common, children are often thoughtlessly cruel to each other, and some children face profound loneliness in spite of being surrounded by people. Indeed, in the United States, it is an all too common occurrence for ostracized young people to commit acts of school violence, which parallel Friend's plan in his adult life to kill all of humanity, except his closest supporters. Friend, therefore, is a nuanced and complex antagonist. His entire life's energy is directed at undoing the wrongs committed against him, and to demonstrating that he is capable of creating relationships in spite of his rejection by those he originally sought as friends. His complex, three-dimensional nature supports the intricate timeline of the movies, jumping back and forth from 1969 to 2017; a more cardboard character would have not provided the depth needed to support the over six-and-one-half hours of screen time.

Redemption

Campbell noted that many stories have an element of redemption, in that the achievements of the mythic hero must always represent an accomplishment that makes up for a wrong, whether or not it is a wrong previously committed by the hero (Campbell and Moyers, 1991). In the later parts of the *20th Century Boys* story, redemption and taking responsibility for one's own actions become focal points of the story. As such, it is a common theme, paralleling many other modern tellings of the myth. The consummately evil Darth Vader, in *Star Wars: Episode VI: Return of the Jedi*, ultimately redeems himself by saving Luke from the emperor. Severus Snape harasses Harry Potter throughout multiple books and films, but is eventually redeemed when he is revealed as a double agent spying on the evil Voldemort. In broader literature, atonement and redemption themes can be found in a wide range of works, such as Coleridge's *The Rime of the Ancient Mariner*, 1798 (Hiller, 2009); Fitzgerald's *The Great Gatsby*, 1925 (Dilworth, 2010); Willa Cather's *Death Comes for the Archbishop*, 1927 (Fisher-Wirth, 1990); and Hemingway's *The Old Man and the Sea*, 1952 (Wilson, 1977); not to mention that redemption from sin forms the basis of Christian theology (Placher, 2009).

Late in the final movie, Friend struggles with whether he should step back from his plan to destroy the world, approaching the emotional line of redemption, but the experiences of his childhood do not allow him to take the final step. Nevertheless, he subconsciously provides a safety valve when he decides not to include the World's Fair venue in his destructive plans. This opens the door for Kanna to stage her musical event that draws hundreds of thousands of people, thus saving their lives with rock music, which we will discuss in detail later.

Kenji, on the other hand, must come to grips with his own youthful misdeed. When Friend is finally unveiled, Kenji realizes that his own actions triggered Friend's vendetta, when Kenji allowed Friend to be blamed for Kenji's theft of a trinket from a shop. Guilt and redemption are often treated as one in mythic imagery because redemption is necessary only as a response to the perception or revelation of guilt (Krishnamurthy, 2007). In this story, a final plot twist reveals that the hero, not the villain, shoulders the guilt and requires redemption because of his own misdeed as a child, resulting in the twisting of Friend's personality and decades of strife with millions of people dead.

New Definitions of "Hero"

Although the theme of ordinary people becoming heroes is common in myth, the heroes of *20th Century Boys* do not all represent the traditional, virtuous everyman. Rather, they draw on modern incarnations of ancient myth, in which the hero is often flawed or not fully worthy of respect. In Greek myth, the hero is defined by the values of both physical strength and mental maturity. Hercules is a good example of a Western mythological hero. Although his father was Zeus, he lived and performed his heroic acts as a human (it was only after his death that he took on the aspects of godhood). Similarly, the Trojan hero Aeneas was the son of Aphrodite/Venus and a human man. When Aeneas died, his mother asked that her son be made immortal, so his mortal parts were washed away by the river god.

In Eastern Taoist tradition, similarly, heroes also live as human and are promoted or elevated to godhood as a result of the peoples' respect for their heroic acts. For example, the 16th century Chinese classic *Investiture of the Gods* includes many mythical figures, based on oral and written traditional stories. The human heroes call upon supernatural beings for assistance in their war. The human heroes eventually become elevated to the status of gods because of their deeds.

Whether or not heroes actually take on the status of gods, ancient heroes have compassion and mercy for human beings and often fight against gods for the benefit of human beings, making them remembered forever for the sufferings endured in order to benefit humanity. In ancient myths around the world, heroes had to accomplish incredible feats, like shooting down suns (Yi Shot Down Nine Suns, N.D.), moving mountains, stealing fire, draining rivers, or otherwise saving mankind, in order to be revered or worshipped.

The incredible or invincible powers described in ancient stories became the foundation for Superman; Captain America, a World War II hero reinvented for the 1960s post-war era, and reinvented again for twenty-first century big-budget Hollywood movies; and other fictional heroes who appeared during the early twentieth-century. Similarly, the character of John McClane, of the *Die Hard* movies, exhibits supreme tenacity and performs extraordinary physical acts to defeat terrorists, fundamentally a mythic accomplishment. Super powers and extraordinary feats have become a common basis for movie heroes in the twenty-first century. Questions of compassion and the welfare of human beings are often secondary in contemporary storytelling, which instead abounds with over-the-top action and explosions. In *20th Century Boys*, Friend knows very well how to manipulate people into following a cult of "heroism" including leading them to believe that he has hero-like super powers. Early in his cult career, he uses a magic trick to appear to float into the air, helping to convince his followers that he possesses such super powers. His death and resurrection is, in effect, the same sort of magic trick, but on a much grander scale.

In addition, the new heroes of the twenty-first century have often lost their self-reliance and confidence because the contemporary world contains rampant ambiguity and imponderables (Rayhanova, 2006). The professional athlete, for example, was traditionally perceived as the 1890s dime novel hero Frank Merriwell (Daniel, 2010), the epitome of late nineteenth century social ideals and virtues. Modern sports stars, however, are often "damaged heroes" characterized by vice and inappropriate behavior (Lines, 2001). Modern heroes, therefore, are still defined by their overwhelming willpower to fight, but also by their vulnerabilities (Fleishman, 1984). The imperfect hero is a more and more common image in contemporary heroic stories (Richardson, 2004). The reluctant heroes of *20th Century Boys* often experience self-doubt and question their worthiness. As outside observers, the audience also sees their flaws, such as those of Kenji's sister who first committed the sin of developing the deadly virus and later redeems herself by developing a cure, at the risk of her own life.

In *20th Century Boys*, the heroism of the characters arises from many sources. They include:

- Traditions descending from ancient Eastern and Western mythology
- Perspectives of good versus evil and particularly the overwhelming power of evil
- The theologies of orthodox and heathen religions
- End-of-the-world prophecies and the ascendancy of conservative religious sects at the turn of the twenty-first century, like Heaven's Gate, the Branch Davidians, and the Peoples Temple
- The 1960s and 1970s counter-culture vision of saving the world with music and love (the era of the earliest scenes in the overall story of the movies)

THE JOURNEY

A key feature of Campbell's framework is The Journey. In *The Hobbit* and *The Lord of the Rings*, Bilbo and Frodo, respectively, leave their homes to pursue an adventure, as do Luke and Anakin Skywalker, in their respective *Star Wars* stories, and as does Harry Potter when he departs for Hogwarts. In Greco-Roman mythology many heroes, like Odysseus and Aeneas, had to visit the underworld, a terrifying place for mortals, and complete a task alone. Campbell says that the hero's call to adventure "signifies that destiny has summoned the hero and transferred his spiritual center of gravity from the pale of his society to a zone unknown" (Campbell, 1947, p. 48). Often, according to Campbell, there is an actual journey, such as the voyages of Jason, Hercules, and Odysseus, but the journey can be symbolic, spiritual, psychological, or a mixture of all of the above. In such stories, nevertheless, the tests endured by the hero are often situated in specific places, such as Bilbo in the camp of the three trolls, the Mirkwood forest, and the lair of the dragon Smaug. This sense of place is pervasive for Kenji, Kanna, and their helpers.

Place

In *20th Century Boys*, the journey of the heroes is psychological, as their experiences drive their developing ethical reaction to the rise of Friend's cult. The actual voyages undertaken by the characters, such as when Kanna follows her missing mother's trail or when Kenji travels to the far north to regain his memory after his disappearance, are part of their character development. Yet, the concepts of "place" and being displaced from one's natural place recur commonly in *20th Century Boys*, and are important in the construction of the characters. Sometimes the place is an actual location, such as the children's grass fort, where their friendships were forged or spurned; the convenience store, where the reluctant hero Kenji wishes he could remain, safe and uninvolved; or Friend's fixation on the venue of the 1970 World Expo, which was the site of one of the few positive elements in his young life, evocative of the hope for the future that he felt was denied to him. This World Expo site, as a place, also becomes the venue where hundreds of thousands of people congregate to be saved from Friend's killer virus.

The signature musical theme of the series, sung in the first movie by Kenji as a street performer and later in another version to rally the people of Tokyo, overflows with images of displacement and of returning home, an idealized emotional place. For example, the lyrics mention walking through narrow streets and alleys, wondering if food from the local deli will still taste the same when the singer finally makes it back home. Home, then, is the focus of Kenji's journey, and with it the friendships, relationships, and safety of home. The places the characters call home are central to the story—Friend's home as a child which becomes a museum for his cult, the living places of the homeless psychic "God," the home of the police detective, the impromptu home of the resistance in the catacombs of the subways, and Kenji's home, both as his sister tells her parents she must leave (displaced to do research to develop Friend's killer virus, we later learn) and as infant Kanna points Kenji to the full *Book of Prophesies*, buried in the wreckage of the burned convenience store.

But place as a function of the journey also manifests itself in *20th Century Boys* as psychological places, and as displacement from preferred psychological places. Freud saw displacement as an unconscious coping strategy in which the mind focuses on objects that feel safe as opposed to those that are dangerous or unacceptable (Nolan, 2011). For example, it is not safe to lose your temper with your boss, but you may lose your temper with someone else, prompted by your feelings about your boss. This process relates to symbolism and metaphoric structures in the mind. As such, the convenience store is not just a physical place for Kenji, but rather defines his character at the launching point of his mythic journey. The store is the epitome of ordinary existence and triviality. The most important things in Kenji's life, initially, are responding to criticism from a convenience store franchise representative and carrying baby Kanna in a backpack to care for her. As such, his psychological place is far from the mental place he needs to reach to become a hero of mythic proportions. When he is ultimately confronted with the need to change, he desperately seeks out his old electric guitar, calling on music to realign and psychologically reposition himself. More broadly, the children also often see their place as beside each other, shown in the heroic pose the children take together as they pretend to be heroes, paralleled by the way they line up when they prepare to confront the deathly robot.

Other psychological places and displacements in the emotional journeys of the characters are driven by friendships and other relationships. Friend's plot to destroy the world is the result of the spurning of his friendship as a child and the resulting psychological displacement from his preferred "place" within the grass fort. The childhood friends coming together as adults are driven by the loyalties stemming from the psychological place of their past relationships, even though in most cases they have not seen each other for 20 years. Kenji and Yukiji still carry the torch for each other, but are displaced from the emotional place they wish they could be. Kenji's best friend, Otcho, comes immediately to Japan from Thailand when his friend calls out of the blue, changing his physical place because of his psychological place. These emotional journeys, based on home, family, and friendships, are therefore central to the way *20th Century Boys* is constructed. As such, they resonate well with Campbell's view of the journey of the hero.

Although much has been written in support of Campbell's work, he also receives significant criticism, primarily that he was looking for similarities in mythic storytelling and not differences, and further that he tended to ignore myths outside the Indo-European tradition (Witalec, 2004). Indeed, Campbell's *The Masks of God, Vol. 2: Oriental Mythology* (1991) does not address archetypal characters in Oriental myth, as such, but rather spends most of its pages contending that Oriental mythology stems from ancient Egyptian culture, *because* he was interested in the similarities, not the differences. In fact, we found no work in the academic literature comparable to Campbell's breadth of analysis concerning Eastern storytelling and rhetorical style. Yet, *20th Century Boys* is clearly a product of both Eastern and Western mythic traditions, modern and ancient. The Eastern traditions are particularly those manifest in the manga inspiration for the graphic novels and movies.

THE RETURN

The final section of Campbell's hero's journey is the return, in which the hero brings a boon for society resulting from the experiences and lessons learned on the journey. Kenji actually returns twice at the end of the 20th Century Boys story. First, he recovers from amnesia and returns to Tokyo in 2017, using trickery to enter the fortified city, and bringing the specific power of his song, "Bob Lennon" (discussed later in the theme Rock Music Saves theWorld), which saves the lives of hundreds of thousands of people gathered for the concert and who would otherwise have died from Friend's virus.

Kenji, however, makes another kind of return when he subsequently uses Friend's equipment to travel into the past and meet the youthful Friend, as well as his own young self. By this time, Kanji understands that it was his own misdeed that perverted Friend, and through his actions, we see an alternate reality in which young Kenji and young Friend become friends and create the Bob Lennon song together. Although the movie is ambiguous about whether this is actual time travel, or a reality created in Kenji's head by Friend's technology, we nevertheless see the adult Kenji intervene and set events on a new course that would not result in the deaths of millions of people around the world, certainly a "boon to society."

We have seen that *20th Century Boys* makes extensive use of Campbell's monomyth, as well as modern and ancient Eastern storytelling traditions. But it also draws upon additional influences and themes that go beyond Campbell and traditional Eastern and Western myth to reflect modern myth.

Trilogy Influences, Themes and Theory

MANGA

The three *20th Century Boys* movies were based on the manga graphic novels of the same name and draw much of their narrative from the manga originals. Manga is the modern descendent of an ancient artistic style that exaggerates features and makes strong use of satire and social commentary. Although referred to as comic books, manga is often not directed toward juvenile audiences. Today, manga is one of the most popular forms of mass entertainment and an agent of socialization in Japan (Ito, 2005). Heroes in manga, however, may differ from traditional Japanese mythological heroes, who possessed strength, skill, and a knack for overcoming problems by using their wits (Davis, 1913). Such heroes were chivalrous and championed the cause of the weak or redressed evil and tyranny. Traditional heroes could occasionally be cunning and were not above criticism, but they had loyalty to purpose and disregard for death. In Japanese legends, Kintaro, a strong boy who fought demons near Kyoto, and Momotaro-san, the "son of the peach" who went to the Demon Island to punish wicked demons (Zabilka, 1955), both exemplified this spirit of the traditional Japanese hero.

In manga storytelling, however, ordinary people, and even people who begin from an unusually low station in life, ultimately become important heroes, often because of innate abilities. Shota in *Shota no Sushi* (1992–1997), Goku in *Dragon Ball* (1984–1995), Conan in *Detective Conan* (1994-), Hanamichi Sakuragi the comic basketball player in *Slam Dunk* (1990–1996), and Doremi Harukaze, the heroine in *Doremi* (1999–2003), are all examples of manga-style heroes who have a "sense of justice" under a seemingly weak nature. Conan, a small, scrawny boy who secretly runs a detective agency, has a strong sense of justice, but whenever he solves a murder, he has to speak via his tall, authoritative looking colleague. The same situation usually applies to other manga heroes, who are often depicted as honest, straightforward, and naïve. Such manga heroes, however, win the ultimate victory using pre-existing special abilities. Shouta frets over learning to make Sushi but in the end receives appreciation from all. Hanamichi Sakuragi had no formal training in the basic skills of basketball, and is laughed at by other professional players, but his unusual "slam dunk" ability wins many games.

Japanese popular culture loves seeing people rise above weak beginnings. A popular TV show called *Saving the Poor* usually starts with someone failing in running a business and follows them to their ultimate success. In the process, the *Saving the Poor* hero will have to take advice from a guardian, usually an "expert" or a "mentor" in the same field. The hero will also have to experience hardship while training for the future success. Such stories are so popular in Japan that they can play the role of a modern myth, i.e., a story told and retold in multiple settings that makes a statement about culture and society.

In *20th Century Boys*, Kenji certainly has a weak beginning. He runs a convenience store that has business problems, takes care of his baby sister, and is awkward in meeting his former classmates at the reunion and in reminiscing with them. Yet, as Kenji's climactic confrontation with Friend springs directly from his sense of justice and his desire to save mankind from the deadly virus.

Even though he does not succeed at the end of the first movie, his innate skill, music, ultimately saves the lives of hundreds of thousands of people in the final movie.

Campbell's characterization of heroes overlaps the manga hero, but in different ways. In the monomyth, the hero is often born with a noble background, but has been exiled or punished and is unaware of his heritage. With the help of an older mentor and companions, the hero eventually acquires the ability and the determination to defeat evil and benefit mankind (Campbell, 1986). Steve Rogers is weak and scrawny before receiving the medical treatment that transforms him into Captain America and is picked for the treatment because of his morality and "sense of justice," the most important character a hero must have in the eyes of the East and the West. In *The Hobbit*, Bilbo succeeds as a burglar largely because of the magic ring he acquires from Gollum, another outside influence leading to victory.

Manga heroes, however, are usually born with their exceptional skill already in place, rather than learning it from outside. They are often laughed at or criticized by others, however, for their clumsiness or ordinary appearance, until at the critical moment, the value of their skill becomes clear. Kenji's rock band was a failure, yet his musical ability saves the people of Tokyo at the end of the story. Kanna shows psychic ability from an early age, which is trivialized as parlor tricks like bending spoons with her mind, yet this ability allows her to resist psychological conditioning by Friend.

Social Commentary

Social commentary is important to the mythic storytelling traditions in both the East and the West. Indeed, our working definition of myth, as stories reflecting ideas or beliefs that offer a lesson to a culture or society, means that both ancient and modern myths speak to our understanding of society. So, social commentary is not foreign to Campbell's monomyth, because ancient myths carried lessons about ancient culture which are often still relevant today. In addition, modern storytelling that functions as myth (Marek, 2008) reflects and helps us understand contemporary society. Just as *20th Century Boys* drew on manga traditions in constructing its heroes, the tradition of social commentary in manga storylines also greatly influenced the story.

This Japanese tradition of social commentary remains a strong element in *20th Century Boys*. Japan is no stranger to intense nationalism and worship of leaders, a history to which other Asian countries are highly sensitive. Friend's cult, which eventually takes over the Japanese government and gains preeminence on the world stage, parallels earlier Japanese history. In addition, history in East Asia is governed by the Confucian tradition, in which history is fixed and absolute, and not subject to interpretation and revision (Sato, 2007). In this tradition, the movie shows the public of Japan easily drawn in by the glamour and charisma of Friend's cult, and later by his "Friendship and Democratic Party," because they are not used to questioning.

Throughout the movies, we see the ramifications of a government grounded in religious values. Although no one calls Friend's government a theocracy, the viewer sees his organization first take control of the Japanese lower house, then the upper house, and later we see Friend's influence on other world leaders, including the American president and the Roman Catholic Pope. The reaction of the viewer to this incursion of religion into government is, of course, intended to be negative, but it echoes the role religious values play in public policymaking in many countries today. The cult, therefore, creates a society of "haves and have-nots." Tokyo itself becomes a walled bastion and only those most loyal to Friend are destined to survive with him when the rest of the world population is killed by the deadly virus. When Kenji and members of the public want to enter the city, a Manga artist counterfeits the pass, further reinforcing the role of Manga in social commentary and justice.

Rock Music Saves the World

Another of the on-going themes underlying all of *20th Century Boys* is the idea of rock music saving the world. As a child in the 1970s, Kenji thinks that rock music will, indeed, save or transform the world. This leads him to become a rock musician in his youth, but also to his disillusionment as nothing seems to change in his culture. When Kenji's dreams are frustrated, he leaves music behind, but when he gains clear understanding of the threat of Friend, his old electric guitar becomes his grounding influence. Later, after Kenji disappears, his recorded song, played anonymously on a radio station, helps the masses of Japan get through tough times, and becomes the focal point for persuading hundreds of thousands of people to come to the world's fair venue to protect them from Friend's deadly virus.

Music has long been associated with myth. Orpheus, who traveled with Jason and the Argonauts, is legendary for his skill as a musician and poet. When the songs of the sirens threatened to lure the *Argo* onto the rocks, Orpheus sang more wonderfully and overcame the sirens' song. Later, when his wife Eurydice died, Orpheus traveled to the underworld and used music to win her release back to the world of the living.

Hollander (2002) directly equated folk music with mythology, suggesting that "folk music and mythology come from the same primal, undifferentiated miasma of what is truly human" (p. 42). Inglis (2007) noted that popular music is a constant source of urban legends and can be seen as a modern variant of the deeper, often religious, myths about legendary places, people, and texts such as Camelot, Atlantis, Confucius, Jesus, the Holy Grail, and El Dorado. However disruptive, however contrived, and however fanciful the popular songs may appear, Inglis argues, their real significance lies not in the details of the particular song, but in their general role as sources of images, ideas, and information which may run counter to, undermine, and challenge "official" discourses. For example, folk-rock music was a ubiquitous part of the American anti-war movement of the 1960s, the era in which *20th Century Boys* begins.

Campbell, himself, addressed the power of the music of that era, after attending a Grateful Dead concert in 1985. "Listen, this is powerful stuff!" he is quoted as saying. "And what is it? The first thing I thought of was the Dionysian festivals, of course. This energy and these terrific instruments with electric things that zoom in. This is more than music. It turns something on in here [the heart]. And what it turns on is life energy" (Joseph Campbell and the Grateful Dead, N.D.).

Many scholars have observed that music actually functions as myth. It is not hard to relate music to our original definition of myth, a story which may or may not be actually true but is often retold, reflecting ideas or beliefs that define a culture or society. Music with lyrics usually has a narrative and even instrumental music typically has a progression of musical ideas or memorable harmonic phrases. The Di-Di-Di-Dah motif of Beethoven's 5th Symphony is highly familiar and many fans can identify popular songs from only a few seconds of their instrumental preludes, the inspiration of the vintage game show "Name That Tune" (1953–1959 and later incarnations).

Music is often used as a metaphor for the universe. In J.R.R. Tolkien's *Silmarillion* (1977) the creation of the universe is an act of heavenly beings in harmony, and evil manifests itself as dissonance. The ancient philosophical concept of "The Music of the Spheres" drew on ancient cosmology in which the Earth was surrounded by spheres on which the heavenly objects resided, moving in musical-type resonance. Music is widely used in religious ceremonies and spiritual events. Therefore, music can be seen as both reflecting and influencing human morality and ethics, and in this way, again, it plays the role of myth.

Kenji's perspective of the power of rock music is rooted in the youth culture of the late 1960s and early 1970s. It was a time when young people were, in effect, waging a crusade to save the world from war and materialism. In the United States, the revolution was political, at one level, stemming from the Vietnam War draft (government conscription of troops) and to racial tensions across the United States. But transcending the political, it was also a social revolution characterized by personal freedom (embodied in the mantra "do your own thing") and emphasizing love, environmentalism, and mistrust of authority.

James Michener described this vision of change in his novel about the 1960s youth culture, *The Drifters* (1971):

> No phrase of the young is more revolutionary than that odd cry "Zap them right back with super-love." If this became a widespread tactic, it could demoralize society as presently constructed. If a southern sheriff puts his police dogs on a group of blacks, and they sing spirituals of forgiveness and pray for him with obvious love, they are going to accomplish miracles. If a college girl can accept being beaten by clubs and then kiss the hands of her assailants and offer them her love, it's going to knock hell out of their program [p. 237].

Rock music was iconic in this youth culture, representing a radical departure from the folk, jazz, and Motown music of the 1950s and early 1960s. The heavy beat of the young people's rock music, the imagery of peace and individualism in the lyrics, and the formerly taboo blunt references to drugs and sex, were in marked contrast to the simpler, more clean-cut music of their parents. The constant reiteration of these themes played the role of a repeating story that became a functional modern myth because it portrayed and defined the values of the youth subculture.

The groundbreaking 1960s musical group the Beatles was at the forefront of the popularity of rock music throughout the world, spreading the idea of uniting people of different cultures through music. For example, in their 1966 song "Yellow Submarine" the band told a story about people defeating evil with love and music. Many other popular musicians around the world followed their lead, supporting the counter-culture of the day, including Bob Dylan; Arlo Guthrie; Joan Baez; Crosby, Stills, Nash & Young; Creedence Clearwater Revival; and the folk-turned-rock band T-Rex, which recorded the title song of the movie series, "20th Century Boy."

In the first scene of *20th Century Boys*, Kenji, as a high school student, stops the schmaltzy music of Paul Mauriat from playing on the school loudspeakers, replacing it with the driving rhythm of T-Rex. "I believed that rock music would change the world, but nothing did," Kenji says in narration over these opening scenes. Later, at the Friend-sponsored musical event, Kenji exclaims that "this isn't rock" but his emotional response is about the social mission of true rock music and not the melody and harmony of the music itself. Shortly before the millennial confrontation with the robot, at the end of the first film, Kanji says, "If you put everything you've got into it, a song can change the world."

For Kenji, therefore, music is the great "boon" of manga tradition that the hero brings to society, but which is not recognized at first. Kenji's musical ability is typical of the innate ability of the manga hero, but it also fits Campbell's framework as Kenji's newfound power that allows the final victory over Friend, i.e., the formerly unrecognized ability transforms into a powerful force that provides the boon to society.

Kenji's signature song, named "Bob Lennon" (named after Bob Dylan and John Lennon), evokes images of "home" in direct contrast with the apocalyptic reality of 2017 and draws hundreds of thousands of people to the one venue in Tokyo, reminiscent of music events connected to social purposes such as Live Aid, Farm Aid, etc. This venue made the people safe from the killer virus. In this way, Kenji's rock song saves the lives of the crowd. But the *20th Century Boys* story includes one more twist on the transformational power of music. At the end of the final movie, we see an alternative reality in which the youthful Kenji and Friend become actual friends and create "Bob Lennon" together, thus canceling the future of Friend's resentment, his cult, and his plot to destroy the world.

From a storytelling perspective, therefore, the beginning and the end of the movie series are tied together closely and we see that the power of music is the boon that, indeed, saves the world. It saves the lives of hundreds of thousands of people, leads to Friend's demise, and even forges the alternate reality in which Friend is not corrupted by hate. Music may be a non-conventional superpower compared to other heroic stories, but in *20th Century Boys*, it represents the Eastern mythic innate ability, as well as the Western mythic acquired power that allows the hero to win the final victory.

Game Theory

20th Century Boys makes extensive use of game theory and explores the ways in which the characters act out a game scenario, affecting the relative power of the characters. This idea of characters playing out a game is not new. In the classic film *Jason and the Argonauts* (1963), the Greek gods play a form of chess with the hero and his companions. Even earlier, Sir Arthur Conan Doyle's nineteenth-century detective Sherlock Holmes often used the catch phrase "the game's afoot." But the application of formal Game Theory to literary works was first proposed by Herbert de Ley (1988) and has since been applied to the interpretation of many such works. In the game perspective, each step in the plot of a literary work is a turn or a round in a game, with characters serving as players or even "game pieces."

Everyday language is replete with metaphors and similes that evoke games or sports. Some such metaphors evoke ideas of teamwork and cooperation, but often they address competition and adversarial relationships (Shields & Bredemeier, 2011). Vying for dominance, controlling competitors, corporate mergers and acquisitions, and economic success in general are often seen in terms of gamesmanship. In effect, analysis of people and organizations as players in a game serves as a modern myth, because the gaming context is often used as a frame of reference, i.e., an often-repeated story, and reflects modern culture and society.

In real life, financial crises, such as the Wall Street crash of 2008, function as games of brinksmanship, in which investors struggle to control the game and make as much profit as they can, but hope to escape the playing field before the market collapses. In politics, game pieces can include the candidates, voters, and special interest groups. Controlling the political game means controlling the discourse and keeping one's opponent on the defensive. Game Theory has even been applied to things like supply chain economics (Cachon & Netessine, 2006), not to mention the strategizing of military scenarios. The "move and counter-move" framework for understanding relationships and endeavors is ubiquitous, illustrated in the cliché "the ball is in your court."

In the media, the *Die Hard* movies, mentioned earlier, represent this kind of game of alternating moves, but many other movies have also used game imagery, including *Butch Cassidy and the Sundance Kid* (1969), *War Games* (1983), *Wall Street* (1987), *The Princess Bride* (1987), and *The Hunt for Red October* (1990), as well as popular novels such as *The Godfather* (1969) and *Jurassic Park* (1990) (Shor, N.D.).

Even in our personal lives, we talk of the "Game of Life" and ideas of move and counter-move are fundamental to our existence. A teenage girl gives a boy her phone number and it is then his move to decide whether to call. A company sends us a bill and the rules say we must send payment, or else the company's next move is collection efforts. Is it the right move to buy a new car or a used car, and how will that affect the other elements of our life game? There are many players when we seek a job promotion, some supportive and some in opposition.

In a game, the players have to observe certain rules, but rules do not always simply provide for fair play and justice. For example, Foucault (1995) saw the shifting of the focus of criminal punishment from the punishing of the prisoner's body, such as in medieval torture, to the punishment or rehabilitation of the prisoner's soul in modern times, as changing the rules of the game. Similarly, literary game players engage in struggles of reward and punishment. The plays of the British playwright Harold Pinter, who received a Nobel Prize in Literature in 2005 (Garai, 2011), use the metaphor of *The Game* as an indicator of competition, to fulfill the power struggle relationship between those in positions of power in his stories and those lacking such power. In Game Theory, therefore, rules are usually the manifestation of complex power struggles found across society, with one party attempting to impose rules on the others. Game imagery is used commonly across society to portray real and fictional situations in which people face adversaries, including even friendly rivalries.

In *20th Century Boys*, the idea of a game is fundamental to the story, beginning with Friend's desire to join the game played by his young classmates, and continued in adult life as he virtually forces his old classmates into his own perversion of their original game. The conflict of the story, therefore, stems from the determination on the part of the classmates to prevent Friend from playing out the game to its conclusion, and to, in effect, again rewrite the rules of the game back to their own version. In this way, the two sides of the game struggle for dominance throughout the three movies.

Using this storytelling framework, the character creating the game and the characters who are players all have rules they must follow. Early in the timeline of *20th Century Boys*, Kenji directs the game as he and his young friends create the story and write their *Book of Prophecies*. But at that same time, the boy who will become Friend yearns to join in Kenji's club and become part of the game. "Play with me," calls the boy to Kenji, whereas Kenji tells another child, Donkey, that "if we play together, that makes you my friend." Friend, however, is ostracized by Kenji's friends, to the point that as adults, they remember incorrectly that the boy died.

In later years, however, Kenji becomes a reluctant pawn in the game being driven by the new game master, Friend. When Kenji and his helpers realize that the last page in their original *Book of Prophesy* does not tell the ending of the story, they must nevertheless move forward to a new level of the game created by their enemy. As adults, Friend reiterates his old calls to "come out and play" or that "it's time to play." But in this case, "play" means the deadly game of Friend sending his robot through the streets to kill people with a deadly virus, with Kenji and his faithful friends trying to counter Friend's move and stop the robot.

At the end of the first movie, the game moves beyond the original story created by Kenji and his friends with Friend solidly the Game Master, forcing the original players to continue to be involved using his own game narrative in the second and third movies, like a new level of a video game. In one sequence, Kanna infiltrates a purported paradise where young people train to be faithful to Friend. The indoctrination actually includes a huge wall-sized video game. Kanna attempts to control the game by refusing to play, hoping to discover the truth behind Friend, but discovers that the only way to find the answers she seeks is to give in and play out Friend's distasteful video game to its finale. Similarly, Yamane, who reconnects with Friend as an adult research scientist, says the virus research was just a game for him, until Kiriko arrived and helped make the virus a reality. Friend may not, however, be aware of his use of Game Theory, his psyche, rather, remaining trapped in the events of his childhood. Therefore, he is not using the game as a tool, but rather is trapped inside it himself, exerting control yet controlled by it. Game Theory, therefore, fits the definition of a modern myth because it is a theme and metaphor that has been employed time after time and makes a statement about culture and society. The makers of *20th Century Boys* used this modern myth as a major framework. But does Game Theory also intersect with Campbell?

We are the protagonists of our own lives. We each want to see ourselves as the hero and our lives often parallel that of Campbell's hero. The Call to Adventure of leaving the protection of our parents' homes is comparable to Campbell's Departure and if there is no overt reluctance, there can still be trepidation in our personal venturing forth into the greater world. Our friends and associates are our Hero Helpers and our teachers and other mentors are our Dumbledore's and Obi Wan Kenobi's. The key events of our lives are the Road of Trials we face on the journey of our Game of Life and these trials often take the form of move and counter-move strategy. Often, we have abilities and skills in our younger years that we strengthen and perfect as time passes so that as our lives mature we hope that our professional work and volunteer service can provide comfort and security to ourselves and our families, but also take the form of a boon that benefits to society as a whole, so that it will be remembered that we made a difference with our lives. So even though we suggested earlier that Game Theory is a storytelling theme that goes beyond Campbell and traditional Eastern and Western myth, it also dovetails well with the monomyth.

Conclusion

We have seen that *20th Century Boys* is a multidimensional story. It begins with a framework that is clearly based on Joseph Campbell's monomyth, but adapts his ancient mythic template to incorporate Eastern traditions and themes. On top of this foundation, the story layers additional storytelling techniques, all based in elements that function as modern myths, to produce a synergy that makes the *20th Century Boys* story complex and intriguing.

But what can we actually learn about the role of myth from this examination of a Japanese movie series? In any literary work, the lessons we truly learn are not so much the straightforward, obvious moral of the story, but from the ways we think about and process the overall narrative. The nuances of the characters, their development, and the issues with which they grapple provide the grist for our mill of analysis and insights, and not everyone produces the same meaning.

We believe that the complexities of *20th Century Boys* mirror the complexities of our cosmopolitan international society. Seemingly minor events can cascade into overwhelming consequences and it often seems that there is no real truth that can be found because people see events and ideas through such different lenses that is often seems that no true consensus can be found. Yet, much of this dissonance is intentional.

When Friend "positions" Kenji and his associates as terrorists in the public mind, he does it by creating a modern myth about them, branding them as terrorists, a news story repeated so frequency that it takes root in society and comes to define peoples' beliefs about Kenji. Indeed, this can be seen as the role of all modern advertising and marketing, one of the foundations of our economy—the creating of public beliefs through repeated telling of the advertising "story" about a given product or service. This is nowhere more true than in politics where the goal of communication is often to create a narrative about an issue or election that favors one side and marginalizes another by repeated telling of the preferred "story." Thus, politics and government make use of the power of modern myth, as Friend himself does expertly. Even science can be interpreted as a myth because of the role it plays. Scientific theory is a "story" about how a particular thing works that is tested and retold time and again, such as the "Standard Model of Physics." Sometimes the story is improved through innovation and creativity, as Einstein did to Newtonian physics, leading to even better understandings of how thing works.

If science is myth, if music is myth, if government is myth, where can we look for truths? In *20th Century Boys*, the answer is that we look inside ourselves and understand how each of these pervasive mythic constructs influences our own ethics and values.

Notes

1. The original manga comics are fairly clear that two different characters appear as Friend during the story, one before Friend's alleged resurrection, and another after, stepping in as the resurrected Friend. The evidence is, however, that the moviemakers intended Friend as a single character throughout the story and stages his death and resurrection as part of playing out his *New Book of Prophesies*. Therefore the films and the mangas are best viewed as two different interpretations of the same story. For purposes of understanding the films, there is no compelling evidence that their narratives are intended to be understood as having two different young associates of Kenji appear as the adult Friend.

REFERENCES

Alexander, J. (2012). Where are all the (good) female superhero movies? Retrieved from: http://ideas.time.com/2012/08/31/where-are-all-the-good-female-superhero-movies/.
BoxOfficeMoJo (N.D.). Japan yearly box office. Retrieved from: http://boxofficemojo.com/intl/japan/yearly/?yr=2008 and http://boxofficemojo.com/intl/japan/yearly/?yr=2009.
Bulfinch, T. (1978). *Bulfinch's mythology*. New York: Avenel Books.
Cachon, G. P., and Netessine, S. (2006). Game Theory in supply chain analysis. In P. Gray (series ed.), *Models, methods, and applications for innovative decision making* (pp. 200–233).
Campbell, J. (1949). *The hero with a thousand faces*. Princeton: Princeton University Press.
Campbell, J. (1986). *The inner reaches of outer space*. New York: HarperCollins.
Campbell. J. (1991). *The masks of God: Oriental mythology* (Vol. 2). New York: Penguin.
Campbell, J., and Moyers, B. (1991). *The power of myth*. New York: Anchor.
Chang, J. (2006). Diversity is not black and white. *Chinese American Forum* 21(3), 37.
Daniel, C. (2010). Improved reflections: American magazines, higher education, and the construction of a middle-class male identity through European comparisons, 1890–1915. *American Educational History Journal* 37(2), 273–290.
Davis, F. H. (1913). *Myths and legends of Japan*. New York: Ballantine.
de Ley, H. (1988). The name of the game: Applying game theory in literature. *SubStance* 17(1), 33–46.
Dilworth, T. (2010). The passion of Gatsby: Evocation of Jesus in Fitzgerald's *The Great Gatsby*. *Explicator* 68(2), 119–121.
Douglas, W. W. (1953). The meanings of "myth" in modern criticism. *Modern Philology* 50(4), 232–242.
Duncan, T. (2005). *Principles of advertising & IMC* (2d ed.). New York: McGraw Hill.
eHow (N.D.). Japanese masks history & meaning. Retrieved from: http://www.ehow.com/about_5376042_japanese-masks-history-meaning.html.
Fisher-Wirth, A. W. (1990). Dispossession and redemption in the novels of Willa Cather. *Cather Studies* 1(1), 36.
Fleishman, A. (1984). Elegiac romance: Cultural change and loss of the hero in modern fiction. *Modern Language Quarterly* 45(3), 308–311.
Garai, D. (2011). Power game in the plays of Harold Pinter. *Indian Journal of Research* 5(6), 78–82.
Greenwood, D. N. (2007). Are female action heroes risky role models? Character identification, idealization, and viewer aggression. *Sex Roles* 57, 725–732.
Hancock, D. (2012). International movie market continues to increase lead over U.S. Retrieved from: http://www.isuppli.com/Media-Research/News/Pages/International-Movie-Market-Continues-to-Increase-Lead-Over-US.aspx.
Herships, S. (2012). Hollywood movies open abroad, then come home. Retrieved from: http://www.marketplace.org/topics/life/hollywood-movies-open-abroad-then-come-home.
Hillier, R. M. (2009). Coleridge's dilemma and the method of "Sacred Sympathy": Atonement as problem and solution in "The Rime of the Ancient Mariner." *Papers On Language & Literature* 45(1), 8–36.
Holander, L. (2002). Folk music, mythology and enlightenment. *American Music Teacher* 52(1), 40–45.
Holman, C. H., and Harmon, W. (1992) *A handbook to literature*. New York: Macmillan.
Irvine, S., and Beattie, N. (1998). Conspiracy theory, pre-millennium tension and *The X-Files*: Power and belief in the 1990s. *Social Alternatives* 17(4), 31–34.

Ito, K., (2005). A history of manga in the context of Japanese culture and society. *The Journal of Popular Culture* 38(3), 456–475. DOI: 10.1111/j.0022-3840.2005.00123.x.
Joseph Campbell and the Grateful Dead (N.D.). Retrieved from: http://www.sirbacon.org/joseph_campbell.htm.
Kaufman, A. (2012). "Avengers" conquer world box office as U.S. audiences wait. Retrieved from: http://articles.latimes.com/2012/may/04/entertainment/la-et-avengers-20120504.
Krishnamurthy, S. (2007). An exploration of the theme of guilt and redemption in the guide by R.K. Narayan and a grain of wheat by Ngugi wa Thiong'o. *NAWA Journal of Language and Communication* 1(1), 105–111.
Leverette, M. (2003). Midriffs, mooks, and myth: Re-imagining Campbell's hero in the post-MTV era. Conference papers of the International Communication Association 2003 Annual Meeting, San Diego, CA.
Line, G. (2001). Villains, fools or heroes? Sports stars as role models for young people. *Leisure Studies* 20(4), 285–303. DOI: 10.1080/02614360110094661.
Marek, M. W. (2008). *Firefly*: So "pretty" it did not die. In D. Whitt and J. Perlich (eds.), *Sith, slayers, stargates & cyborgs: Modern mythology in the new millennium* (pp. 99–120). New York: Peter Lang.
Merton, R. K. (1936). The unanticipated consequences of purposive social action. *American Sociological Review* 1(6), 894–904.
Michener, J. (1971). *The drifters*. New York: Random House.
Minamoto Yoshitsune (N. D.). In *Encyclopedia britannica online*. Retrieved from http://www.britannica.com/EBchecked/topic/383453/Minamoto-Yoshitsune.
Nolan, R. (2011). Defenses. Retrieved from: http://www.psychpage.com/learning/defenses.html.
Ono, S., Woodward, W. P., and Sakamoto, S. (2004). *Shinto the kami way*. Tokyo: Tuttle.
Perkins, D. (1999). *Encyclopedia of China: The essential reference to China, its history and culture*. New York: Checkmark Books.
Placher, W. C. (2009). How does Jesus save? *Christian Century* 126(11), 23–27.
Rayhanova, B. (2006). The concept of the hero in modern Arabic prose. *Middle Eastern Literatures* 9(2), 169–178. DOI: 10.1080/14752620600814343.
Richardson, N. (2004). The gospel according to Spider-Man. *Journal of Popular Culture* 37(4), 694–703. DOI: 10.1111/j.0022-3840.2004.00094.x.
Sato, M. (2007). The archetype of history in the Confucian ecumene. *History and Theory* 46, 218–232.
Shields, D., and Bredemeier, B. (2011). Contest, competition, and metaphor.*Journal of the Philosophy of Sport* 38(1), 27–38.
Shor (N.D.). Game theory in film, music, and fiction. Retrieved from http://www.game-theory.net/popular/.
Siegel, M. (1985). Foreigner as Alien in Japanese Science Fantasy. *Science Fiction Studies* 12(3), 252–263.
Tofighian, O. (2010). Beyond the myth/philosophical dichotomy: Foundations for an interdependent perspective. *Forum Philosophicum* 15, 175–189.
Tolkien, J. R. R. (1977). *The silmarillion*. Boston: Houghton Mifflin.
Wang, D. (2008). "Thematic archetypes" and new era fiction. *Social Sciences in China* 29(4), 113–127. DOI: 10.1080/02529200802500417
Wilson, G. R., Jr. (1977). Incarnation and redemption in "The Old Man and the Sea." *Studies in Short Fiction* 14(4), 369.
Witalec, J. (ed.). (2004). *Twentieth-century literary criticism*, vol. 140. Toronto: Gale Cengage.
Wright, W. M. (2009). Greco-Roman character typing and the presentation of Judas in the fourth gospel. *Catholic Biblical Quarterly* 71(3), 544–559.
Yi shot down nine suns (N.D.). In Aboutwww. Retrieved from http://chineseculture.about.com/library/extra/story/blyrh11051999.htm.

Zabilka, G. (1955). *Customs and culture of Oki-Nawa* (Rev. Ed.). Tokyo: Charles E. Tattle Company.

Zeitchik, S. (2012). Movie projector: James Bond's "Skyfall" will blow up the box office. Retrieved from: http://articles.latimes.com/2012/nov/08/ entertainment/la-et-mn-james-bond-skyfall-box-office–20121108.

A Change of Scenery

The Southern, the Western and the Evolution of the Frontier Myth in Justified

Aaron Duncan

The camera opens on a man dressed in tan suit and a Stetson cowboy hat walking through a posh Miami resort. He takes a seat at a table across from a wealthy looking man who is eating lunch and proclaims, "The airport is a good forty-five from here, but I figure you will be alright if you leave in the next two minutes." The audience soon learns that the man in the Stetson is United States Marshal Raylan Givens and the wealthy man eating lunch is drug kingpin Tommy Bucks. We then learn that Bucks killed an innocent man while Givens was forced to watch and, as a result, the Marshal has given Bucks twenty-four hours to leave town, or be shot on sight. Givens take a seat across from Bucks at his table and reminds him of his deadline to leave town. Bucks declines to leave and instead attempts to draw down on Givens. Proving he is the fastest gun in Miami, or at least the fastest one at table, Givens outdraws Buck and shoots him dead in the heart.

This is the opening scene of the first episode of the FX's hit television show *Justified* that debuted in 2010. The scene tells the audience a lot about the character of Raylan Givens and the mythic arc of the show. We learn quickly that Givens is not a man to be trifled with, willing to do whatever it takes to get justice. However, there is something about the scene that does not fit with the traditional narrative of the Western: the setting. This gunfight does not take place at the O.K. Corral or in some smoke-filled tavern of the Old West. Instead, this battle is set on the pool deck of a fancy Miami resort. The heroes and the villains remain the same, but the scene in which they are placed is different.

Although the setting for the initial scene is sunny and decadent Miami, it soon changes to Eastern Kentucky with its mountain ranges and rustic population. The majority of *Justified* takes place in rural Kentucky, which may, in superficial ways, resemble the Western frontier but has important key differences. I argue that the location of the South changes not only the setting of the narrative, but the values and meaning associated with it. *Justified* transforms the Western into a new type of mythic narrative, which I will refer to as "the Southern." The Southern draws critical elements from the traditional Frontier Myth but adapts them to the unique setting of the American South. Based on the stories of best-selling author Elmore Leonard, *Justified* follows the life of U.S. Marshal Raylan Givens after he is reassigned from Miami to his birthplace in Eastern Kentucky. The series has garnered both critical and popular acclaim, but I wish to examine it because it represents a shift in narrative storytelling. Most importantly, the Southern is representative of the tension between modern American culture and traditional Southern culture.

The phrase "the Southern" was coined by film writer and director Quentin Tarantino. Tarantino utilized the term to characterize his latest cinematic effort, *Django Unchained* (2012), which, while stylized to look like a classic Western film, takes place deep in the American South. Tarantino states that his film is a Southern because its form parallels that of the spaghetti Western, but its subject matter deals with the historical issue of Southern slavery (Hiscock, 2007). When discussing this new genre of film he stated:

> I want to do movies that deal with America's horrible past with slavery and stuff but do them like spaghetti westerns not like big issue movies. I want to do them like they're genre films, but they deal with everything that America has never dealt with because it's ashamed of it, and other countries don't really deal with because they don't feel they have the right to [36].

The Southern then refers to a narrative which borrows from many of the traditional elements of the Western, but deals with subject matter specific to American Southern culture, in particular aspects of that culture which conflict with the values of the larger American culture. I examine *Justified* as a means of investigating the modern telling of the Southern. *Justified* takes the cowboy lawman, in this case Raylan Givens, and transports him deep into the heart of the American South. I argue that the tension that exists between Givens and the South is representative of larger tension between modern American culture and traditional Southern culture. I will also argue that the transformation of the Western to the Southern alters key elements of the Frontier Myth.

The Frontier Myth

The Frontier Myth is an enduring myth deeply connected to the American psyche. McLure (2000) writes, "The American West in the popular imagination has always been a region of endless possibilities, a vast, magnificent, ideal stage for the national drama of liberty, equality, and the pursuit of happiness" (p. 457). Although the West has long since been conquered, the myth survives in America's consciousness. Harter (2004) claims, "The frontier narrative functions as a textual guide that directs the formation of not only individual identities (e.g., the farmer as the lone hero) but also organizational form (e.g., the proclivity for structures that privilege individualism)" (p. 89). The Frontier Myth is vital to our understanding of the shaping of America and its continued growth. The myth was used by both Presidents Franklin Roosevelt and John F. Kennedy, who reconstituted myths about American progress to forward their political agendas in the form of the New Deal and the New Frontier, respectively.

The Frontier Myth has been told in modern times through the genre of the Western. Western films have exerted a powerful influence over America's collective consciousness. Loy (2001) argues that Westerns shaped American culture and taught values to its audience. For example, through the actions of the hero we learn that people are basically good, success requires hard work, leadership is important, and "crime does not pay!" (Loy, 2001, p. 6). Rushing (1989) contends that the myth has evolved over time to fit changing circumstances, but nonetheless is ever present. From classic Western films *My Darling Clementine* (1946), *High Noon* (1952), and *Shane* (1953) to classic television shows like *Gunsmoke* (1955) and *Bonanza* (1959). These films also dealt with important issues of their time. *High Noon* was an allegory for McCarthyism written by the soon to be back-listed Carl Foreman (Caparros-Lera & Alegre, 1996).

I argue in this essay that the television show *Justified* exemplifies the traits of this new genre of narrative and demonstrates the evolution of the Frontier Myth. Changes and alternations to the classic Myth of the Frontier, particularly with regard to the setting, are important because they are reflections of larger cultural shifts and changes. Rushing (1989) writes, "I argue that the evolution of the frontier must be understood as a cultural variant of a larger evolution of the archetypes inherent in the myth" (p. 1). Rushing's work examined the films *Alien* (1979) and *Aliens* (1986), which shifted the setting of the myth from the Old West to outer space. Rushing argued that this change of scenery allowed for the creation of new type of female heroine not bound by the patriarchal structures of the traditional Western. Similarly, I contend that shifting the setting from the Old West to the modern South has important implications not only for the evolutions for the characters of the story but also for the central tension that drives the narrative.

Many elements of the traditional Frontier Myth are present in *Justified*. Rushing (1986) notes that the most iconic character of the Frontier Myth is the lawman. According to Rushing, the cowboy lawman is daring, noble, ethical, and romantic. In Western films and television shows, the cowboy lawman is personified by men like Wyatt Earp and Matt Dillon. Raylan Givens appears to be cut from the same cloth as his fellow Marshals. Portrayed by Timothy Olyphant, Givens is tall, handsome, daring, and strong. In addition to the badge and gun he wears on his hip, Givens' other chief attire consists of cowboy boots, blue jeans, and his trademark Stetson hat.

The audience learns in the first scene of the pilot episode that Givens is a violent man and willing to kill when needed. Tommy Bucks declined to leave Miami and attempted to draw down on Givens, but ends up shot dead. This scene firmly establishes Givens' code of ethics and legitimizes him as fast drawing cowboy lawman. It also demonstrates that Givens has another key attribute of Western heroes: he is good with a gun, a talent reaffirmed throughout the series. Indeed, he does not hesitate to draw his gun or use it. As Raylan matter of factly states, "I don't pull my side arm unless I am going to shoot to kill. That's its purpose: to kill. So that's how I use it" (Season 1, episode 1). The title of the show, *Justified*, refers to Givens' defense to the repeated inquires about his many shootings. Marshal Givens believes firmly that all his shootings and killings are "justified."

However, despite similarities between *Justified* and the traditional Western story, the series alters the Myth of the Frontier in important ways. The most obvious change that occurs is with regards to setting: the Old West is traded for the hill country of Eastern Kentucky. This change in setting alters not only the location of the series, but also changes the central tension that drives the narrative. Rushing (1983) states, "The fundamental values of the American Western myth exist in the paradoxical form of Individualism vs. Community" (p. 14). The classic lone cowboy hero is uncomfortable with the civilizing efforts of modernization, and although he saves the community, he cannot remain a part of it. This is epitomized by the classic western *Shane*, where the title character saves the town, but immediately leaves afterwards. In the Southern the tension remains, but is transferred. The tension exists not between the individual and the community, but rather the individual and Southern culture. The character of Raylan Givens is not seeking to flee civilization; he only wishes to flee the South. We learn as the series evolves that Raylan joined the Marshals as a way to escape his backwoods, crime infested home in Harlan County, Kentucky. However, Raylan's shooting of Tommy Bucks draws the ire of his superiors and, as punishment, he is shipped back to his home state. Raylan enjoys living in the city and has no desire to return to his rural roots in Kentucky.

This shift in tension is important because it reflects a larger cultural shift. The Frontier Myth, as exemplified by the classic Western, reflected our cultural desire to conquer new lands and spaces and tame the wilderness. The tension between the cowboy and the community reflected the tension created between the desire for individual freedom and the need to be part of a community to survive. In the Western, the cowboy is trying to escape civilization, but in the Southern, Givens wishes only to escape Southern culture. The desire of Marshal Givens to be freed from his cultural heritage is reflective of the larger cultural desires of modern America to be freed from the legacy of the Old South. Like Raylan, we may embrace superficial elements of Southern culture, such as penchant for using the term "Ma'am" and tipping his cap whenever he meets a lady, but we are uncomfortable with the historic legacy of the region which hits a unique cultural nerve.

The Old South and the New

Perhaps no region in the modern world is so linked to its mythology as the American South. The mythology of the region is potent, profuse, and at times paradoxical (Tindall, 1989). However, despite its strong influence on the shaping of America, the South has not been subject to the same level of mythological analysis as the American West. The South occupies a unique and often uneasy place in both America's history and consciousness. This is due in large part to the U.S. Civil War and its lasting legacy. Symbols of the confederacy, such as the "Stars and Bars" flag, are still present and representative of the Old South with which many Americans living outside the South find distasteful. Jasson (2003) concluded that despite its location within the borders of the lower forty-eight states, the South is often constructed and viewed as the "other." hooks (2000) explained that othering occurs when members of the mainstream work to push a group of people to the margins of society. She states, "To be in the margin is to be part of the whole but outside the main body" (p. ix). The Old South is thus presented as being at the fringes of American society and not representative of the culture as whole. Even seemly positive images of the South are often presented in fashion that distances the region from the rest of America. Jasson explains, "By contrasting itself with a racist, violent, poor, intolerant, and xenophobic South, America comes to know itself as personifying the opposite traits; hence Americans are enlightened, peaceful, prosperous, tolerant, and cosmopolitan" (p. 350). Groups portrayed as the other lack the power and status of members of the in-group and thus their discourse is often silenced or simply not heard (hooks, 2000). The culture and traditions of the region may be celebrated within the South, but the rest of the country remains distant and at times outwardly disdainful of them (Hutson, 1993).

A reading of the mythology of the American South reveals that there are the prominent mythological strains which are in tension with each other: the Myth of the Old South and the Myth of the New (Jasson, 1993). The Old South is a reflection of the values that America wishes to contrast itself against characterized by images of racism, poverty, intolerance, and violence. Depictions of the Old South may focus on the Southern aristocracy and plantations, but we are always reminded that "away from the white columns and gentility, there existed Po' White Trash: the crackers, hillbillies; sandhillers, rag, tag, and bobtail; squatters" (Tindhall, 1989, p. 5).

Conversely, the New South is constructed by the steps it takes away from the Old South (Jansson, 2003). The term "New South" was first used in 1862 by a Union solider but was popularized by *Atlanta Constitution* editor Henry Grady. Grady used the term to symbolize rejection of traditional Southern values and mores and the embracing of national values and morals (Mixon, 1989). The New South not only embraces the values of progress and tolerance, but also seeks greater prosperity through industrialization. The New South attempts to put aside the agrarian lifestyle of the Old South in favor of the industrial lifestyle of the North. *Justified* strikes at the core of the tension between the old and the new. The show's protagonist Raylan Givens embraces superficial aspects of the Old South's culture, such as his choice of dress, music, and love of Kentucky whiskey, but rejects the central values of Old Southern culture. I argue that his struggle to escape the rural South and his personal history with the region is emblematic of our nation's larger cultural shift to replace the traditions, values, and history of the Old South with those of the New South.

Characters of the Old West and South

Justified reaffirms many of the stereotypes of the Old South through its different characters. Frequently, Southern characters are portrayed as racists, backwards, uneducated, and uncivilized. Characters like Dewey Crowe, Devil, and their white supremacist friends display ample amounts of racism and stupidity. The ignorance of these characters is often mined for laughs. For example, in season three episode four, Dewey Crowe becomes mistakenly convinced that he has four kidneys. The few intelligent Southern characters depicted are either members of the law enforcement community, such as Raylan, chief deputy Art Mullen and fellow deputy Rachel Brooks, who are intent on bringing order and civility to the area, or criminals who are adapt at exploiting the unintelligent members of their community as exemplified by Boyd Crowder, Arlo Givens, and Mags Bennett.

While the hero is an important character in the Western, he is far from alone. Women also play an important role in telling the Frontier Myth. The two most prominent women in the myth are the "good girl" and the "bad girl," who together serve to represent the paradox facing the hero (Rushing, 1983). The "good girl" typically comes from the East and represents civilization, community, and refinement. She often appears as the schoolmarm or rancher's daughter. The "bad girl" works either in the town's saloon or brothel and typically represents the desire for freedom and rebellion against the community. Perhaps most importantly, the "good girl" is dependent on men for her survival. She is weak and timid, and she faints or falls to pieces when trouble occurs. The "bad girl" by comparison is a stronger; she is from the West and although she still depends on men, she is more independent and self-sufficient. Plus, she represents something sinful and taboo. Put another way, the women represent classic characters of ancient myth, the virgin and the harlot. In classic western *My Darling Clementine* the "good girl" is personified by civilized and gentile Clementine Carter, while the saloon working poker cheat Chihuahua offers us the perfect example of the "bad girl."

While, there are a variety of characters that exist in Southern mythology, but one of particular importance is the "Southern Belle." The Southern Belle occurs frequently in Southern mythology and is at the forefront of its most enduring narratives. In essence she is the "good girl" of the western myth, but with a southern twist. She is epitomized by the character Blanche DuBois in *A Streetcar Named Desire*. The Southern Belle is "modest, submissive, frail, pious, given more to moral than to intellectual capabilities, whole-heartedly devoted to her family, and, above all, sexually pure" (Joyner, 1974, p. 67). The Southern lady has limited participation in the public sphere and instead is focused on issues related to her sex and gender. The Southern Belle ought to embody motherhood and is called upon to exemplify "true womanhood" (Heyse, 2010). In many respects, the Southern Belle is similar to the character of the "good girl" from the Myth of the Frontier, as both are depicted as outwardly attractive and ladylike but are also physically and mentally weak. However, the "good girl" hails from the industrialized city, while the Southern Belle comes from the rural plantation.

The mythology surrounding the Southern Belle is both confining and historically inaccurate. Southern women before, during, and after the Civil War took on a variety of duties that would be stereotypically defined as "man's work" (Joyner, 1974). The documentary *Southern Belle* (2012) explained that the mythic figure of the Southern Belle was created in the 1880s in an attempt to help cope with the loss of the Civil War. Southern masculinity was severely harmed by the Confederacy's defeat, and in order to restore it, the figure of the Southern Belle was created. Despite historical documentation that Southern women prior to this era were educated and even involved in politics, the Southern Belle is portrayed as physically and intellectually submissive, and in need of male protection. According to the film, this rhetoric provided justification for organizations like the Ku Klux Klan, who argued that the gentile Southern Belle needed protecting from the dangerous black man.

The archetypes of the southern white male characters are no less stringent than those of their white female counterpart. Southern men are nearly uniformly domineering patriarchal figures. Smith and Wilson (2004) noted that while the feminine southern male does exists they are almost exclusively represented by unsympathetic characters, such as the southern aristocrat Ashley Wilkes in *Gone with the Wind*. The majority of images of southern white men represent them as being "violent rednecks" or beer-guzzling "good old boys" (Smith & Wilson, 2004, p. 189). The poor white southern male has been labeled throughout history as a hillbilly, redneck, or simply poor white trash. Although Smith and Wilson did concede that the meaning of the term redneck was altered to a "semipositive affirmation" in the late twentieth-century, due in large part to the work of comedians Jeff Foxworthy and Larry the Cable Guy.

Justified presents us with numerous depictions of both stereotypes. The Crowder clan is prototypical of the violent redneck stereotype. In the pilot episode of the series Boyd Crowder blows up an African American church with a rocket launcher. Although never shown, we learn that Bowman Crowder often beat his wife Ava. The patriarch of the Crowder family is Bo Crowder, leader of his own gang of violent redneck thugs known affectionately as "Crowder's Commandos." Bo is the former crime boss of Harlan County who begins the series in prison but is eventually released. Soon after he restarts his criminal practices which include the making and dealing of drugs, murder, and racketeering. In one particularly brutal episode in season one Bo murders all of Boyd's followers, and although he initially decides to spare his son's life, he later changes his mind. In the final episode of season one, Bo is shot to death by members of a Miami drug cartel.

Boyd is angered by the murder, in part because he wanted to be the one to kill his father.

The stereotypical "good old boy" may be less violent than his relative the redneck but he is still a testosterone-fueled, hyper-masculine caricature of southern manhood (Smith & Wilson, 2004). In addition to generally being depicted as sexist and racist the "good old boys" are often depicted as drunks. Characteristically good old boys love hunting, fishing, NASCAR, guns, drive pickup trucks, and drink copious amounts of cheap beer (Kraft, 2012). The character of Stanley Kowalski in *A Streetcar Named Desire* embodies this stereotype. Stanley enjoys playing poker, smoking cigars, and drinking. His drinking also leads to many of his violent outbursts and abuse of the females around him.

In recent years an archetype has developed of the "new southern man" (Smith & Wilson, 2004). The new southern man is characterized not by his association with the rural south, but his inhabitation of urban southern communities like Atlanta and Nashville. He is depicted as a kinder and gentler, more sanitized version of the traditional southern gentleman. Smith and Wilson state, "Populated by Jimmy Carter, Bill Clinton, and Forrest Gump and set to a soundtrack by Shania Twain and Alan Jackson, the modern South attempts to maintain links to its traditional past while creating a business and social climate conducive to a global consumer society" (p. 192). I will contend later in this essay that Raylan Givens is representative of the emerging archetype of the "new southern man."

Myth of the Southern

Justified is set in Eastern Kentucky, but within that area the characters encounter two very different scenes. The two primary settings are the city of Lexington and rural Harlan County. It is unclear how many miles separate the two localities, but for all intents and purposes, they are worlds apart. Lexington represents the new South and is depicted as industrialized, sophisticated, and civilized. The residents of the town live in nice houses, drive on paved roads, and wear business attire and work in professional jobs. When violence does occur in the city, it is seen as out of place and troublesome. Actions are taken to swiftly rectify the problem.

It is important to note that Harlan is a county and not a city. Harlan lacks the population size and density to be considered a city. The rural setting of Harlan County serves as the embodiment of Old South. Unlike Lexington, the residents of Harlan are spread out across a wide area, and close neighbors are few and far between. While some people live in houses, others live in trailer parks or rustic cabins. Their dwellings are located off mostly unpaved dirt roads and they wear simple clothes that often appear to be dirty.

Most of the men in the area either work in the coal mine or are involved in petty criminal activity. The women are housewives, prostitutes, or waitresses. Crime is commonplace in Harlan County, and the residents would rather handle the situation themselves than involve law enforcement. In fact, calling the cops to report a crime is enough to get you killed. This is in part for good reason, since all of the various officers of local law enforcement are corrupt and in cahoots with various criminal elements.

The character of Raylan Givens has trouble committing to either setting. He refuses to move home to Harlan, but he also refuses to commit to living in Lexington. For much of the series, Raylan lives in a hotel, which is representative of his transitive nature and his hope that soon he will be headed back to Miami or some other locale. Harlan County represents the Old South and Lexington the New South, but Givens would rather be free of both of them. Although he prefers Lexington to Harlan, he does not wish to remain in either. He moved to Lexington against his will, and often speaks of escaping it and going somewhere else, somewhere farther away from Harlan County. Unfortunately, for him, he has yet to escape either place. Raylan does not seem to dislike Lexington, but he does dislike its close proximity to Harlan. During the final scene of season two, the Brad Paisley song "You'll Never Leave Harlan Alive" (2001) plays in the background. The song describes roots there, but expresses the hopelessness of escape. The series is ongoing, so we do not yet know whether Raylan Givens will escape Harlan alive, but if he fails to do so, it will not be for a lack of effort.

Urban Cowboy

When we first meet U.S. Marshal Raylan Givens, it is easy to mistake him for a modern day Wyatt Earp or Matt Dillon. He is tall, handsome, and strong. He wears cowboy boots, blue jeans, and is never without his gun or his trademark Stetson hat. Of all the pieces of his attire, it is Raylan's hat that is most iconic and worthy of discussion. The hat is referenced by several characters and even plays into key plot points of the series. In the episode "Hatless" from season one, Raylan loses his hat in bar fight and must try to get it back. The importance of the hat is reiterated throughout the episode because whenever anyone who knows Raylan sees him, they inquire about the missing hat. In season three, the smalltime criminal Dewey Crow uses a similar hat to impersonate Raylan and rob a local drug dealer. Later in the season, a state trooper is shot from behind when Raylan's dad, Arlo Givens, mistakes the trooper's hat for Raylan's.

Raylan's Stetson hat also serves to differentiate him from the other characters. The hat makes him stand out in part because it seems out of place. The hat makes Raylan look like he belongs riding next to John Wayne and Clint Eastwood on the western frontier rather than of the hills of Eastern Kentucky, and is therefore critical to connecting Raylan to the Myth of the Frontier. Traditionally, all cowboys are supposed to have a hat: ten-gallon, straw or otherwise. The characters portrayed by John Wayne, Clint Eastwood, and Will Rogers were defined in part by their hats. However, Raylan's Stetson makes him look out of place in the South, a fact reinforced by the show's other characters who feel the need to constantly comment on his distinct head gear. Additionally, no other character in the series is ever shown wearing a cowboy hat of any kind.

Despite his attire and his penchant for settling disputes with this gun, Raylan Givens is not made in the mold of the Western cowboy. The cowboy of the Old West is too much of an individual to exist in the confines of civilization and thus must always seek to leave it (Rushing, 1983). However, as previously mentioned, Raylan seeks out civilization and spurns the openness of the country. When Raylan is told that he is being forced to leave Miami and return to Kentucky, he responds, "Ah damn, I grew up in Kentucky, I don't want go back there" (Season 1, episode 1). His preference for the city over the country makes Raylan more of an urban cowboy than a Western one. Raylan serves as the representation of the new southern man. One who is more comfortable in the urban environment than the rural, preferring to distance himself from the historical legacy of poverty, sexism, and racism that have come to define the Old South.

A Troubled Past

Raylan's disdain for the Old South, as represented by Harlan County, is one of the focal points of the series. The advantage of television over film is that it allows more time to fully delve into the backstories of the characters. One of the central elements early episodes of the series revolve around is attempting to explain why Raylan has such contempt for the place he grew up. Why does Raylan hate the Old South? Even though his father Arlo does not appear in the series until episode five of season one, the audience is made well aware of the tension between father and son before then. Whenever Raylan ventures into Harlan in early episodes of the series, locals continually ask him if he has been by to see his father, and he continually tells them he has not. In episode five, when he does finally go to see his father, it is only because

Arlo has been arrested and needs Raylan to bail him out. We soon learn this is not the first time that Arlo has been arrested and that he makes his leaving as a con man, petty thief, and drug trafficker. Arlo is the personification of all the negative qualities of the Old South. In short, Arlo is the embodiment of the stereotype of the southern good old boy. He is poor, uneducated, frequently drunk, and dishonest.

Raylan goes out of his way to avoid his father whenever possible, and for good reason. Arlo not only fails to protect Raylan when given the chance, he repeatedly puts him in harm's way. In the final episodes of the first season, Arlo attempts to turn Raylan over to crime boss Bo Crowder in order to save himself, knowing full well that Bo intends to kill Raylan. In season three, the deterioration of their relations has reached a point that Arlo is even willing to murder his own son. In the final episode of the season, Arlo shoots a state trooper believing him to be Raylan. Not surprisingly, Raylan has little love for his father, as demonstrated by him shooting Arlo in the leg during season one and his indifference to Arlo's increasing mental deterioration from Alzheimer's. This is to say nothing of the fact of Raylan's choice to rebel against his outlaw father by choosing to become a marshal.

We are told little of about Raylan's mother Frances Givens, other than that she died when he was still a boy. Adding to the family tension is that fact that after Frances's death, Arlo married her sister Helen. Raylan was raised by his outlaw father and step-mother/aunt. Although, it should be noted that Raylan does appear to love Helen and credits her with giving him the money and opportunity to escape Harlan. He is deeply troubled by her murder in later episodes of the series and blames Arlo for her death. Helen's murder further entrenches his hatred of Harlan, and all that it represents.

Given his family history and the seemingly inescapable poverty of Harlan, it is not hard to understand Raylan's disdain for the place. He also seems to have a sordid history with many of the residents of Harlan. For example, we learn that during a youth baseball game, he crippled his future nemesis Dickie Crowder by breaking his leg with a baseball bat. He also worked in the coal mines with his future "frenemy" Boyd Crowder, and both men where almost killed in a mining accident. Other characters in the series also seem to have problems with Raylan that are attributed to some past deed or a general disliking of his status as an officer of the law. His decision to join the Marshal Service is interpreted by many of the characters as a betrayal of the community. This, coupled with his decision to flee Harlan for the big city, reinforces the belief in residents of Harlan that he is no longer fully one of them. In other words, Raylan is the new urbanized South and they fight against him in hopes of preserving the old rural South.

A Father and a Boss

While Wyatt Earp did not have to answer to anyone for his actions, Raylan does. When he angers his supervisors in Miami, Raylan is forced to return to Kentucky and answer to Chief Art Mullen. Their relationship is one of supervisor and supervisee, but also that of father and son. It is not uncommon for the modern cowboy lawman to have a boss, as in the cases of the likes of Clint Eastwood's Dirty Harry and Bruce Willis's John McClane in the *Die Hard* series, but the authority figures they encounter are adversarial in nature and often hinder their success. Chief Mullen works to get Raylan out of trouble, often defending him to the U.S. attorney's office and the FBI. He also offers him fatherly advice on everything from how to control his temper to what it is like to be a father. In contrast, Raylan's real farther Arlo is a poor, uneducated, "backwoods" criminal who cannot even be trusted to love his son. Art, on the other hand, is an educated, decorated officer of the law who goes out of his way to protect Raylan, even saving his life at the end of season two. Staring down the barrel of corrupt sheriff Doyle Bennett's gun, Raylan is seconds away from dying when Chief Mullen arrives with the cavalry. Arlo frequently places Raylan in harm's way only to have Art rescue him from it. In one telling scene, Raylan and Art are on stake out sitting in a car together. Art is offering Raylan advice about his life, when Raylan interrupts saying, "Art, I've already got a daddy." Chief Mullen responds, "I've met your daddy." Raylan then concedes, "Fair enough. Continue" (Season 3, episode 11). Art serves as Raylan's surrogate father and represents the New South we are told to love. Here we see Raylan explicitly rejecting his old father and the Old South, for a new father and a new South.

Shotguns, Moonshine and Southern Feminism

In many ways *Justified* reinforces the negative stereotypes that have come to represent the Old South. This is important because as White (1987) reminds us narratives are never neutral. He explains that the production of narratives "entails ontological and epistemic choices with distinct ideological and even specifically political implications" (pp. ix-xi). Consequently, *Justified*'s narrative can be analyzed in relation to larger cultural myths. Rowland (1990) explained one essential function of myth is to "symbolically solve the problem facing the society, provide justification for a social structure, or deal with a psychological crisis" (p. 103). In this way the Southern works to reinforce negative stereotypes about the South and, in so doing, provides justification for the larger culture's condemnation the Old South. *Justified* depicts the South as intolerant, ignorant, uneducated, poor, and unsophisticated.

However, the series does challenge one important aspect of traditional mythology of the Old South: the depiction of the Southern Belle. The women of the show do not exemplify the qualities of the meek and modest Southern Belle. Instead, they show themselves to be powerful, strong, determined, and above all else, resourceful. The female characters of the Southern also fail to fit into the Frontier Myth's black and white categories, creating a false dichotomy of female characters being either "good girls" or "bad girls." The women in of the Southern are more complex and nuanced. The most prominent of these characters are Ava Crowder, Winona Hawkins, U.S. Marshal Rachel Brooks, and season two arch villain Mags Bennett. Each of these women rejects both the Myth of the Southern Belle and the classification of either being "good girl" or "bad girl" in their own unique ways. They all possess both good and bad traits and exist somewhere in the gray between black and white.

Of all the female characters in the series, the character of Ava Crowder most closely resembles the prototypical "bad girl." She works in bar, runs a prostitution ring, and although she is Raylan's girlfriend in season one, in later seasons, becomes the girlfriend of criminal mastermind Boyd Crowder. Ava is also seen frequently cooking and taking care of the men in her life. However, Ava rejects many of the limiting aspects of this myth. She is far from helpless. We learn in the first episode of the series that her husband Bowman Crowder was abusive towards her. While the typical Southern Belle or female character in a Western would likely have take this abuse passively, Ava responds by shooting her husband while he is eating his dinner. Later, Raylan is concerned that the Crowder family will take revenge on her for the killing of Bowman and that she ought to allow him to protect her. She responds by telling him, "I'm a big girl, Raylan. I've been taking care of myself long before you rode in to town on your white horse" (Season 1, episode 11). She defends herself throughout the series with everything from a shotgun to a frying pan.

In contrast to Ava, who most closely resembles the "bad girl," the character of Winona Hawkins, Raylon's ex-wife, most closely fits the characteristics of the "good girl." Unlike Ava, Winona is opposed to violence and attempts to extricate Raylan from violent situations. Like the traditional good girl, she is representative of civilization. Ava is not from Harlan and resides in the more urban city of Lexington. While she does have a southern accent, it is less noticeable than the more rural characters. Most the characters in the show work in blue-collar jobs, but Winona works as a court reporter. She dresses in business clothes that distinguish her from the residents of Harlan. She is also depicted as physically weak and dependent on Raylan to save her.

Yet, there is a key aspect of the traditional good girl narrative Winona does not conform to—she is not dependent on men for her happiness. In the first episode of the series we learn that Winona is Raylan's ex-wife who left him years before. Later, in the first season, Winona divorces her second husband Gary Hawkins, and reconciles with Raylan becoming pregnant with his child. However, unable to accept the violence present in Raylan's life, and unable to change him, she chooses to leave him again in season three. Winona possesses her own sense of identity and is not limited or defined by the men in her life.

U.S. Marshal Rachel Brooks, played by African American actress Erica Tazel, is another character who does not fit into any of the stereotypical categories offered by either the Myth of the Frontier or the traditional archetypes Southern mythology. The notion of either an African American or female officer of the law does not fit with the traditional Frontier Myth, and the notion of a female African American U.S. Marshal in the South is truly ground breaking. While narratives can reinforce mythic tropes they can also serve to redefine them. Moreover, mythic narratives have the power to subvert and reinvent tired genres (Cochran & Edwards, 2008). The character of Rachel Brooks is particularly important when one considers evidence exists that depictions of African American women in popular culture, influence dominate group members' judgments and interaction with African American women in real life situations (Brown-Givens & Monahan, 2005). Two prominent archetypes about southern African American women persist in popular culture, the jezebel and the mammy (Brown-Givens & Monahan, 2005; Kelley-Romano, 2008; Larson, 1994).

Both the jezebel and mammy archetypes developed out of slavery, and continue to define African Americans in negative and limiting ways. The jezebel archetype portrays African American women as having uncontrollable sexual appetites and as the seducers of white men. While the mammy archetype depicts African American as subservient care givers who are often depicted having or taking care of children (Kelley-Romano, 2008; Larson, 1994). Marshal Brooks fails to fall victim to either of these stereotypes. Unlike, Ava and Winona, Marshal Brooks has no love interest in the series, and is never shown as a sex symbol or as a mother or caregiver. She is neither reliant on, nor subservient to, her male counterparts in the Marshal Service. Unlike the Southern Belle she does not need a man to get her out of trouble, and in fact, is usually seen coming to the aid of Raylan. While Raylan is emotional and often goes into situations half-cocked, Rachel is always calm, cool, and calculated. A fact recognized by Chief Art Mullen when he stated, "She's the best Marshal I've got." An incredulous Raylan replied, "You realize I'm sitting right here?" Chief

Mullen calmly responded, "I do" (Season 2, episode 4). No one ever told Wyatt Earp, Matt Dillon, or any of John Wayne's characters that they were second best. Brooks is both a women and a Southern African American, meaning that the depiction of her as superior to her white male counterpart is especially meaningful.

Of all the characters in the series, perhaps none is more unique or interesting than Mags Bennett. There is no female character in the traditional Frontier Myth that she is comparable with, and to compare her to the Southern Belle is laughable. Mags is clearly not a good person, but she does not fit the model of the saloon girl either. It is hard to believe that anyone would refer to the 60-year-old Mags as a girl. She is old, overweight, and plain in appearance. While Ava and Winona are slender, attractive, and feminine; Mags is none of those things. She does not appear in any way to be feminine, forsaking makeup and wearing pants held up with a tool belt. Actress Margo Martindale portrayed Mags Bennett and described the character like this: "Mags Bennett didn't care that she was fat. I care that I'm fat, but I could let that part of it go. I didn't wear [any] makeup except for the spots on my face. My hair had to be the worst it's ever been; I just made it as bad as it could be. There was great freedom in that" (Lacob, 2011). Mags did not subscribe to any of the social conventions or confines of the traditional Southern Belle. She was the head of the fearsome Bennett family and Raylan's chief adversary in season two. Frontier lawmen are supposed to feud with other men, not female senior citizens.

The closest Southern archetype Mags comes to embodying is that of the matriarch. However, the portrayal of Mags differs from the traditional matriarch in key ways. Like the traditional matriarch Mags is head of her family and she is without a man in her life. It is briefly mentioned that her husband died years ago, leaving behind her and her three sons. Mags is not controlled by men or dependent upon them; instead her sons are controlled by and dependent on her. However, as Larson (1994) noted the traditional Southern matriarch is African American often depicted as domineering, but also nurturing. Mags is Caucasian and while she is domineering she is far from nurturing. Perhaps the most defining scene of the series for Mags involved her disciplining her slow-witted son Coover. In the scene, she discovered that he was going behind her back to participate in a scam that had inadvertently endangered the family's marijuana growing and dealing business. Mag's justice comes in the form of a ball peen hammer, which she uses to break Coover's hand. Out of love, she tells him that she has decided to not hurt his shooting hand, but if he crosses her again, she will break that one, too. Not breaking both of her son's hands is as close to nurturing as Mags gets. Larson also explained that the Southern matriarch is supposed to possess a morality that makes her superior to men. Mags is certainly more intelligent than most of the men she encounters but she was also a murderer, drug dealer, and con artist. Finally, she defies the matriarch archetype in another key way. According to Smith and Wilson (2004) "Several modern American films (*Steel Magnolias, Fried Green Tomatoes, Divine Secrets of the Ya-Ya Sisterhood*) have explored this Southern matriarchal legacy as a passing of cultural values from woman to woman, emphasizing a construction of the feminine sphere as quite distinct from the world of men" (Smith & Wilson, 2004, p. 190). Mags possesses none of these traditional attributes and values of Southern women and her sphere of influence is over her masculine sons. Mags does befriend a young girl Loretta, whose father she killed, but Loretta is taken from her by the police before Mags can fully bond with her. Although, it is clear that Mags sees Loretta as the daughter she never had and gives her special privileges not afforded to her sons, one must remember that she murdered Loretta's father and repeatedly lied to her about his whereabouts.

In addition to being weak and dependent on men, the Southern Belle and women of the traditional Frontier Myth are also unintelligent and emotional. When dramatic events occur, they fall to pieces and act irrationally. The men in these stories either end up having to comfort them, in the case of the good girl, or slap some sense into them, in the case of the bad girl. Mags, on the other hand, is unemotional and logical. What she lacked in formal education, she more than made up for with her cunning and street smarts (since Harlan County does not have many paved roads, we might in this case call them country smarts). She is one the most powerful people in the area, and in addition to her country store, she also operates a large business dealing marijuana. Mags also made her own moonshine called "apple pie" which is sometimes laced with a deadly poison. Mags would share some apple pie with her victims, then watch as they realized they had been poisoned. She explained to Loretta's father, Walt McCready, "It [the poison] was already in the glass, not in the jar." Still, she is not entirely cold hearted telling the poisoned man that dying will allow him to be with his deceased wife and that he will "get to know the mystery" (Season 2, episode 1). In the finale of season two, she even out wits Raylan. Two of Mags' sons have been killed and she has been shot in the leg. She invites Raylan to have a glass of apple pie with her, and for a moment, we are led to believe that she has poised him Mags reveals that this time, she took the poisoned glass for herself and that now she gets "to see her sons" and gets "to know the mystery" (Season 2, episode 13).

The series also subverts the Myth of the Southern Belle in another key way. In the traditional telling of the myth, the Southern Belle is attacked by

African American men and needs to be protected by the white Southern gentlemen. However, in *Justified*, just the opposite is true. In Harlan County, most of the African Americans live in Nobles Holler, an isolated area accessible by only one bridge. Free African Americans were driven to Nobles Holler generations ago, as its isolated location makes it easily defensible from attack from white supremacists and members of the KKK. It also turns out that Nobles Holler is the place where white women go when they need protection from their abusive husbands. The audience learns that for decades white women seeking refuge would flee to Nobles Holler because it was the only place they would be safe. Their husbands were either too afraid to venture across the bridge or would be turned back by the Holler's male residents if they did attempt to across. We learn that Raylan's mother once sought shelter here, as did Ava Crowder. Nobles Holler is controlled by Ellstin Limehouse, who appears to be every bit as intelligent as other characters in show. We learn in season three that Nobles Holler is not only a safe haven for abused women, but also serves as a sort of rural bank. Even the tough as nails Mags Bennett seeks out Limehouse to protect her money. Upon her death Limehouse safely delivers her fortune, nearly three million dollars, to the young child Loretta. The notion that African American men are the true protectors of Southern white women is subversive to the traditional mythology of the Old South. It appears that white women of Harlan County trust the African American men of Nobles Holler with both their personal and financial safety.

Conclusion

Justified has many of the elements of the traditional Western. The show features outlaws, untamed wilderness, gunfights, and a cowboy lawman hero. On the surface, *Justified* appears to be a modern telling of the Frontier Myth, but critical elements of the traditional myth have been subverted and altered, creating the new narrative of the Southern. In the traditional telling of the Frontier Myth, the cowboy comes from the rural setting into the city. Although he succeeds at vanquishing the villain from the city, he cannot remain there and must return to the untamed Western frontier. Raylan Givens certainly dresses and looks the part of the cowboy and often acts it too, but his relationship with the city and frontier is the opposite of the Western cowboy. Givens prefers the city to the country, and although his work often takes him into the rural landscape of Harlan County, he does not stay there. He retreats back the city and to civilization whenever possible.

While much of the depiction of the Old South in the series is negative, there are aspects of it that can be seen as positive. Specifically, *Justified* rejects the Myth of the Southern Belle and the confines of the "good girl" and "bad girl" in favor a more nuanced and resourceful depiction of Southern women. In particular, the character of Mags Bennett demonstrates the power of the matriarch in Southern culture. She commanded her sons and was feared and respected by the residents of Harlan County. Ava Crowder may possess the beauty and sweet accent of Southern Belle, but she possesses a strength and power not found in the likes of Blanche DuBois. If Blanche had possessed Ava's penchant for dealing with her problems with a shotgun, then *A Streetcar Named Desire* would have had a very different ending. The narrative of the Southern rejects the Myth of the Southern Belle and offers a picture of Southern feminism more in line with the historical role of women in Southern history. *Justified*'s narrative also rejects the idea that African American men are threats to female Southern virtue and instead shows them as its protectors. The Southern narrative as told through the television series critiques the mythology of the Old South, and in doing so, empowers the previously marginalized groups of women and African American men.

The tension that drives the Southern is not a tension between individualism and community, rather it a tension between traditional Southern culture and the larger American culture. Myths evolve as the result of changing cultural conditions, and in so doing, reveal aspects of our national psyche that may otherwise be overlooked. Through the character of Raylan Givens, *Justified* presents us with the personification of the New South, and through the criminals of Harlan County, reflects the personification of the Old South. The war between the Old South and the New takes place every week during the series. Although Raylan inevitably wins his gunfights and battles with individual criminals, he can never fully control Harlan County. Nor can he completely break from his roots and escape the pull the Old South has over him. For all his talk of wanting to leave Kentucky, he is never able to do it. And while his decision to become a Marshal has alienated him from his community, he is still more accepted there than his Northern colleagues. Other members of law enforcement in the show frequently complain about being unable to connect to or be accepted by the residents of Harlan and thus are forced to rely on Raylan when they need to obtain information. In many ways, Raylan is stuck in a Southern purgatory pulled between Old and New South. Raylan's struggle is emblematic of a larger struggle taking place in the contemporary South. At the same time, the forces behind the emergence of the New South cannot fully dispense with the heritage and tradition of the Old South. Like Raylan, the larger American culture may wish to escape the heritage and past of the South, but it can never truly divorce itself from it.

The Myth of the Frontier has evolved over time to create a new myth, which I refer to as the Southern. More investigation ought to be done into the emergence of the Southern in the larger American culture. America appears increasingly ill at ease with the legacy of the Confederacy and history of the Old South. New reality television shows have even developed which do nothing more than mock Southern people for being unintelligent and uncivilized. Shows like *My Big Redneck Wedding, My Big Redneck Vacation,* and *Redneck Island* ask us to laugh at rather than with the South. *Redneck Island* is a take off of the popular show *Survivor,* and puts contestant in situations that only a redneck would face. For example, on the premier episode of the show, contestants use duct tape to remove the back hair off one of their fellow participants. The term "redneck" as used in these shows can be seen as being synonymous with the more derisive terms hick, yokel, or idiot. The derision with which Southern culture is increasingly viewed is noteworthy, and further explanation of the causes, manifestations, and future of this phenomenon is warranted.

References

Brown-Givens, S. M., and Monahan, J. L. (2005). Priming mammies, jezebels, and other controlling images: An examination of the influence of mediated stereotypes on perceptions of an African American woman. *Mediated Psychology* 7, 87–106.

Caparros-Lera, J. M., and Alegre, S. (1996). Cinematic contextual history of *High Noon* (1952, dir. Fred Zinnemann). *Film-Historia* 4, 37–61.

Cochran, T. R., & Edwards, J. A. (2008). *Buffy the vampire slayer* and the quest story: Revising the hero, reshaping the myth. In D. Whitt & J. Perlich (eds.), *Sith, slayers, stargates, & cyborgs* (pp. 145–169). New York: Peter Lang.

Harter, L. M. (2004). Masculinity(s), the agrarian Frontier Myth, and cooperative ways of organizing: Contradictions and tensions in the experience and the enactment of democracy. *Journal of Applied Communication Research* 32, 89–118.

Heyse, A. (2010). Women's rhetorical authority and collective memory: The United Daughters of the Confederacy remember the South. *Women & Language* 33, 31–53.

Hiscock, J. (2007, April 27). Quentin Tarantino: I'm proud of my flop, *The Telegraph.* Retrieved from http://www.telegraph.co.uk/culture/film/starsandstories/3664742/Quentin-Tarantino-Im-proud-of-my-flop.html.

hooks, b. (2000). *Feminist theory: From margin to center* (2d ed.). Cambridge, MA: Sound End Press.

Hutson, C. K. (1993). Cotton pickin', hillbillies and rednecks: An analysis of black oak Arkansas and the perpetual stereotyping of the rural South. *Poplaur Music and Society* 17, 47–62.

Jansson, D. R. (2003). American national identity and progress of the New South in *National Geographic* magazine. *Geographical Review* 93, 350–369.

Joyner, N. (1974). The myth of the matriarch in Andrew Lytle's fiction. *The Southern Literary Journal* 7, 67–77.

Kelley-Romano, S. (2008). Makin' whoopi: Race, gender, and the Starship *Enterprise*. In D. Whitt & J. Perlich (eds.), *Sith, slayers, stargates, & cyborgs* (pp. 170–189). New York: Peter Lang.

Kraft, A. (2012, August 5). The good ole' boy portfolio. Retrieved September 23, 2012, from http://beta.fool.com/leglamp/2012/08/05/the-good-ole-boy-portfolio/8589/.
Lacob, J. (2011). Emmy's stealth frontrunner. Retrieved June 17, 2012, from http://www.thedailybeast.com/articles/2011/08/24/margo-martindale-interview-on-justified-emmys-mags-bennett-more.html.
Larson, S. G. (1994). Black women on *All My Children*. *Journal of Popular Film & Television* 22, 44–48.
Loy, P. R. (2001). *Westerns and American culture, 1930–1955*. Jefferson, NC: McFarland.
McLure, H. (2000). The wild, wild web: The mythic American West and the electronic frontier. *The Western Historical Quarterly* 31, 457–476.
Mixon, W. (1989). New South myth. In C. R. Wilson and W. Ferris (eds.), *Encylopedia of southern culture*. Baton Rouge: Louisiana State University Press.
Rowland, R. C. (1990). On mythic criticism. *Communication Studies* 41, 101–116. doi: 10.1080/10510979009368293.
Rushing, J. H. (1983). The rhetoric of the American western myth. *Communication Monographs* 50, 14.
Rushing, J. H. (1986). Mythic evolution of "The New Frontier" in mass mediated rhetoric. *Critical Studies in Mass Communication* 3(3), 265.
Rushing, J. H. (1989). Evolution of "The New Frontier" in *Alien* and *Aliens*: Patriarchal co-optation of the feminine archetype. *Quarterly Journal of Speech* 76, 1–24.
Smith, G. M., and Wilson, P. (2004). Country cookin' and cross-dressin': Television, southern white masculinities, and heirarchies of cultural taste. *Television & New Media* 5, 175–196.
Tindall, G. B. (1989). Mythology: A new frontier in southern history. In P. Gerster & N. Cords (eds.), *Myth and southern history: The new south* (2d ed.). Champaign: University of llinois Press.
White, H. (1987). *The content of the form: Narrative discourse and historical representation*. Baltimore: Johns Hopkins University Press.

PART 2
RIGHT OR LEFT OF CENTER

The Mythology of Suffering and Redemption in the Discourse of Al Qaeda

JASON A. EDWARDS

Since the attacks of September 11, 2001, a cottage industry has developed of scholars and pundits who attempt to explain the motives of terrorist groups like Al Qaeda (see Habeck, 2007; Pape, 2006; Stern, 2004). Most of these accounts are pejorative in nature. They assail Islam as a backwards and uncivilized faith, where violence is its fundamental tenet (for examples see Bawer, 2007; Benjamin and Simon, 2003; Gabriel, 2002, 2007; Phares, 2008; Pipes, 2003; Spencer, 2005, 2007). In the field of communication studies, the scholarship conducted has been from the angle of understanding how the President of the United States and the press portray Muslims, instead of studying groups like Hamas, Hezbollah, and Al Qaeda and their accompanying motives (for exceptions see Cronick, 2002; Mater, 2008; Rowland and Theye, 2008; Winch, 2005).

This lack of scholarship could be for a variety of reasons including: language and cultural barriers, unfamiliarity with how to study such groups, and/or disinterest on the part of scholars. However, one study by Rowland and Theye (2008) has laid some important groundwork. These authors argue that the key to understanding terrorist motives is to analyze their discourse, what they call the "symbolic DNA of terrorism" (p. 53). This symbolic DNA is structured, at its core, by mythic narratives and these authors proceeded to chronicle the use of specific mythic themes. Kluver (1997) noted it is the job of the scholarly critic to define the mythic narrative(s) embedded in the discourse of rhetors and nations, explaining the rhetorical motivations for their actions. In this chapter, I seek to build upon the work of Rowland and Theye (as well as others), while taking up Kluver's charge of the critic, by providing an account and analysis of the themes embedded within the discourse of Islamist groups like Al Qaeda. Fundamentally, I argue Islamist groups, like Al Qaeda, use mythic themes, specifically suffering and redemption, to justify terrorist violence, inspire and motivate their supporters, and explain their actions and purposes to global audiences. These mythic themes are accompanied by various rhetorical tactics in disseminating their message to the larger world. Through this analysis, I try to "make sense" of Islamist argumentation, which affords greater understanding and the possibility to create blueprints in countering such discourse.

In order to examine this argument I begin by offering a theoretical road map of myth and public discourse. I then explore a large sampling of the rhetoric of Osama bin Laden—his fatwas and public statements made since the 1990s—to deconstruct and analyze his use of the suffering and redemption myth. Prior to his death and even after, bin Laden's discourse is/was the most visible and considered to be the most central of Islamist leaders, at least in terms of transnational movements. His rhetoric tapped into fundamental discontent many Muslims have toward a variety of communities, both external and internal to Islam. Because his rhetoric was the most visible of all Islamist leaders and responded to fundamental feelings of Muslim discontent his rhetoric is the ideal case study to interrogate. That centrality makes his rhetoric the ideal case study to interrogate. Finally, I draw conclusions from this analysis.

A Theoretical Overview of Myth, Suffering and Redemption

Myth is a common form of discourse. The work of comparative mythologist Joseph Campbell (see 1949) demonstrates that myths are apart of all cultures, peoples, and nations. At their most basic, myths are narratives, but not all narratives are myths. For example, a narrative of the happenings of one's day is not mythic because it does not contain coherent plotlines filled with heroes, villains, and sidekicks; and it does not articulate a society's beliefs, dilemmas, and values (Rushing and Frentz, 2005). Myths offer a way to frame the reality of a society's situation as seen by a person, group of persons, organization, or nation. Contained within these narratives are lessons and values that appear as deep truths to participants of a particular culture.

Myths perform a variety of functions, two of which are important to this study. First, myths help us make sense of the world. They allow people to see their place in the social order of the universe (Nimmo and Combs, 1980). This function becomes most apparent when some form of disorder or the belief of disorder befalls a community. All individuals and communities are struck by some sense of chaos in their lifetimes. Disorder can come in the wake of a natural disaster, an attack by another nation, an illness, a downturn in the economy, or other disturbances to the regularity of life. From this vantage point, the world looks too complicated to grasp—too much information, too many countries, and too many factors to manage all at once. It is here that myths offer a sense of stability and structure. They provide a means of coping with the disturbances around us. Myths work to clarify challenges that are a threat to our universe, opportunities that may pose a threat to our success, and the limitations within which we must work to accomplish an objective. For example, after the collapse of the Soviet Union many states had to rebuild their sense of nationalist identity to create a modern state. Around 1991 political leaders within the Ukraine, as it attempted to form a new government, used the myth of the Cossack in creating this national identity. The Cossacks were renowned for their heroic endeavors to drive out their enemies and bring renewed freedom to their peoples. The time of the Cossack is often viewed as a golden age within Ukrainian history. Ukrainian political leaders asserted they were carrying on the traditions of the Cossacks in the government that was being formed. The historic legacy of these venerated heroes would live on, just in a different context, for the 20th century. Connecting the present to the past gave Ukrainian leaders a semblance of legitimacy. They were connecting Ukrainians to their storied past, which would serve as a buffer to the political, cultural, and social chaos occurring within other former Soviet states.

Second, myths perform an identity function. Myths offer people a worldview that helps them see the world as a whole instead of in pieces (Roy and Rowland, 2003). This worldview generates a strong sense of identification. In this sense, myths provide the people of a community with a form of "social glue" (Nimmo and Combs, 1980, p. 13). Myths work to hold a group together by providing the basis for peoples of diverse backgrounds to find common ground with each other. This common ground defines who "we" were, are, and will be (Kluver, 1997; Starr, 1973). Often a particular myth can unite a small or larger group around a common ideal, one that can be expanded further if the group accepts a specific casting of the myth. For instance, the myth of divine election holds that a community, such as the United States with its belief in exceptionalism, collectively believes it has an exclusive place within the overall order of communities. This community is special or "chosen" and destined for a unique mission that will demonstrate its exceptional nature over other communities (Cauthen, 1997, 2004). The sense of chosenness, within this mythic narrative, serves to provide individuals and communities a sense of identity and place.

A type of myth that encapsulates both of these functions is a myth of suffering and redemption. George Schopflin (1997) asserted that through this myth a "nation by reason of its particularly sorrowful history, is undergoing or has undergone a process of expatiating its sins and will be redeemed or, indeed, may itself redeem the world" (p. 29). Myths of suffering and redemption tell a story of a nation that is powerless to stem its suffering, but that it will one day be compensated for this powerlessness through some form of redemptive act, typically in heaven. This type of myth is common amongst nations within Central and Eastern Europe. For example, a central mythic narrative for the Serbian nation centers on the Battle of Kosovo in 1389.

According to legend, Serbia's leader Prince Knez Lazar was visited by the Archangel Gabriel on the eve of the battle. Gabriel had come with a message from God and gave Lazar a choice. Lazar could choose to defeat the Ottomans in battle and create an earthly kingdom for Serbians. However, he could also choose to lose the battle, subjugating Serbs to Ottoman rule, but guaranteeing Serbs forever had an exalted place in heaven. Ultimately, Lazar chose a heavenly kingdom over an earthly one. Although Serbs "suffered" five hundred years of Ottoman rule, Lazar's choice guarantees Serbians will be redeemed in the afterlife and he is viewed as a national hero (see Beider, 2002; Doder and Branson, 1997; Kaplan, 1996). Over the years, this myth has been recast by other Serbian leaders to justify their political actions. Slobodan Milosevic was one of the most recent leaders to use it as he ascended to the presidency in the Serbian republic in 1989 (Edwards, 2003). Milosevic actively wrapped himself in the memory of Knez Lazar. He asserted Serbians could find an earthly redemption through his leadership. Milosevic pledged if Serbians could unify they could overcome the ever-growing cracks that were apparent in Yugoslavia's union. Serbia would emerge a victor and throw off the shackles of subjugation once and for all.

Similarly, Osama bin Laden's rhetoric told the story of Islam's suffering and reaches far back into history. However, the increase of globalization in the post–Cold War world has in many respects fragmented Islamic communities. The unity of a transnational movement of Islam is made more difficult and perpetuates Muslim suffering that bin Laden describes. Concomitantly, the benefits of globalization—transnational media, increased interdependence and integration, and social networks—provides the opportunity for the Islamic community to unite like never before. Bin Laden's discourse holds the key to how Muslims can achieve redemption on earth, not just in heaven.

Al Qaeda's Mythic Narrative of Suffering and Redemption

Up until his death in 2011, Osama bin Laden issued fatwas, gave interviews, and presented speeches to a variety of audiences. Other Al Qaeda leaders have since taken up the mantle of leadership. When bin Laden spoke he asserted it was on behalf of the *ummah*, the true Islamic community. For bin Laden, Islam was a "nation" united by faith. Territorial borders marking each nation-state in the Muslim world were boundaries imposed by former colonial powers and reinforced by tyrannical governments. What made a "true" member of his nation was his/her adherence to what the Al Qaeda leader believed were the true tenets of Islam (a topic discussed later in this chapter). Unfortunately, there were forces that did not allow Islam to unite as one *ummah*. Rather, bin Laden claimed Muslims suffer because of a lack of unity imposed upon them by forces opposed to Al Qaeda's leader. As he pointed out in his 1996 fatwa, "the people of Islam had suffered from aggression, iniquity, and injustice imposed on them by the Zionist-Crusaders alliance and their collaborators" (5). This short passage revealed the source of all of Islam's suffering: the external "Zionist-Crusaders alliance" enemy, consisting of Israel, the United States, and the West in general and the internal enemy of "collaborators" that manifest from a number of sources. Over the next few pages, I outline and analyze how bin Laden described and depicted these sources of suffering.

External Enemies: The United States, Israel and the West

A close reading of bin Laden's discourse revealed he encased Islam's suffering in a rhetorical strategy of scapegoating. Recall myths provide a sense of order and identification for the world around us. According to language theorist Kenneth Burke (1961) human beings create hierarchical order through language. We produce symbolic universes naturally and do so to make sense of who we are and what the world is like around us. Inevitably, however, those orders will be violated. Burke termed these violations as "guilt." Guilt is an undesirable state of affairs and needs to be extricated immediately. One of the means to rid one's symbolic universe of guilt is through victimage, more commonly referred to as scapegoating. Scapegoating involves creating an "us versus them" mentality where rhetors blame others for the corruption and inadequacy of modern life, a violation of their universes (Carter, 1996; Roy, 2004). Keen (1986) argued that "we scapegoat and create absolute enemies, not because we are intrinsically cruel, but because focusing our anger on an outside target, striking at strangers, brings our tribe or nation together" (p. 27). People scapegoat because it supplies them with a channel to direct their anger, uniting a certain group so they can act against any force that may cause it harm. In this sense, scapegoating is a projection tool. This projection is what Burke (1973) calls a curative device. It is curative in the sense that a rhetor chronicles, diagnoses, and projects the ills of the nation upon the enemy. Metaphorically speaking, the rhetor who scapegoats is a "doctor" describing "medicine" to his community that will restore it back to health. That "doctor" is redeeming and restoring order to the symbolic universe of that patient. Osama bin Laden was, proverbially speaking, a "doctor" of Islam. His universe was not one particular nation-state, but all of Islam. His rhetoric "diagnosed" what he believed were the causes of the *ummah*'s illnesses and the results that impede the unity of Islamic world.

For this Islamic "doctor," the primary cause of Muslim pain was a cabal of Western enemies that included Israel and the West—primarily Western European nations and most importantly, the United States. A typical example of bin Laden's depiction of Islam's external enemy can be found in a 1997 interview with CNN. In that interview, bin Laden argued a holy war against the United States was necessary because

> the U.S. government is unjust, criminal, and tyrannical. It has committed acts that are extremely unjust, hideous and criminal whether directly or through its support of the Israeli occupation of the Prophet's Night Travel Land (Palestine). And we believe that the U.S. is directly responsible for those who were killed in Palestine, Lebanon, and Iraq.... It transgressed all bounds and behaved in a way not witnessed before by any power or any imperialist in the world [8].

For the Al Qaeda leader, America was *the* center of his holy war. The United States committed more "tyrannical" acts against Muslims than "any power" or "imperialist in the world." Putting the blame squarely on American shoulders for Islamic suffering offered Al Qaeda with a focus for its movement. Identification of a specific enemy allowed like-minded Muslim groups and individuals to rally to its banner. It offered "social glue" upon which a larger movement can be built. Unity was found in opposition to the enemy. The fact that a clear and centralized enemy was identified suggested bin Laden declared and fought his war with an end game in mind: defeating the United States and its proxies. By doing that, by driving the "Zionist-Crusader alliance" away from the Muslim world, bin Laden advocated his plan to arrest Muslim agony and the ultimate redemption of the Islamic world.

In his discourse, bin Laden advocated Muslim oppression did not begin with the United States. Rather, he maintained Muslims have been oppressed by external enemies for decades. According to the Al Qaeda leader's (2001) logic, there have been a series of events over the past one hundred years that on the surface look like isolated geo-political events, but really they are "links" in a chain to a "long series of crusader wars against the Islamic world" (40). The chain of events of which bin Laden spoke began "following World War I" where the "whole Islamic world fell under the crusader banner—under the British, French, and Italian governments.... Since then, and for more than 83 years, our brothers, sons, and sisters in Palestine have been badly tortured" (42–43). Here and throughout his discourse, bin Laden gave significant weight to the word "crusader." All of his enemies were painted with the broad "crusader" brush. His invocation of the word "crusader" linked his war with the West to the historical crusades of Christians—which were primarily under the banners of "British, French, and Italian governments"—and Muslims over the Holy Land. By tagging these current conflicts as a form of "crusade" bin Laden implied there was a seamless narrative within the history of Islam. Bin Laden's battle was merely another chapter in the long and violent history the Muslim world and the West had together. Moreover, his use of "crusader" implicitly suggested a similar outcome of the historical crusades. The historical Crusades lasting from the 11th to the 13th centuries, for the most part went badly for Christian warriors. The Holy Land remained under Muslim rule for hundreds of years. Similarly, bin Laden believed the fight in these new "crusader wars" would end with the same result: Muslims would drive out the "Zionist-Crusader alliance," regain the Holy Land, and achieve redemption denied to Islam for almost a century.

Redemption could be achieved by defeating Islam's most dangerous enemy, the United States. However, before Muslims could join his cause they must know and understand what kind of diabolical enemy they were fighting. To that end, bin Laden accused America and its allies of a litany of crimes against Islam and the world at large. According to the Al Qaeda leader, the United States had a "horrific and bloody history of murdering humans" (2007a, 18). For example, "in the Vietnam War" American leaders declared that to be a "necessary and crucial war" but the United States "murdered two million villagers" (2007a, 18). In 1982, the United States directly harmed the Islamic nation by permitting the "Israelis to invade Lebanon with the aid of the American sixth fleet" (2004, 4). Bin Laden described his memory of the attack including "moving scenes—blood, torn limbs, and dead women and children; ruined homes everywhere, and high rises being demolished on top of their residents; bombs raining down mercilessly on our homes" (2004, 4; see also 1996, 1997, 2000, 2002). With the end of the Cold War, the United States continued to wage war against Muslim nations. In 1991, the United States went to war with Iraq. The result of the first Gulf War, including the sanctions imposed upon

Iraq afterward, resulted in the deaths of over "600,000 Iraqi children due to lack of food and medicine" (1996, 95). After September 11, 2001, the United States waged war against Afghanistan and Iraq causing "fear, destruction, killing, hunger, illness, displacement, and more than a million orphans in Baghdad alone, not to mention hundreds of thousands of widows" (2007a, 15).

Not only did America commit violent acts against the Muslim world, but it openly colluded with other allies in an international struggle against Islam. For example, bin Laden argued America's ally the "Russian bear" "annihilated the Chechen people in their entirety and forced them to flee to the mountains where they were assaulted by the snow and poverty and diseases (2001, 49). In Bosnia, "Europe" and the "United Nations" did nothing as "our brothers have been killed, our women have been raped, and our children have been massacred" (2001, 52). In Kashmir, Muslims have been "subjected to the worse forms of torture for over 50 years. They have been massacred, killed, and raped" continually by the West (2001, 59). Indonesia has been divided by the "crusader Australian forces" where they separated "East Timor which is part of the Muslim world" (2001, 69). In recent years, bin Laden (2009, 2) accused the "NATO alliance" of "deputizing Ethiopia" to attack Somalia, vanquishing Islamist fighters, and replacing them with a government that was friendly to America. Ultimately, bin Laden maintained the Muslim world was

> facing a universal Crusade.... There is Somalia on the southwestern wing, and the Crusaders have invaded land, air, and sea. From the direction of the west, there is another Crusader march, this one against the Sudan and advancing from Darfur.... In the north, in the blessed Aqsa Mosque, there are Zionist armies for over 60 years, and Crusader ships facing Gaza, and other Crusader armies in the south of Lebanon. And in the east, there is a Crusader invasion led by America against Afghanistan, and another against Iraq, in addition to the military bases spread throughout our countries [2009, 2–3].

The reader should take note of two items that demonstrate, at least according to bin Laden, the extent of Muslim suffering. Initially, notice the expanse of the "Crusader march" touches three different continents and nearly every corner of the Muslim world. Specifically, "the Crusader invasion led by America" was being fought in: Afghanistan, Bosnia, Chechnya, Gaza, Indonesia, Iraq, Lebanon, Palestine, Somalia, and Sudan. Naming these specific theatres of war suggested the expanse of the assault means that there is no escape for any Muslim. Islam was under siege from all directions. According to bin Laden, these battlegrounds were evidence of a "universal crusade" by the West against Islam. It provided motive for bin Laden's followers and all true Muslims to recognize the suffering caused by the West, arrest it, and redeem the *ummah* before it was overcome by invasion.

Additionally, note how bin Laden described the crimes committed by the United States and their Western proxies against Islam. Americans contributed or caused Muslims to be "annihilated," "assaulted," "killed," "raped," "massacred," and "tortured." Because of America's actions, Muslims had "bombs rained down" upon their houses; been "forced to flee," into the mountains where they faced "poverty" and "disease; "600,000 Iraqi children" have been killed, over a "million" people displaced and "hundreds of thousands of widows" were created from America's actions. The United States and its allies cause nothing but "fear, destruction, killing, hunger, illness, and displacement." Plainly, these words described countless hardship imposed by the West upon the *ummah*. But bin Laden's rhetoric had a deeper logic to it. His discourse connoted images of a barbaric, cruel, and heartless people who have no regard for human life. So much so that if people found even small kernels of truth within his rhetoric then his message was: one cannot be a true Muslim and at the same time identify and align oneself with the Zionist-Crusader alliance. If one supported the United States and its allies, then that person tacitly supported the "Crusader invasion led by America." By implication that person was just as guilty as the West and cannot consider him/herself to be a "true" Muslim. Any identification with the Crusaders extended the suffering of the people of Islam. Consequently, that person was an enemy of the true faith and must be expunged from the Islamic universe, lest that tacit compliance cause more Islamic agony. In the next few pages, I outline more specifically how bin Laden constructed who was responsible for this tacit compliance.

Internal Enemies: Various Islamic States, Leaders and Organizations

As noted in the previous section, Osama bin Laden believed his central enemy to be external, but he also consistently railed against an internal enemy within the Islamic *ummah*. According to bin Laden (2002, 50) "all the Muslims are brothers." Yet bin Laden had an extremely narrow view of what constituted Muslim brotherhood. In a 2002 interview with *Al Jazeera*, he told his interviewer "everyone that supports Bush, even with one word, is an act of great treason" (72). Bin Laden asserted that "everyone supporting America, even medically, is considered renouncing Islam" (75). In a 2008 audio recording, bin Laden stated that any Arabs that "gave support to Annapolis" committed "one of the ten prohibitions of Islam" (9). All Muslims "should hate them, curse them, and endeavor to disown them ... even if it may be difficult in certain locations" (9). For bin Laden, any assistance given by Muslims to

America or to other entities opposing bin Laden have "followed the path of the *Munafiqeen*" (2007, 10). *Munafiq* is an Arabic word that translates as religious hypocrite. Accordingly, any Muslim advocating for peace, democracy, and/or allegiance to an Islamic government opposed to bin Laden was automatically cast as someone who lies outside the true Islamic faith. According to his logic, the *munafiqeen* perpetuated Islamic suffering because they undercut bin Laden's movement to move Islam to its "true" traditions, while at the same time hampering his war against Islam's external enemies. Just as the Crusader-Zionist alliance must be defeated, true Muslims should "hate," "curse," and "disown" these religious hypocrites to end Islamic hardship and accelerate Islam's return to its proper form.

Bin Laden's rhetoric was harsher for specific internal enemies within the Islamic community. For example, the Al Qaeda leader's 1996 fatwa declared war on America for their actions in Saudi Arabia. Yet the document also made an explicit argument that Saudi Arabia was a complicit partner with the United States or as he put it "an agent of the U.S." (1996, 50; see also 1997, 4). In his fatwa, bin Laden recorded the sins of the Saudi regime. Saudi Arabia's primary offenses consisted of "suspension of the Islamic Sharia'ah law and exchanging it with man made civil law" and "the inability of the regime to protect country, and allowing the enemy of the *Ummah*—the American crusader forces—to occupy the land for the longest of years" (16). Those that opposed Saudi crimes, bin Laden pointed out, attempted to petition the Saudi government peacefully. In 1992, a "Memorandum of Advice" was created by Islamist scholars and given to King Fahd. This memorandum provided "medicine" that could cure the ails of Saudi society. However, "its content was rejected and those who signed it and their sympathizers were ridiculed, prevented from travel, punished, and even jailed" (31). The Saudi regime went so far as to use the army to "protect the invaders, and further deepening the humiliation and betrayal" of Islam (52).

In other addresses to the Muslim world, bin Laden demonstrated his disdain for other Muslim governments such as Pakistan. In 2007, Pakistani President Pervez Musharraf ordered an assault on the Red Mosque in Islamabad because, according to Musharraf, it became a place that taught and exported Islamic extremism. In the attack, dozens were killed and the mosque was severely damaged. After this event, bin Laden declared in a speech to the Pakistani people that its "government and army have become enemies of the Ummah" (2007b, 10). For bin Laden, the raid on the Red Mosque "demonstrated Musharraf's insistence on continuing his loyalty and submissiveness and aid to America against Muslims and this is one of the ten nullifiers of Islam" (2007b, 7). Furthermore, bin Laden accused Musharraf of throwing "away the cause of Kashmir" and restraining "those fighting to liberate it, in accordance with the wishes of the Hindus and the Nazarenes." Musharraf "opened his bases and airports to America for invading Muslims in Afghanistan," "attacked the people of Swat," "attacked the people of Waziristan," "extraditing hundreds of Arab Mujahideen," and refusing to "rule by the religion of Islam in all of life's affairs, like politics, economy, social life, and other matters" (10). Bin Laden also has harsh words for regimes in Egypt, Lebanon, Iraq, Yemen, Indonesia, and Jordan because of actions taken against Muslims or assistance given to the United States and its allies.

Even *Al Jazeera*, the most popular news organization and the CNN of the Islamic world, was cast as a villain in bin Laden's account of Muslim suffering. In 2007, bin Laden's supporters issued a statement saying that Al Jazeera "did manipulate the speech of Sheikh Osama bin Ladin, may Allah preserve him, and how did they divert the message from its designated point" (Al Fajr Media Center, 2007, 1). According to the Al-Fajr Media Center, Al Jazeera presented "so-called scholars" to counter bin Laden's message. These scholars "alter the truth, spread hatred about the Mujahadeen, and took part in the war against them. At the same time, they are in good terms with the apostates and their allies (2007, 2). Moreover, Al Jazeera's "editors in chief counterfeited the facts" of bin Laden's speech perpetuating lies that are spread to the larger Islamic community about his intentions. Ultimately, Al Jazeera is a channel that "has an outstanding record in the betrayal of the Umma, the unfaithfulness to our Deen and a tool in the hands of the Kufr" (4). (Deen, in this context, translates as "way of life" and Kufr translates as "disbelief," but I would suggest it would mean disbelievers and/or deceivers.)

In these discursive examples regarding Saudi Arabia, Pakistan, and *Al Jazeera* the reader should notice two important items. First, all three examples depict the people involved with these entities as "bad" Muslims. Roy (2004) noted nationalist rhetors often label their enemies as "traitors" to the nation. Bin Laden was certainly a nationalist rhetor—Islam is a transnationalist nation united by religion, but a nation nonetheless—who argued these entities were "traitors" because they all had "an outstanding record in the betrayal of the Umma," including the "suspension of Shari'ah law and exchanging it for man made civil law," allowing the enemy to "occupy" Muslim lands, protecting "invaders," assisting in the killing of thousands of Muslims, spreading "hatred," generally being "unfaithful" to Islam, and ultimately a "tool" in the hands of the external enemy. All of these actions count as "one of the ten nullifiers of Islam." Moreover, bin Laden argued these "bad" Muslims gave preferential treatment to Islam's enemies over normal Muslims. For example, bin Laden railed against Saudi Arabia's leaders because they "protect the invaders." Pakistan put the needs of Kashmiri Hindus above those of Kashmiri Muslims by giving away the issue of "Kashmir." *Al Jazeera* used "so-called scholars" to "alter the truth" of Islam. *Al Jazeera* privileged lies above truth. The "invaders," Kashmiri Hindus, and "so-called scholars" were all privileged communities that these traitorous Muslims were protecting. By portraying a set of "bad" Muslims who gave preferential treatment to certain communities, bin Laden provided his supporters with a viable channel in which to direct their anger. His rhetoric demonstrated that there were not only external enemies, but internal ones as well. Accordingly, these supporters could take action to stop the suffering of the Muslim *ummah*, purge these traitors from their universe, and restore order to the Islamic universe. Ultimately, bin Laden's identification of these bad Muslims offered an implied path for "good" Muslims to unite and redeem the Islamic nation.

The Means to Redeem Islam

For the past few pages, I have analyzed how bin Laden described and depicted his enemies. His scapegoating strategy was a symbolic means to arrest Islam's suffering, purge it of its enemies, and restore it back to its most pure and true form. However, bin Laden also offered a specific material means to redeem the Muslim community. For the Al Qaeda leader, the only real way to get rid of its external and internal adversaries and find salvation was through jihad.

Jihad is a concept within Islamic theology that can have several different meanings and is open for contentious debate amongst Islamic scholars. In its most basic terms, jihad is defined as exerting one's efforts, to resist or struggle for something in the name of Allah. It can be used to describe one's own personal struggle against his/her own vices or can be a struggle against some external force (Esposito, 2005; Firestone, 1999; Peters, 1996). In bin Laden's public discourse, jihad was always coupled with violent struggle against its enemies. For bin Laden, jihad was the fundamental duty of all Muslims (see his statements in 1996, 1997, 2000, 2002, 2007a, 2007b, 2007c). It was, as he stated, the "acme of this religion" (1997, 20). Conducting jihad was an "act of worship" (2007b, 19). According to bin Laden's logic, when Muslims committed violent acts against their foes they were practicing Islam. Those armed fighters were considered the most pious. Accordingly, they would receive a more exalted place in heaven. Consequently, true redemption could only come through one's earthly actions.

The primary object of this violent struggle was, as noted earlier, the United States. Time and again, the Al Qaeda leader repeated that a basic obligation of Islam was to stand up to Americans and fight them through aggression. As he put it, "clearly after Belief there is no more important duty than pushing the American enemy out of the holy land" (1996, 37; see also 2002, 18). In this instance, the "holy land" was Saudi Arabia, but bin Laden did not stop there. He insisted that "driving away jihad against the U.S. did not stop with its withdrawal from the Arabian Peninsula, but rather it must desist from aggressive intervention against Muslims in the world" (1997, 10). Peaceful coexistence with America was not possible. According to bin Laden, "there can be no dialogue with occupiers except through arms" (2000, 9). Americans only "understand the language of attacks and killings" (2002, 26). Through jihad, bin Laden stated, a "balance of terror ... between the two parties, between Muslims and Americans" would be established for the first time (2002, 27). Note the Al Qaeda's leader use of the phrase "balance of terror." bin Laden's inherent message was there had been in imbalance in the amount of terror the United States created for Islam. Jihad was the mechanism to strike back, to beat the Americans at their own game. It afforded Muslims the first and best opportunity to drive United States from the "Arabian peninsula" and get them to "desist from aggressive intervention" in the Muslim world.

To justify jihad, bin Laden relied on two rhetorical strategies: citing verses of the Quran and appropriating/interpreting historical events for his own purposes. For someone who argued that he was doing Allah's work, it was not surprising bin Laden invoked the Quran to sanctify violence. Throughout his public rhetoric, bin Laden quoted at length from the Quran and Islam's other holy documents to provide a rationale for his actions. As I am not versed in the intricacies of the Quran, I will not hazard an interpretation of bin Laden's use of Islam, which I imagine many, if not most, Islamic scholars would find his use of holy scripture to be suspect at best. What I find to be more interesting was bin Laden's use of collective memory. Collective memory is a particular way to understand the past and by its nature is selective and partial. Shawn and Trevor Parry Giles (2002) argued that society's collective memory is constructed like a mosaic with some memories having more resonance than others. Because collective memory is selective and partial it is managed in important ways by rhetors for strategic purposes (Bostdorff and Goldzwig, 2005; Browne, 1999; Edwards, 2007, 2009). Specifically, bin Laden used collective memory through historical analogy. He compared the situation Al Qaeda faced against its external and internal enemies with struggles Muslims fought in the past. For example, in his 1996 fatwa, bin Laden invoked the memory of Ibn Taymiyyah. Ibn Taymiyyah was a thirteenth-century Islamic scholar who may be best known for his fatwa against the Mongol rulers of his time (Janin, 2007). According to Taymiyyah, Muslims had an obligation and a duty to fight the Mongols because they ruled according to secular (man-made) law instead of law coming directly from the Quran. Bin Laden (1996) observed:

> Ibn Taymiyyah, after mentioning the Moguls (Tatar) and their behaviour in changing the law of Allah, stated that: the ultimate aim of pleasing Allah, raising his word, institution his religion, and obeying his messenger (Allah's blessing and salutations upon him) is to fight the enemy, in every aspects and in a complete manner; if the danger to the religion from not fighting is greater than that of fighting, then it is the duty to fight them even if the intention of some of the fighter is not pure [38].

Bin Laden used Taymiyyah as an authorizing figure. An authorizing figure is a historical figure that rhetors call upon to justify a specific set of actions. In different cultures, different historical heroes resonate more than others. For example, in Cuba, Fidel Castro used the exploits of the great Cuban leader, Jose Marti, to justify a number of his principles, policies, and positions during his reign as Cuba's leader (Rice, 1992). In the United States, Republicans and Democrats invoke the memory of President Harry Truman when advocating and justifying a variety of foreign policy positions (Edwards, 2009). Appealing to the memory of important historical figures endows that rhetor's discourse with more authority. Through the use of the authorizing figure, the rhetor

> demonstrates that the orator and the authorizing figure are doing similar work, despite major differences in the circumstances they may face. In other words, when a policy is proposed and/or passed, the rhetor can invoke the memory of that historical hero to demonstrate this policy and/or principle is in accordance with what s/he had done in the past ... the communicator's discourse suggests that if the authorizing figure were alive they would not only approve of the rhetor's policy, but may have enacted similar ideas [Edwards, 2009, p. 459].

Ibn Taymiyyah justified jihad based upon the Mongols refusal to rule via Sharia law. He argued Muslims had a duty to oppose the Mongols disregard for Islamic law at every turn. Similarly, bin Laden argued he fought against Islam's external and internal enemies because of their attempts to turn away Islam from Sharia to secular based law. Accordingly, bin Laden calls for all true Muslims to aggressively oppose those forces that fight against the basic tenets of Islam. The Al Qaeda leader's call for jihad was in line with other great minds of Islamic jurisprudence. His fight was no different than the one Taymiyyah sanctioned seven centuries before. In that light one can surmise bin Laden thought of himself as a twenty-first century version of Ibn Taymiyyah. By engaging in jihad the late twentieth and twenty-first century Muslims would be able to throw off the yoke of their oppressors, just as they did seven hundred years earlier.

Bin Laden took his historical analogizing one step further by comparing his situation with other "successful" jihads. He often discussed how Muslims drove out the British out of Muslim lands in the 1930s, the Soviets out of Afghanistan in the 1980s, the Americans out of Lebanon in 1983, and Americans out of Somalia in 1994 (see bin Laden, 1996, 2002, 2007b, 2007c). Speaking specifically about the United States, bin Laden (1996) asserted:

> Your most disgraceful case was in Somalia, where after vigorous propaganda about the power of the USA and its post Cold War leadership of the new world order you moved tens of thousands of international force, including twenty-eight thousands of American soldiers into Somalia. However, when tens of your soldiers were killed in minor battles and one American Pilot was dragged in the streets of Mogadishu you left the area carrying disappointment, humiliation, defeat, and your dead with you. [President]Clinton appeared in front of the whole world threatening and promising revenge, but these threats were merely a preparation for withdrawal. You have been disgraced by Allah and you withdrew; the extent of your impotence and weaknesses became very clear [68].

Clearly, bin Laden spoke of the U.S. debacle in Somalia in October 1993. For bin Laden, this event confirmed America's "impotence and weaknesses." In turn, it gave the Al Qaeda leader license to believe the United States could be easily defeated if it were attacked en masse. Because jihad drove the Mongols from the Middle East, the British from Lebanon, the Soviets from Afghanistan, and the United States from Lebanon and Somalia, engaging in violent action is the most logical and straightforward means to drive Islam's enemies out of their power structures. Bin Laden (1996) assured his audiences this sustained armed struggle would "re-establish the normal course" of Islam and achieve redemption for the Islamic *ummah*.

Conclusions

In this essay I have attempted to make sense of Islamist discourse by closely examining the discourse of a central figure in the Islamist movement, Osama bin Laden. After reviewing his rhetoric, I argue a fundamental narrative that underwrites it is a myth of suffering and redemption, where he uses various rhetorical strategies including scapegoating and the invocation of historical memories. These strategies provided an account of the suffering he argued Muslims currently endure, symbolically purified them from his Islamic universe, and gave supporters an object to focus their anger upon. Moreover, he offered a precise means to arrest their suffering through violent jihad. It was only through this armed struggle that Islam can return to its normal path, otherwise it would be destroyed.

This analysis suggests that mythic themes and the rhetorical strategies found here are part and parcel of larger mythic narratives. Although I argue that bin Laden's rhetoric is fundamentally underwritten by mythic themes of suffering and redemption, the implicit claim of all of his discourse is that Islam suffers because it has been polluted by a modern, secular world. For Islam to truly thrive, it must return to its origins. This return to its origins, its roots, is what Roy and Rowland (2003) call a myth of return. They defined myths of return as a narrative of where a people have been stripped of their dignity by some malevolent force and can only regain that dignity by returning to values and ideals that "defined their birth as a people" (p. 231). Bin Laden's rhetoric was a chronicle of suffering that has stripped Muslims of their fundamental dignity. What bin Laden's rhetoric lacked was a full and fervent discussion of what a return to origins entailed. He certainly hinted at it by castigating Islamic governments who have turned away from Sharia law. That, however, was the extent of his discussion. He spent more time justifying why like-minded supporters should oppose his external and internal enemies. Yet there was no doubt bin Laden advocated Islam return to its origins. The mythic themes of suffering and redemption work symbiotically with the mythic theme of return. Accordingly, future research may focus on analyzing all of these themes together to map out underlying motives, which will differ from group to group.

Ultimately, however, a greater contribution this analysis may make is merely making sense of bin Laden's rhetoric and the commonalities it shares with other Islamist groups and other groups that feel, real or imagined, marginalized. Trying to understand what underwrites the larger goals of these groups is fundamental to countering their work, because it ultimately leads to tragedy. If one doubts the power of scapegoating, one only needs to think about atrocities committed within Germany, Cambodia, Rwanda, Bosnia, and Darfur. Aside from the mass killings, a common link that all of these sites share is the violence that ensued was engendered through scapegoating. Perhaps Abhik Roy (2004) put it best when he wrote:

> Rhetorical scholars have a moral responsibility to deconstruct these messages and advice policy makers concerning the dangers of such discourse. The analysis of hateful nationalist rhetoric and identification of strategies of scapegoating the "other" are certainly productive moves that will help generate more humane ways of building nationalism and national identity. Although rhetoricians may not be able to stop the violence that is perpetuated in the name of nation building, the development and application of critical techniques that evaluate nationalist rhetoric will certainly help in identifying potential danger spots [p. 330].

Rhetorical scholars not only have a responsibility to "deconstruct these messages" but all scholars should engage in this charge to "generate more humane ways" of interaction in a world that grows more integrated on a daily basis.

REFERENCES

Al-Fajr Media Center (2007, October 24). Statement regarding *Al-Jazeera*'s deceitful manipulation of the speech by Shakyh Usama Bin Laden. Retrieved October 10, 2008, from http://www.nefafoundation.org/documents-aqustatments.html.
Bawer, B. (2007). *While Europe slept: How radical Islam is destroying the West from within*. New York: Anchor.
Benjamin, D., and Simon, S. (2003). *The age of sacred terror: Radical Islam's war against America*. New York: Random House.
Bieber, F. (2002). Nationalist mobilization and the stories of Serbian suffering: The Kosovo myth from 600th anniversary to present. *Rethinking History* 6, 90–122.
Bin Laden, O. (1996, August). Bin Laden's fatwa. Retrieved October 10, 2008, from http://www.pbs.org/newshour/terrorism/international/fatwa_1996.html.
Bin Laden, O. (1997, March). Transcript of Peter Arnett interview of Usama Bin Laden, CNN. Retrieved October 10, 2008, from http://www.nefafoundation.org/documents-aqustatments.html.
Bin Laden, O. (2001, November 3). Bin Laden rails against crusaders and UN. Retrieved October 10, 2008, from http://news.bbc.co.uk/q/hi/world/monitoring/media_reports/1636782.htm.
Bin Laden, O. (2002, February 5). Transcript of Bin Laden's October interview. Retrieved October 10, 2008, from http://archives.cnn.com/2002/asiapcf/south/02/05/binladen.transcript.index.html.
Bin Laden, O. (2004, January 4). Bin Laden statement. Retrieved October 10, 2008 from http://www.nefafoundation.org/documents-aqustatments.html.
Bin Laden, O. (2004, November 5). Osama Bin Laden's speech to the Muslim world. Retrieved October 10, 2008, from http://www.memri.org/bin/opener.cgi?Page=archives&ID=SP81104.
Bin Laden, O. (2007a, September 8). The solution. Retrieved October 10, 2008, from http://www.nefafoundation.org/documents-aqustatments.html.
Bin Laden, O. (2007b, September 20). Come to jihad: A speech to the people of Pakistan. Retrieved October 10, 2008, from http://www.nefafoundation.org/documents-aqustatments.html.
Bin Laden, O. (2007c, November 29). Message to the peoples of Europe. Retrieved October 10, 2008, from http://www.nefafoundation.org/documents-aqustatments.html.
Bin Laden, O. (2008, March 20). The way for the salvation of Palestine. Retrieved October 10, 2008, from http://www.nefafoundation.org/documents-aqustatments.html.
Bin Laden, O. (2009, March 19). Fight on, champions of Somalia. Retrieved May 10, 2009, from http://www.nefafoundation.org/documents-aqustatments.html.
Bostdorff, D.M., and Goldzwig, S.R. (2005). History, collective memory, and the appropriation of Martin Luther King, Jr.: Reagan's rhetorical legacy. *Presidential Studies Quarterly* 35, 661–690.
Browne, S.H. (1999). Remembering Crispus Attacks: Race, rhetoric, and politics of commemoration. *Quarterly Journal of Speech* 85, 169–187.
Burke, K. (1961). *The rhetoric of religion*. Berkeley: University of California Press.
Burke, K. (1973). *The philosophy of literary form: Studies in symbolic action*. Baton Rouge: Louisiana State University Press.
Carter, C.A. (1996). *Kenneth Burke and the scapegoat process*. Norman: University of Oklahoma Press.

Cauthen, B. (1997). The myth of divine election and Afrikaner ethnogenesis. In G. Hosking and G. Schopflin (eds.), *Myths and nationhood* (pp. 107–131). New York: Routledge.

Cauthen, B. (2004). Covenant and continuity: Ethno-symbolism and the myth of divine election. *Nations and Nationalism* 10, 19–33.

Cochran, T.R., and Edwards, J.A. (2008). Buffy the Vampire Slayer and the quest story: Revising the hero, reshaping the myth. In J. Perlich and D. Whitt (eds.), *Sith, slayers, stargates, and cyborgs: Modern mythology in the new millennium* (pp. 145–169). New York: Peter Lang.

Cronick, K. (2002). The discourse of President George W. Bush and Osama Bin Laden: A rhetorical analysis and hermeneutic interpretation. *Forum: Qualitative Social Research.* http://www.qualitative-research.net/fqs (Accessed April 1, 2009).

Doder, D., and Branson, L. (1999). *Milosevic: Portrait of a tyrant.* New York: Free Press.

Edwards, J.A. (2003). Bringing an earthly redemption: Slobodan Milosevic and t the national myth of Kosovo. A paper presented at the 2003 National Communication Association Conference, Miami, FL.

Edwards, J.A. (2007). Staying the course as world leader: Bill Clinton's use of historical analogies. *White House Studies* 7, 53–71.

Edwards, J.A. (2009). Sanctioning foreign policy: The rhetorical use of Harry Truman in presidential discourse. *Presidential Studies Quarterly* 39, 454–472.

Esposito, J. (2005). *Islam: The straight path.* Oxford: Oxford University Press.

Firestone, R. (1999). *Jihad: The origin of holy war in Islam.* Oxford: Oxford University Press.

Gabriel, M.A. (2002). *Islam and terrorism: What the Quran really teaches about Christianity, violence and the goals of the Islamic jihad.* New York: Creation House.

Gabriel, M.A. (2007). *Culture clash: Islam's war on the West.* New York: Charisma House.

Habeck, M. (2007). *Knowing the enemy: Jihadist ideology and the war on terror.* New Haven: Yale University Press.

Janin, H., and Kahlmeyer, A. (2007). *Islamic law: The sharia from Mohammed's time to the present.* Jefferson, NC: McFarland.

Kaplan, R.D. (1996). *Balkan ghosts: A journey through history.* New York: Vintage.

Keen, S. (1986). *Faces of the enemy: Reflections on the hostile imagination.* New York: HarperCollins.

Kluver, A. (1997). Political identity and national myth: Toward an interculturalunderstanding of political legitimacy. In A. Gonzalez and D.V. Tanno (eds.), *The International and Intercultural Communication Annual* (pp. 47–70). Thousand Oaks, CA: Sage.

Matar, D. (2008). The power of conviction: Nasrallah's rhetoric and mediated charisma in the context of the 2006 war. *Middle East Journal of Culture and Communication* 1, 122–137.

Nimmo, D., and Combs, J.E. (1980). *Subliminal politics: Myth and mythmakers in America.* Englewood Cliffs, NJ: Prentice-Hall.

Pape, R. (2006). *Dying to win: The strategic logic of suicide terrorism.* New York: Random House.

Peters, R. (1996). *Jihad in classical and modern Islam.* Princeton, NJ: Markus Weiner.

Phares, W. (2008). *The war of ideas: Jihadism versus democracy.* New York: Palgrave Macmillan.

Pipes, D. (2003). *Militant Islam reaches America.* New York: W.W. Norton.

Rice, D.E. (1992). *The rhetorical uses of the authorizing figure: Fidel Castro and Jose Marti.* Westport, CT: Praeger.

Rowland, R.C., and Theye, K. (2008). The symbolic DNA of terrorism. *Communication Monographs* 75, 52–85.

Roy, A. (2004). The construction and scapegoating of Muslims as the "other" in Hindu nationalist rhetoric. *Southern Communication Journal* 69, 320–332.

Roy, A., and Rowland, R.C. (2003). The rhetoric of Hindu nationalism: A narrative of mythic redefinition. *Western Journal of Communication* 65, 225–248.

Rushing, J.H., and Frentz, T.S. (2005). The mythic perspective. In J. Kuypers (ed.), *The art of rhetorical criticism* (pp. 241–269). New York: Allyn & Bacon.

Schopflin, G. (1997). The functions of myth and a taxonomy of myths. In G. Hosking and G. Schopflin (eds.), *Myths and nationhood* (pp. 19–35). New York: Routledge.

Spencer, R. (2005). *The politically incorrect guide to Islam (and the Crusades)*. New York: Regnery.

Spencer, R. (2007). *The truth about Mohammed: Founder of the world's most Intolerant religion*. New York: Regnery.

Starr, J. (1973). *Ideology and culture*. New York: Harper Row, 1973.

Stern, J. (2004). *Terror in the name of God: Why religious militants kill*. New York: Harper Perennial.

Winch, S. (2005). Constructing an "evil genius": News uses of mythic archetypes to make sense of Bin Laden. *Journalism Studies* 6, 285–299.

Mothers and Monsters
The Return of the Great Goddess in George R. R. Martin's A Song of Ice and Fire

SHARON DEE GOERTZ

George R. R. Martin's sprawling five-novel fantasy-epic *A Song of Ice and Fire*, begun in 1996 and projected to continue at least through two more novels, is set in a land called Westeros that resembles medieval Europe. Since the story focuses on wars and political struggles in a world where women are supposed to stay in the home and out of politics, the reader might expect that his female characters will be minor and stereotyped. And indeed, early on, Martin's women do seem to fall into the stereotypical categories of nubile victim, bitchy seductress, faithful wife, and devoted mother. The latter is an especially hidebound stereotype, based on the medieval ideal of the Virgin Mary but alive and well in American culture today. In fact, the myth of the ideal self-effacing and self-sacrificing mother is enjoying a resurgence as part of the backlash against feminism, according to Susan Douglas and Meredith Michaels in *The Mommy Myth: The Idealization of Motherhood and How It Has Undermined Women* (2004) and other scholars, such as Crittenden (2000, reissued 2010), Warner (2006), Almond (2011), and Badinter (2012). Martin's mothers, however, surprise us by breaking out of this stereotype and becoming powerful players in the game of thrones. Particularly, he creates four characters who are both literal and symbolic mothers, each instrumental in their factions' political struggles, and who blend the characteristics of nurturers, killers, sex objects, and sexual predators: Catelyn Stark, Cersei Lannister, Melisandre, and Daenerys Targaryen. These characters break down the comfortable stereotype of idealized motherhood and restore it to its ancient, pre–Christian, dynamic complexity. Martin enriches his exploration of mothering by infusing the story with symbols of the Neolithic mother goddess that draw on a variety of interpretations of this figure. I will first describe these different theories of the mother goddess that have been put forth by anthropologists, Jungian and feminist scholars, and then apply these theories to Martin's novels. Martin infuses his narrative with both characters and symbols reminding us of the great mother, making motherhood an integral part of the game of thrones and challenging the narrow ideology of the ideal mother.

The Great Mother Goddess

The importance and antiquity of a mother goddess figure in human culture has been widely documented and analyzed by such scholars as Erich Neumann, Joseph Campbell, Marija Gimbutas, Anne Baring, and Jules Cashford. The earliest three-dimensional representations of the human figure are of women, typically with enormous breasts, hips, and bellies (in a time before McDonald's made this body type easy to achieve). These female figures, and their later, slimmer counterparts, are named the Great Mother, the Great Goddess, or more neutrally, the Goddess. Gimbutas (1989) posited about twenty years ago that these Neolithic sculptures, such as the famous robust nude called the "Venus of Willendorf," descend from even older images of the mother goddess (p. xix). And indeed, a recent issue of *Archaeology* magazine lists one of the "Top 10 Discoveries of 2012" as identifying the date of an image of a vulva to at least 37,000 years ago, making it "Europe's oldest engraving" (Swaminathan, 2013, p. 29). The fascination with women's body parts relating to generation and sexuality can thus be traced back thousands of years before *Playboy*, *Cosmopolitan*, Victoria's Secret, or *The Song of Ice and Fire*. Exactly what these figures meant to the ancient people who made them has been interpreted differently by different scholars. Gimbutas (1989), for example, describes the multiple roles of this figure in Neolithic times as

> the birth-giver, portrayed in a naturalistic birth-giving pose; the fertility-giver influencing growth and multiplication, portrayed as a pregnant nude; the life or nourishment-giver and protectress, portrayed as a bird-woman with breasts and protruding buttocks; and the death-wielder as a stiff nude [p. xix].

She includes the role of the bringer of death with the more pleasant nurturing roles of bearing and feeding children and promoting fertility. Moreover, many of these images also convey a distinct erotic charge. Martin taps into this rich source of myth from the first page in the series, when in the midst of a decidedly unfeminine scene, he inserts a reference to breast-feeding. He has saturated the series with characters and images associated with motherhood that can be related to the concept of the Great Goddess.

THE TRIPLE-GODDESS: MAIDEN/MOTHER/CRONE

Within the world of *A Song of Ice and Fire*, Martin invites us to think back to the Great Goddess by including a fictionalized version of her worship within the text. The most prominent of the religious systems Martin creates is the "Sept," the state sponsored religion of Westeros based on a seven-personed god. The Sept itself is more or less gender equal: of the seven faces of god, three are female (Maiden, Mother, and Crone), three are male (Father, Warrior, and Smith), and one is no gender (the Stranger, who represents Death). In this analysis, obviously, I am most concerned with the Mother, though the Maiden, Crone, and the Stranger also play an important role in Martin's conception of the Great Mother. Two points to note about the three overtly female aspects. First, as is the case in so much of female stereotyping, the three female figures are defined by the woman's sexual/generative body (Creed, 1993), with aspects representing the virginal adolescent female, the woman who has born children, and the woman who has passed through menopause. (Note that there is no image for either a sexually active woman who has no children or a celibate woman.) Second, Martin did not invent these categories; they are common in the analysis of female deities worldwide and are three aspects of the Great Goddess figure, though the Sept splits off the Crone's death-bringing function and gives it to the Stranger. Marija Gimbutas (1989), however, replaces the second category with "nymph," and she and Baring and Cashford (1991) also replace Neumann's term "Great Mother" with "Goddess" to broaden the archetype to include more than its sexual and generative aspects. Gimbutas describes this triple-aspect divinity: "The moon's three phases—new, waxing, and old—are repeated in trinities or triple-functional deities that recall these moon phases: maiden, nymph, and crone: life-giving, death-giving, and transformational; rising, dying, and self-renewing" (p. 316). This symbolism is "built around the understanding that life on earth is in eternal transformation" (p. 316), since each is a phase of a woman's life and are therefore always in flux and inseparable from each other. In Martin's Sept, however, each aspect represents a separate quality: the Mother "gives the gift of life" and "loves her little children"; the Crone "is very wise and old"; the Maiden "lives in every lover's sigh" (Martin, 2000, p. 531). More simply, the Mother represents mercy, the Maiden innocence, the Crone wisdom, and the Stranger death—so scary that it is shunned altogether. The Mother is so closely associated with mercy that characters use the phrase

"Mother have mercy" reflexively. Though Martin creates a multi-aspected deity that potentially limits the role a woman can play according to her stage in life, it is clear that this is the Westerosi's stereotyping, not Martin's: while he has many female characters that could be described as either maidens, mothers, or crones, most of them break through these boundaries. For example, he includes maidens who are warriors (Arya, Brienne, Asha), mothers who are ruthless politicians (Catelyn, Cersei, Daenerys), and crones who are murderers (Mirri Maz Duur, the Queen of Thorns).

THE GODDESS SPLIT IN TWO

Erich Neumann, in *The Great Mother: An Analysis of the Archetype* (1963), proposes another theory of the goddess figure that is helpful in analyzing Martin's mothers. Neumann describes two types of archaic images of the female, the first being positive "in which the woman contains and protects, nourishes and gives birth" (p. 120). The feminine principle is here reduced to a nurturing vessel. The characteristics of the positive aspect correspond with our idealized version of motherhood and correspond closely to the Mother of the Sept or the Virgin Mary. The second image, the Terrible Mother, however, is negative and represents the "anguish, horror, and fear of danger that the Archetypal Feminine signifies" (p. 147). In his Jungian approach to the goddess, Neumann describes the Terrible Mother as the "symbol for the unconscious" (p. 148), the terrifying darkness within ourselves. In the heroic struggle of the ego to establish itself in the course of individual development, the Terrible Mother embodies annihilation and all the terrors that it implies: "Thus the womb of the earth becomes the deadly devouring maw of the underworld.... This Terrible Mother is the hungry earth, which devours its own children and fattens on their corpses" (p. 149). The goddess becomes a sexual predator: "The yawning, avid character of the gullet and the cleft represents in mythological apperception the unity of the Feminine, which as avid womb attracts the male and kills the phallus within itself in order to achieve satisfaction and fecundation" (p. 171). Neumann continues, "Thus the Terrible Goddess rules over desire and over the seduction that leads to sin and destruction" (p. 172). One vivid representation of this sexually destructive goddess is the *vagina dentata*: "the destructive and deathly womb, [which] appears most frequently in the archetypal form of a mouth bristling with teeth" (p. 168). Martin frequently describes his female characters with the fearsome teeth and claws denoting this symbol.

To update this concept of the negative aspect of the feminine, Barbara Creed (1993) analyzes female monsters in contemporary horror movies. She asserts that "All human societies have a conception of the monstrous-feminine, of what it is about woman that is shocking, terrifying, horrific, abject" (p. 1). She uses Julia Kristeva's concept of the "abject" to analyze the horrific images of the Terrible Mother reborn in contemporary films such as *The Exorcist* (1973), *Carrie* (1976), *Alien* (1979), *The Brood* (1979), and *The Hunger* (1983). Simply put, Kristeva's concept of "abjection" draws on the common meaning of the word as the state of being contemptible or miserable and adds to it the idea of being outcast from society, representing that which must be excluded from the human. It includes all that is considered spiritually impure and must be ritually cleansed, for example, all sorts of bodily fluids. In horror movies, the abject underlies the depiction of the monstrous and includes "the following religious 'abominations': sexual immorality and perversion; corporeal alteration, decay and death; human sacrifice; murder; the corpse; bodily wastes; the feminine body and incest" (p. 9). Creed's succinct description of the twelve-year-old girl Regan who is the main character in *The Exorcist* illustrates almost all of these abject characteristics:

> She spews green bile, utters foul obscenities, tries to fuck her mother, causes inanimate objects to fly, rotates her head full circle on her neck, knocks two men to the floor with one punch, tries to castrate a priest, murders two men, and in her spare time masturbates with a crucifix [1993, p. 31].

From a cultural perspective that considers the spiritual superior to the body, the sexual and reproductive functions of women makes them suspect, as Creed explains: "In Kristeva's view the image of woman's body, because of its maternal functions, acknowledges its 'debt to nature' and consequently is more likely to signify the abject. The notion of the material female body is central to the construction of the border in the horror film" (p. 11). Thus Creed's view brings the Terrible Mother into the twentieth century as the monstrous-feminine with its focus on "woman's reproductive and mothering functions" (p. 14). I will use these theories of the two aspects of the Great Mother to analyze several of Martin's mothers.

Martin's Mothers

Of the many families or "houses" vying for possession of the Iron Throne, four stand out, and each of them has a mother as a major player: the Starks, the Lannisters, the Baratheons, and the Targaryens. (If *A Song of Ice and Fire* is indeed a fantasy based on the Wars of the Roses—a struggle for the English throne in the years 1455–1485—then the names "Stark" and "Lannister" echo the major contenders in that conflict: York and Lancaster.) The Starks get the most sympathy from the reader: we get to know most of them intimately as point of view characters, and even though they are not perfect, they have qualities we admire: courage, loyalty, and a strong sense of justice. Early on, each of the five Stark children (Robb, Sansa, Arya, Bran, and Rickon) and their illegitimate half-brother (Jon Snow) acquire as a pet a "direwolf," a sort of saber-toothed version of a wolf that seems supernaturally fated to bond with them. The natural connection the Stark children have to these beasts, semi-mythic even in the world of Westeros, also ennobles them in the reader's mind. In dramatic contrast to the Starks, the wealthy, manipulative, beautiful Lannisters come off initially as greedy, whiny villains, although over the course of the series, we come to respect and even like some of the members of that family. Cersei Lannister is married Robert Baratheon who is the king in the first book. However, since Robert had usurped the Mad King, Aerys Targaryen, his hold on the throne is suspect. Robert dies in the first book, and the rumored illegitimacy of his children sets off the conflict for control of the throne between the Lannisters and the two remaining Baratheon brothers, each of whom claims the throne. Meanwhile, the last surviving children of Aerys Targaryen, Viserys and Daenerys, live in exile, hoping to gain enough support to retake the throne. Mothers associated with each of these groups play prominent roles in the plot: Catelyn Stark, Cersei Lannister, Melisandre (advisor to Stannis Baratheon), and Daenerys Targaryen.

Catelyn Stark represents the positive side of the Great Mother for the most part. She loves her five children deeply, protecting them with her life while not trying to overprotect or consume them, as her sister Lysa does with her son Robert (as he is called in the novels, though his name has been changed to Robin for the HBO series). When a killer tries to stab her son Bran, Catelyn grabs the dagger with her bare hands and holds him off long enough for Bran's direwolf to kill the attacker. Then she goes on a quest to seek the person behind the attack and boldly makes a citizen arrest of the man she thinks is responsible, Tyrion Lannister, and inadvertently ignites the struggle between the Lannisters and the Starks. Later, her anguish at hearing of the supposed deaths of her youngest children Bran and Rickon leads her to the possibly foolish step of releasing captive Jaime Lannister in the desperate hope that he can extract her daughters Sansa and Arya who are being held hostage by the Lannisters. Even though her sternness and lack of love for her husband's bastard son, Jon Snow, make it seem like she has little of the Mother's mercy, a closer look reveals that she does. She is constantly seeking a peaceful resolution to the game of thrones. Moreover, she takes pity on bereaved maiden/warrior Brienne and becomes a second mother to her.

The fact that none of Catelyn's efforts seem to make things better for her children underscores one of the mythic aspects of motherhood—grief and helplessness before fate. In this way, her story recalls the archetypal stories of grieving mothers: Demeter and Niobe from Greek mythology, and Mary, mother of Jesus. When Catelyn visits her sister in the first book in the series, she sees a waterfall called "Alyssa's Tears," based on a myth invented by Martin of a woman who cries endlessly for the loss of her children: "Catelyn wondered how large a waterfall her own tears would make when she died" (1996, p. 360). Alyssa's story is reminiscent of the Greek myth of Niobe, who boasted of her many children and then lost them all to an irate goddess, as Ovid recounts: "Utterly bereft now, she sank down surrounded by the bodies of her sons, her daughters, her husband, and grief turned her to stone.... There she wastes away, and even now, tears trickle from her marble face" (1955, p. 142). The connection between Catelyn and this Niobe-like figure foreshadows her loss of all her children (as she thinks) as well as her resurrection as "Lady Stoneheart" later in the series.

Catelyn reaches the peak of her grief and despair in *A Storm of Swords* when she sees her son Robb betrayed and killed at the "Red Wedding," a wedding that she helped plan in an effort to make peace and firm up good relations with the treacherous Frey family. At this point, her despair at the deaths or imprisonment of all her children tips her characterization over to the Terrible Mother aspect of the Great Goddess. She takes revenge for the death of her son by killing her own hostage, and the Terrible Mother takes over as her fury turns inward:

> She tugged hard on Aegon's hair and sawed at this neck until the blade grated on bone. Blood ran hot over her fingers.... Finally someone took the knife away from her. The tears burned like vinegar as they ran down her cheeks. Ten fierce ravens were raking her face with sharp talons and tearing off strips of flesh, leaving deep furrows that ran red with blood. She could taste it on her lips [2000, p. 583].

Even though Catelyn is killed and thrown in the river after this, supernatural forces combine to revive her and she reappears in the fourth book as "Lady Stoneheart," also known as "Mother Merciless" (2005, p. 631). But even earlier in the series she had already shown this side of herself when she defends Bran in the first book: "The hand [of the attacker] over her mouth clenched more tightly, shutting off her air. Catelyn twisted her head to the side and managed to get a piece of his flesh between her teeth. She bit down hard into his palm.... She ground her teeth together and tore at him, and all of a sudden he let go" (1996, p. 111). The use of teeth, talons, and sharp weapons signal her connection to the Terrible Mother in her aspect as *vagina dentata*. Martin complicates and makes three-dimensional this admirable woman by giving her characteristics of the Terrible Mother.

On the other hand, Cersei Lannister is easily identified early on in the series as a representation of the Terrible Mother. Not only are her actions those of a villainess (she cheats on her husband with her twin brother Jaime, defends her son Joffrey's monstrous actions, plots to kill her husband King Robert— and that is just in the first book), she also symbolically fulfills both Neumann's description of the Terrible Mother and Creed's definition of the monstrous-feminine. Through her name, Martin associates her particularly with Circe (one of Neumann's "Ladies of the Beasts"), the witch from Homer's *The Odyssey* who seduces men and then turns them into animals. Cersei turns men into animals metaphorically by seducing them and then manipulating them. The language used to describe her betrayal of her husband—she has "cuckolded" him and "put horns on his head" suggests that she has transformed him into an animal. The Greek Circe is also one of the representations of the fearsome *vagina dentata*: the teeth of wolves and lions surrounding her in Homer's and later painters' depictions of her symbolize the *dentata*, as Neumann points out. By the second book, *A Clash of Kings*, her dwarf brother Tyrion describes her in terms of the *vagina dentata*:

> Tyrion reflected on the men who had been Hand [the King's chief advisor] before him, who had proved no match for his sister's wiles. *How could they be? Men like that ... too honest to live, too noble to shit, Cersei devours such fools every morning when she breaks her fast* [1999, p. 337].

Moreover, the particular language with which Tyrion describes the men who are not equal to Cersei signals her abjectness, linking her to the monstrous-feminine. When Tyrion says that these men were *"too noble to shit,"* he is drawing a line between the abject (which includes himself and Cersei) and the purified. Another abject bodily fluid that Cersei is connected with is menstrual blood. When Sansa begins menstruating in the second book, far from her own mother, it is Cersei who counsels her on the subject of the abjection of women: "The blood is the seal of your womanhood. Lady Catelyn might have prepared you. You've had your first flowering, no more" (1999, p. 571). Sansa demurs, saying it is less flowery than messy to become a woman.

> Queen Cersei laughed. "Wait until you birth a child, Sansa. A woman's life is nine parts mess to one part magic, you'll learn that soon enough ... Joffrey has always been difficult. Even his birth ... I labored a day and a half to bring him forth. You cannot imagine the pain, Sansa" [1999, p. 571].

Of course, incest also marks Cersei as abject. When Catelyn learns in the second book of the accusation that Cersei's children were all fathered by her twin brother Jaime, she can scarcely believe that this woman, whom she believes responsible for the death of her husband and brother-in-law is "guilty of such monstrous crimes" (1999, p. 357). In the world of Westeros, where murder is common, incest damns Cersei more thoroughly in Catelyn's eyes than even the murder of her husband and brother-in-law.

Even though Cersei is despicable, Martin allows her some sympathy from the reader. He places at least some of the blame for her behavior on her victimization by a patriarchal society that subjects her actions to male control at every turn. Even Eddard "Ned" Stark, best friend and loyal subject of Cersei's husband, King Robert Baratheon, sympathizes with her. Ned knows that her husband is a drunkard and an abusive womanizer. Cersei's father, Tywin Lannister, forced her to marry Robert as a political maneuver, as arranged marriage in the upper classes is a Westerosi tradition. So, after she is widowed, she is still not free of male domination: her father plans to marry her off to someone else, again for political reasons. Cersei is forced to play the role of demure maiden when it is the last thing she is.

By the fourth book, *A Feast for Crows*, Martin starts giving Cersei her own point of view chapters, and although much of what goes on in her mind is damning, we do get her side of the story. She recalls that she was so similar to her twin brother Jaime that she could masquerade as him, and she notes how differently she is treated when she is thought to be a boy. She and others compare her to her father Tywin a number of times; like him, she wants power and is ruthless. In this way, she resembles Norwegian playwright Henrik Ibsen's famous character Hedda Gabler, who gains a measure of sympathy from the audience even though she does heinous things. In Ibsen's play, it is clear that had she been a man, Hedda would have been a great general like her father, but with a woman's narrow field of action, especially in the late nineteenth century, her power can only be used for petty and pathetic manipulation.

Like Cersei, Melisandre, the mother associated with the house of Baratheon, skillfully seduces and manipulates men. As a priestess of the Red God, R'hllor, she has convinced one of Robert Baratheon's brothers, Stannis, that he has been chosen by her god to rule Westeros. Her intentions might actually be good— her point of view chapters show that she believes that she can protect Westeros from the dreadful Others by putting Stannis on the throne, but her methods, which include murder by magic and public burning, are heinous. Martin connects her explicitly to the Terrible Mother in *A Clash of Kings* (1999), in which she gives birth in obstetrical detail to what seems to be an evil spirit:

> Panting, she squatted and spread her legs. Blood ran down her thighs.... Davos saw the crown of the child's head push its way out of her. Two arms wriggled free, grasping, black fingers coiling around Melisandre's straining thighs, pushing,

until the whole of the shadow slid out into the world and rose taller than Davos, tall as the tunnel, towering above the boat [p. 468].

The spirit kills Lord Renly, the third Baratheon brother, another contender for the throne, in the heart of his armed camp, eliminating him from the game of thrones. Melisandre uses the generative power of the Terrible Mother most directly of all these characters to destroy her enemies. Still, Martin avoids stereotyping her as a one-dimensional destroyer of men by giving her point of view chapters that reveal her sincere motives.

Of all the mothers, Daenerys Targaryen has the most significant and complex story arc. She starts out as seemingly another passive teenaged girl (a "maiden") who is victimized by the patriarchal system of Westeros. And, indeed, both Martin and the HBO series producers also exploit the vulnerable female body of the character (not to mention the young actress playing her). We first meet Daenerys as a point of view character early on in the first book, which signals her centrality in the narrative. But otherwise, she is unpromising as a player in the game of thrones. When she is first introduced, Daenerys, or Dany, is a victim of her sadistic brother Viserys, the last surviving heir of the slain king of Westeros, who marries her off at thirteen to Drogo, a nomadic king of the Mongol-like Dothrakis, selling her in order to make a political alliance that he hopes will allow him to invade Westeros. Martin exposes the brutality of this exchange, suggesting that arranged marriage is legalized rape. Viserys treats Daenerys abominably, sexually humiliating her and enacting the "male gaze," turning her into an object through his possessing gaze:

> He studied her critically. "You still slouch. Straighten yourself." He pushed back her shoulders with his hands. "Let them see that you have a woman's shape now." His fingers brushed lightly over her budding breasts and tightened on a nipple. "You will not fail me tonight [when her future husband Drogo will also objectify her by "studying her critically"]. If you do, it will go hard for you. You don't want to wake the dragon, do you?" His fingers twisted her, the pinch cruelly hard through the rough fabric of her tunic. "*Do you?*" he repeated.
> "No," Dany said meekly [1996, p. 24].

Martin is at least in part trying to condemn the patriarchal system that allows women to be prodded and sold at the will of their male relatives, yet the presentation is a two-edged sword that also allows the reader to voyeuristically exploit Dany. Her cowed acquiescence in her status would seem to set her up as a figure to be visually consumed by the male gaze of the audience. Yet she develops into a much more interesting character, not only becoming a major player in the game of thrones, but also mythologically complex and interesting. In the character of Daenerys, Martin unites four aspects of the Sept—Maiden, Mother, Crone, and Stranger—as well as Neumann's Good Mother and Terrible Mother into one powerhouse character. And since her story has not ended, we cannot be sure exactly how or if Martin is going to resolve the tensions in her character. Moreover, we are not sure if she will be able to fulfill her potential as uniter of Westeros, or even if she *should* be the one to end up on the Iron Throne. (Judging from the imagery used so far regarding thrones, I would guess that if Daenerys does win, she will promptly melt the Iron Throne into plowshares.)

The story of how Dany transforms from exploited maiden to "Daenerys Stormborn, the Unburnt, *khaleesi* and queen, Mother of Dragons, slayer of warlocks, breaker of chains" in book three (2000, p. 816) is filled with mythic symbol and ritual. Her transformation begins in the first book on the day of her wedding, which might be expected to be another example of her victimization, when she is given two significant gifts. First, she is given three dragon eggs, thought to be petrified and merely ornamental. But Daenerys, like Viserys, is a Targaryen and therefore has the "blood of the dragon," and so her eggs do not remain stone-like for long. Repeating this mantra to herself—"I am the blood of the dragon"—helps her survive the ordeal of the wedding night (which is less of an ordeal in the book than in the HBO version) (1996, p. 88). Second, her new husband, Drogo, a *khal* (king) of the horse-riding Dothraki people, gives her a horse. When she rides this filly, "for the first time in hours, she forgot to be afraid. Or perhaps it was for the first time ever" (1996, p. 87).

> As she turned to ride back, a fire pit loomed ahead, directly in her path.... A daring she had never known filled Daenerys then, and she gave the filly her head.
> The silver horse leapt the flames as if she had wings [1996, p. 88].

This daring "flight" foreshadows a flight on one of her hatched dragons that does not occur until the end of the fifth book, *A Dance with Dragons*. Nevertheless, with these tokens of supernatural aid, Dany officially embarks on her own hero's journey, which corresponds closely to Campbell's monomyth. Martin deepens and complicates Dany's role as mother by combining it with role as hero. The next stage in her transformation begins when she discovers she is pregnant midway through book one. Soon after, she begins to distance herself from her brutal, yet pathetic, brother and move closer to the true dragons:

> Dany curled up on her side, pulling the sandsilk cloak across her and cradling the [dragon's] egg in the hollow between her swollen belly and small, tender breasts. She liked to hold them. They were so beautiful, and sometimes just being close to them made her feel stronger, braver, as if somehow she were drawing strength from the stone dragons locked inside. She was lying there, holding the egg, when she felt the child move within her ... as if he were reaching out, brother to brother, blood to blood. "*You* are the dragon," Dany whispered to him, "the *true* dragon" [1996, p. 331].

It is Dany herself who becomes the true dragon, but only after she passes a series of tests. One such test is to travel to the Dothraki's sacred city, Vaes Dothrak, to be presented to a panel of crones, the widows of other *khals*. Martin embeds this scene in imagery of the Great Mother: the city itself is called "the Mother" (p. 327), which lies in the shadow of the "Mother of Mountains" and on the banks of a lake called "the Womb of the World" (p. 412). Dany's successful performance of the ceremony of eating a wild stallion's heart, raw, wins the approval of the crones, who proclaim that not only is she carrying a healthy boy-child, but that he will be the *"stallion who mounts the world"* (p. 413). The place names link Dany with the Great Mother. In the same chapter, her brother Viserys finally crosses the line when he tries to steal her dragon eggs and harm her fetus. His attack leads her to report the threat to her husband, who then executes Viserys in a particularly horrible but appropriate way by pouring molten gold over his head. Afterwards, Dany is "curiously calm": "He was no dragon.... Fire cannot kill a dragon" (p. 418), no more than it can kill Dany.

In the final image of the first novel, Daenerys hatches and suckles the dragons in a *tour de force* of mythic storytelling. The deaths of her husband Khal Drogo and her newborn son leave her in a precarious position. His men refuse to follow her, until, in a magic trial by fire, she claims her own hereditary status as the last of the ancient Targaryen kings: *"The fire is mine. I am Daenerys Stormborn, daughter of dragons, bride of dragons, mother of dragons...."* She walks into her husband's funeral pyre, which Martin describes using imagery associated with birthing and nursing: "Sweat ran down her thighs and between her breasts.... The painted leather [of her discarded vest] burst into sudden flame as she skipped closer to the fire, her breasts bare to the blaze, streams of milk flowing from her red and swollen nipples" (pp. 672–673). The ancient dragon eggs that she has put into her husband's pyre hatch and she is found among the ashes of the pyre, phoenix-like, "unhurt. The cream-and-gold dragon was suckling at her left breast, the green-and-bronze at the right. Her arms cradled them close" (p. 673). Significantly, the patriarchal Dothraki bow before her, "and Dany had only to look at their eyes to know that they were hers now, today and tomorrow and forever, hers as they had never been Drogo's" (p. 674). As with Melisandre, Dany's supernatural generative power gives her political power that otherwise she would not have had. Moreover, in this scene, she has become the monstrous-feminine. The abjectness of her maternal body also links her to the image of the Terrible Mother.

For a time, Dany's story arcs steeply upward. In *A Storm of Swords*, she leads her small tribe bravely through the desert, Moses-like, to rest at the ruins of an ancient city. By then, rumors of her dragons have made her a celebrity and she travels to Quarth to try to exploit her fame. Her group gathers strength as she moves from city to city conquering, freeing slaves, and leaving more equitable governments in her wake. The grateful freed slaves adore her as a universal mother:

> "*Mhysa!*" they called. "*Mhysa! MHYSA!*" They were all smiling at her, reaching for her, kneeling before her. "*Maela*," some called her, while others cried "*Aelalla*" or "*Qathei*" or "*Tato*," but whatever the tongue it all meant the same thing. Mother. They are calling me Mother [2000, p. 487].

The fact that Dany, whose biological child has died, is purely a symbolic mother intensifies her association with the goddess.

By early in the fifth book, however, she has come to a standstill. Her good intentions for her metaphoric children have failed, as Catelyn's did. And she comes to see the danger inherent in "waking the dragon." She starts referring to herself as "Mother of monsters" and berating her failure to foresee the "price of power" (2011, pp. 159–160). Her story is not nearly over, however. In another *tour de force* of storytelling, Martin breaks the stalemate by having Dany's escaped dragon return and start wreaking havoc at a gladiator-style contest. Dany heroically leaps into the fighting pit and rides Drogon out of the city to safety, in a scene with unmistakably sexual overtones: "Drogon's wide black wings beat the air. Dany could feel the heat of him between her thighs. Her heart felt as if it were about the burst. *Yes*, she thought, *yes, now, now, do it, do it, take me, take me, FLY!*" (2011, p. 699)—and then goes missing for the next 200 pages. The language suggests part of the hero's journey as described by Campbell (1968), where the apotheosis of the hero is the mystical union with the goddess (or here, the heroine's mystical union with the god): "The mystical marriage with the queen goddess of the world represents the hero's total mastery of life" (p. 120). Significantly, she had named this particular dragon after her beloved husband Drogo. The flight is just the beginning, though, of another series of ordeals that Dany must overcome in order to move to the next level. When we leave her at the end of the fifth book, she is eating seared horsemeat along with her dragon when she is confronted by a group of Dothraki led by a rival. "To go forward I must go back," she thinks (p. 942), but we must wait for the next installment to see what happens.

By combining the qualities of the good mother (mercy, protectiveness of her children) with the abjectness of bodily fluids and the association with monsters in the form of the dragons, Martin has reunited in Daenerys the two halves of the Great Goddess that Neumann insisted on splitting asunder. Gimbutas (1989) complains about this split, which she asserts is not part of the original worship of the Goddess: "A complete division into a 'good' and a 'terrible' Mother never occurred: the Life Giver and the Death Wielder are one deity" (p. 316). Moreover, Dany's parthenogenic hatching of the dragons resembles the self-sufficiency of the archaic goddess: "There is no trace of a father figure in any of the Paleolithic periods" (p. 316). Gimbutas attributes the change from the Great Goddess as an autonomous figure to merely a wife, or worse, demon, dominated by a male god to the "repeated disturbances and incursions by Kurgan people [a term she applies to a nomadic warrior tribe, much like the fictional Dothraki] ...which put an end to the Old European culture roughly between 4300 and 2800 BC changing it from gylanic [a culture with gender equality] to androcratic and from matrilineal to patrilineal" (xx).

> We are still living under the sway of that aggressive male invasion and only beginning to discover our long alienation from our authentic European Heritage—gylanic, nonviolent, earth-centered culture [xxi].

The hyper-masculine culture of the Dothraki, which ghettoizes its feminine side in its only settled community, Vaes Dothrak, is much like the Kurgan people that Gimbutas blames for repressing the "authentic" heritage of the Goddess culture. Perhaps Martin is purposely updating the myth to promote a return to the kind of peaceful, goddess-worshipping culture that Gimbutas hypothesizes. Certainly, the goal of many of the mothers in this series is peace. The point is that all the Martin's mothers combine to some degree both positive and negative characteristics of the archetypal feminine. Daenerys, especially, brings a balance to the nurturing and fearsome sides of the Great Mother. It remains to be seen whether Martin imagines that this balance can bring peace to the troubled world of Westeros. Since the trouble that Westeros faces—political infighting that distracts the Westerosi from addressing looming environmental disaster —mirrors our own in twenty-first century America, observing their struggles can be instructive.

Symbols of the Great Mother

In addition to creating characters that represent the Great Goddess in her various aspects, Martin imbues the books with symbols representing the Great Mother: particularly pervasive are dungeons, crypts, caves, sewers, and thrones. To examine every one, or even most, of these images is beyond the scope of this chapter, but some key symbols recur in the series.

Except for thrones, all of these images are associated with the abject side of the Mother Goddess: namely, excrement, death, and decay. Certainly the dungeons of the king's castle in King's Landing, the Red Keep, fulfill that purpose. The lowest of the four levels of the dungeons, as described in the third book, is a place of unspeakable torment and death: "Once a man is taken down to the fourth level, he never sees the sun again, nor ears a human voice, nor breathes a breath free of agonizing pain" (2000, p. 875). Even so, this underground labyrinth also serves its symbolic function as womb when Varys, the eunuch councilor, helps Tyrion Lannister to escape to a new life through its secret tunnels. Likewise, though sewers are nasty places, Daenerys makes use of them to conquer the oppressive slave society of Meereen and free the slaves into a new life.

Bran Stark, a young boy who is prematurely separated from his biological mother, Catelyn, is particularly associated with these symbolic wombs. The crypt of Winterfell is a dim and gloomy place filled with the dead, yet Bran and his guardians successfully hide there to escape death at the hands of several enemies. Bran then embarks on a journey to the far north to be healed of the injury that Jaime Lannister inflicts on him in the first book. To reach the end of his journey to the north, Bran must pass through a gate and enter a cave that both symbolize his transformation from a crippled boy to a supernatural figure, a Greenseer, who can fly with crows and run with wolves. To get to the haunted forest beyond the Wall in the third book, Bran must first pass through a magic door at the bottom of a well. The door has a face, and when the proper words are spoken, it opens its mouth for Bran and his party: "Its lips opened, wide and wider and wider still, until nothing at all remained but a great gaping mouth in a ring of wrinkles" (2000, p. 638). Clearly, this is a womb image. We do not see Bran again until the fifth book when he finally makes his way to a cave that seems to be filled with "great white snakes" and "stone teeth" (2011, p. 176), which are both images associated with the Terrible Mother. However, the snakes turn out to be roots of the great weirwood forest that is growing above the cave. "Weirwood" is a particular kind of tree associated in the books with the "old gods" and the "children of the forest." Although the old religion is not overtly matriarchal, it is connected to the worship of the Great Goddess through its connection to nature and peace, a less hierarchical culture than the one the First Men and then the Andals, both invaders, imposed on Westeros.

Even more significant is the image of the man that Bran meets in this cave: "a pale lord in ebon finery sat dreaming in a tangled nest of roots, a woven weirwood throne that embraced his withered limbs as a mother does a child" (2011, p. 177). Bran is soon sitting on a similar weirwood throne, drinking the sap of the tree, and learning to use his powers as a Greenseer. He is not entirely happy with this fate, and the reader does not know quite what to think of it either, but foreshadowing elsewhere in the book suggests that the only way Westeros will be able to survive the coming winter and the incursion of the Others is through the help of the children of the forest, so we tend to see these images as positive ones.

In the throne image above, Martin uses a simile to connect the throne to a mother. Significantly, so does Neumann (1963):

> As mother and earth woman, the Great Mother is the "throne" pure and simple, and, characteristically, the woman's motherliness resides not only in the womb but also in the seated woman's broad expanse of thigh, her lap on which the newborn child sits enthroned.... It is no accident that the greatest Mother Goddess of the early cults was named Isis, "the seat," "the throne," the symbol of which she bears on her head; and the king who "takes possession" of the earth, the Mother Goddess, does so by sitting on her in the literal sense of the word [p. 99].

With this in mind, the title phrase of the first book, *A Game of Thrones*, which Martin repeats throughout the series at least once a book, takes on a deeper meaning, as do the physical thrones that appear in the books. If the throne symbolizes the lap of Mother Earth, then it helps explain why literal as well as symbolic mothers are so prevalent in the books. Bran's weirwood throne, natural and rooted to the earth as it literally is, begins to look like a legitimate seat of power. Contrastingly some of the other thrones in the series, especially the Iron Throne so hotly contested in Westeros, begin to take on even darker connotations. Martin created a striking image in the Iron Throne, which has been realized brilliantly in the HBO series and used subsequently on the HBO themed cover of the first book. The first Targaryen king, an invader from the east, had it forged from "the swords laid down by his enemies" (1996, p. 386). Martin describes it through Eddard Stark, who as the Hand, the King's chief counselor, sits on it in the king's absence:

> He sat high upon the immense ancient seat of Aegon the Conqueror, an ironwork monstrosity of spikes and jagged edges and grotesquely twisted metal. It was, as Robert had warned him, a hellishly uncomfortable chair.... The metal beneath him had grown harder by the hour, and the fanged steel behind made it impossible to lean back [1996, p. 386].

The weapons seem to make the throne a masculine object: they symbolize a man's physical and political dominance over other men, and certainly the hard metal seat does not immediately remind one of a mother's lap. However, the ancient association of a throne with the Great Mother asserts itself through the metaphor "fanged." Aegon's Iron Throne has skewed the image of a throne to the side of the Terrible Mother, who is often depicted with devouring fangs, a "mouth bristling with teeth," the *vagina dentata* (Neumann 1963, p. 168). The throne seems to bite certain sitters, especially the heinous ones. For example, the Mad King Aerys, last of the Targaryens, was cut repeatedly by the throne, as described in *A Feast for Crows*:

> By the end the Mad King had become so fearful that he would allow no blade in his presence, save for the swords his Kingsguard wore.... Yet still the blades tormented him, the ones he could never escape, the blades of the Iron Throne. His arms and legs were always covered with scabs and half-healed cuts [2005, p. 232].

Likewise, the throne nips another heinous king, Joffrey Lannister Baratheon. Even before young King Joffrey, child of Cersei and Jaime, ascended the throne, he exercised his power with a sadistic pleasure. After his father dies, he delights in ordering executions, most notably Eddard Stark, the most honorable character in the book. When a prisoner captured during the battle for King's Landing in book two denounces him before the court as an "abomination born of incest,"

> Joffrey lurched to his feet. "*I'm* king! Kill him! Kill him now! I command it." He chopped down with his hand, a furious, angry gesture ... and screeched in pain when his arm brushed against one of the sharp metal fangs that surrounded him.... "Mother!" he wailed....
> The throne denies him!" [the accuser] cried. "*He is no king!*" [1999, p. 687].

Interestingly, Joffrey whines to his real mother here and earlier in the book when Arya Stark's direwolf bites him. As the natural symbols of the Terrible Mother try to annihilate him, he turns to his own terrible mother.

Likewise, the Iron Throne torments Cersei herself. In a horrifying dream in book four, Cersei imagines herself devoured by the *vagina dentata* of the Iron Throne, an appropriate punishment worthy of Dante's *Inferno*:

> The barbs and blades of the Iron Throne bit into her flesh as she crouched to hid her [nakedness]. Blood ran down her legs, as steel teeth gnawed at her buttocks.... The more she struggles the more the throne engulfed her, tearing chunks of flesh from her breasts and belly until they were slick and red, glistening [2005, p. 46].

By the epilogue of the fifth book, Martin makes explicit the Throne's animal malevolence:

> Behind the table where the five members of the king's small council were seated, the Iron Throne crouched like some great black beast, its barbs and claws and blades half-shrouded in shadow. Kevan Lannister could feel it at his back, an itch between the shoulder blades. It was easy to imagine old King Aerys perched up there, bleeding from some fresh cut, glowering down [2011, p. 944].

One last throne, which is described in book three, warrants a look. The harpy throne in Meereen, one of the three slavers' cities that Daenerys conquers, shares the ugly Terrible Mother connection with the Iron Throne and a more explicit connection to the feminine. The harpy, symbol of the Ghiscari empire that has made its fortune in a graphically brutal slave trade, is a monster with a woman's head and the body and talons of an bird of prey—a bristling reminder of the *vagina dentata*. Dany will have none of it: "She had taken one long look and commanded it be broken up for firewood. 'I will not sit in the harpy's lap,' she told them. Instead she sat upon a simple ebony bench" (2000, p. 805). Dany's choice of a "simple ebony bench" instead of a throne is significant and could be interpreted in several ways. It suggests that she sees her leadership as something other than taking possession of Mother Earth, as sitting on a throne indicates. It suggests that she does not look at her leadership as dominance over others. It suggests that even though she herself embodies characteristics of the Terrible Mother that she does not wish to use the image of death-dealing to terrify her subjects.

Conclusion

Symbol hunting is a dangerous sport; the danger is in imposing symbols where none exist. The only thing more dangerous is overburdening a story with symbolic overtones. Martin avoids this by using a scrupulous realism that relies less on the supernatural than a typical fantasy novel. Each of his characters who displays characteristics of the Great Goddess is also a fully realized three-dimensional character blending the good and terrible sides of the figure. Moreover, Martin is careful to use his symbols in a natural way so the repeated womb images that subliminally remind us of the Great Goddess are unobtrusive. Of course Bran would take refuge in a cave in the far north, for example; it offers shelter and protection from the elements as well as the Others.

But what Martin seems to be showing is that a male-dominated culture that splits the Great Goddess into two with the result being the demonization and control of women's sexuality has turned Westeros into a wasteland. The fifth book repeatedly reminds us that the senseless and brutal struggle for the Iron Throne has destroyed crops throughout Westeros in the face of a looming long winter of famine. His solution seems to be to reunite the good and terrible sides of the Mother Goddess in the figure of Daenerys Targaryen to achieve a Daoist-style balance between yin and yang, life and death, feminine and masculine, spirit and body. In the midst of this very political story set in a world where the masculine virtues of strength, fighting skill, and aggression are valued at the expense of innocence, mercy and wisdom, Martin makes motherhood a major theme. He creates mothers who are both politically powerful and intensely concerned with their children, and through their struggles reacquaints us with our ancient, complicated Mother while offering us food for thought about possible solutions to our own seemingly intractable problems.

With the women's movement of the 1970s, America seemed to be groping toward a balance between masculine and feminine values that would encourage both women to work outside the home and men to express their nurturing side. However, maternal love has never been held in the same esteem as paternal power, otherwise men who stay at home to raise their children would be given more respect and childcare workers would be paid more money. Moreover, women today who have children and work either through choice or necessity are facing renewed pressure to stay home to provide "ideal" care for their children. As Douglas and Michaels (2004) argue, the "new momism"—an idealized view of motherhood—"may be as bad, or worse, as the [rigid gender roles] that chained mothers to their Maytags in 1957 ... the problem with the new momism is that it insists that there is one and only one way the children of America will get what they need: if mom provides it. If dad 'pitches in,' well, that's just an extra bonus. The government? Forget it" (p. 27). Douglas and Michaels are not the only ones sounding the alarm: more recent books by scholars such as Barbara Almond (2011) and Elisabeth Badinter (2012) also outline the renewed emphasis on mother's self-effacement and self-sacrifice. Almond warns that "the idealization of motherhood has continued into the present and grown in intensity.... Fierce and demanding pressures surround contemporary mothering" (p. 5). Badinter agrees: "Feminist ideology and contraception might have ... opened up the parameters [for motherhood], but there are now opposing efforts to push women toward a more constrictive model of the good mother" (p. 26). Martin's mothers, however, offer a much more varied and richer portrait of what the role entails. In fact, Martin might be directly satirizing the new momism in one of his least likable mothers, the overprotective and insane Lysa Arryn. She seems to represent "attachment parenting," which sends mothers back into the home to nurse their children for extended periods. This particular form of new momism was the subject of a controversial May 21, 2012, cover of *Time* magazine picturing a woman breastfeeding her three-year-old son next to the headline, "Are you MOM ENOUGH? Why attachment parenting drives some mothers to extremes...." The accompanying article takes a fairly neutral approach to attachment parenting, but it does raise the question of the possible damage done to working mothers: this promotion of intense mother-child bonding "can send anxious moms into guilt-induced panic.... So is attachment parenting a misogynist plot to take women out the workplace and put them back in the home full time?" (Pickert,

p. 34). Since breastfeeding is a cornerstone of attachment parenting, gender roles are reestablished and nurturing returns to being the domain and duty of the mother (despite the gender-neutral term "parenting").

If we Americans could adopt a true balance in the way we define gender roles and motherhood, no longer splitting the Great Goddess into two irreconcilable aspects, women would not have to feel like they had to choose between being "the selfless nurturer or the wicked stepmother" (Thurer 1994, xxvi). But beyond offering working mothers psychological relief, this balance could have wide-ranging political implications. If political leaders valued compassion more and dominance less, we might have sensible gun control laws, for example. If we had a less conflicted view of women's sexuality, we would not be so conflicted about reproductive rights to birth control and abortion. And we might be able to see motherhood and caregiving as truly powerful. As Shari Thurer says of the Great Goddess, "God used to be a mother who worked outside the home" (1994, p, 1). Martin's characters restore the full range of mythic powers to mothers: mercy, love, and nurture are intermingled with assertiveness, political savvy, and strength. Who knows? Maybe Martin's re-visioning of motherhood will encourage us to elect a "Mother of Dragons" president someday.

References

Almond, B. (2011). *The monster within: The hidden side of motherhood.* Berkeley: University of California Press.
Badinter, E. (2012). *The conflict: How modern motherhood undermines the status of women.* New York: Macmillan.
Baring, A., and Cashford, J. (1991). *The myth of the goddess: Evolution of an image.* New York: Viking.
Campbell, J. (1968). *The hero with a thousand faces.* Princeton: Princeton University Press.
Campbell, J. (1988). *The power of myth with Bill Moyers.* New York: Doubleday.
Creed, B. (1993). *The monstrous-feminine: Film, feminism, psychoanalysis.* London: Routledge.
Crittenden, A. (2010 [2000]). *The price of motherhood: Why the most important job in the world is still the least valued.* New York: Picador.
Douglas, S. J., and Michaels, M. W. (2004). *The mommy myth: The idealization of motherhood and how it has undermined women.* New York: Simon &Schuster.
Gimbutas, M. (1989). *The language of the goddess.* London: Thames and Hudson.
Martin, G. (1996). *A game of thrones.* New York: Bantam.
Martin, G. (1999). *A clash of kings.* New York: Bantam.
Martin, G. (2000). *A storm of swords.* New York: Bantam.
Martin, G. (2005). *A feast for crows.* New York: Bantam.
Martin, G. (2011). *A dance with dragons.* New York: Bantam.
Neumann, E. (1963 [1955]). *The great mother: An analysis of the archetype.* (R. Manheim, trans.). Princeton: Princeton University Press.
Ovid. (1955). *Metamorphoses.* (M. Innes, trans.). London: Penguin.

Pickert, K. (2012, May 21). The man who remade motherhood. *Time*, 32–39.
Swaminathan, N. (2013, January/February). Europe's oldest engraving. *Archaeology* 66(1), 29.
Thurer, S. L. (1994). *The myths of motherhood: How culture reinvents the good mother.* Boston: Houghton Mifflin.
Warner, J. (2006). *Perfect madness: Motherhood in the age of anxiety.* New York: Riverhead.

Myth and Meaning-Making in Showtime's *The L Word*

JUDY BATTAGLIA

Set against the glittering city lights of Los Angeles, the flitting of skirts around ankles, the clicking of heels on pavement, the crowded freeways darting to and fro, and the crashing waves of the Pacific Ocean, a group of women inhabit a place known as "The Planet"; a liminal, seductive coffee-shop-turned-nightclub along Santa Monica Boulevard. This clique, the cast of characters on Showtime's *The L Word (2004–2009)*, appeared to viewers to be much like any other series ensemble. However, hidden beneath the glamour and grandeur of the depicted West Hollywood lifestyle are deep-seated myths about female sexuality.

The television viewing audience for the *L Word* was comprised of diverse populations (The Nielsen Company, 2009). The show's series finale, in its sixth season drew 756,000 viewers, the second highest rated episode, behind only the two-part pilot that raked in 761,000 viewers according to the Nielsen ratings. When the show premiered it was "broadcast to critical acclaim and instant popularity"; as an article by Alison Glock (2005) from the *New York Times* pointed out audiences were "suddenly able to watch lesbian characters not only living complex, exciting lives, but also making love in restaurant bathrooms and in swimming pools. There was no tentative audience courtship. Instead there was sex, raw and unbridled in that my-goodness way that only cable allows" (p. 35).

This essay examines the myths of the Amazon, Medusa, Sorceress/Temptress, and Vampire in relation to Showtime's pioneering television series *The L Word*, created by Ilene Chaiken. A discussion about how these myths contribute to our understanding of feminine sexuality through the lens of feminist ideological criticism will be provided. Applying mythological metaphors to marginalized social groups can elucidate structures of domination, subordination, and rearticulated power transfers. Sexuality permeates the various locales of Los Angeles, which functions as a symbol of the ultimate postmodern metropolis. By situating the drama here, the creators and the viewers are able to co-construct a safe space, a rhetorical space, to challenge the hegemonic (domination by consent) myths that we often take for granted.

The setting of Los Angeles allows for a dynamic interplay of temptation, deviance, defiance and mystery (if not, sorcery) to unfold. The urban canvas of Los Angeles functions in *The L Word* as a beautiful yet atypical backdrop for the suburban drama that unraveled (from 2004 to 2009, and presently on iTunes and Amazon) in the heart and homes of West Hollywood. The L.A. setting is a battleground for the characters and a unifying place in which the women are both literally and figuratively given their own "planet." By living in L.A. and frequenting "The Planet," *The L Word* ladies are given a rhetorical space outside the mainstream majority to exist without threat, therefore allowing audiences the opportunity to vicariously question and challenge hegemony and heteronormativity—defined by postmodern theorists Michel Foucault (1981) and Judith Butler (1999) through the concept of the "heterosexual matrix."[1]

"Pretty Little Ladies": The Cast of Characters in Showtime's The L Word

The L Word focused on a group of successful Los Angeles lesbians, their friends and their surrounding community. For the purpose of this essay on myth, six primary characters with two primary story arcs are discussed. The first arc is the love triangle between Dana Fairbanks (Erin Daniels), a professional tennis player, her partner Tonya—who is also her publicist/manager (Meredith McGeachie) and her best friend Alice Pieszecki (Leisha Hailey), a radio broadcaster for an alternative news station. The second storyline that will be examined in relation to its mythical connections is Jennifer Schechter (Mia Kirsher) and her introduction into this new queer world through the characters of Tina Kennard (Laurel Holloman) and Marina Ferrer (Karina Lombard).

Dana Fairbanks

Dana Fairbanks has recently come out of the closet with the support of her friends, particularly her best friend Alice. Coming from a conservative background, her family is a bit resistant to her newfound identity. Tonya is Dana Fairbanks' partner. She is an agent and a publicist and she becomes Dana's manager. Soon after the pair started dating it was revealed that Tonya was only using Dana for her money, power and fame and Tonya quickly replaces Dana with Melissa Rivers who plays herself in the series.

ALICE PIESZECKI

Viewers are first introduced to Alice (Dana's best friend and secret lover), with her bleached blonde pixie haircut and whimsical, capricious nature, on rides like Ferris wheels and carousels—enjoying a day of leisure on the Santa Monica pier. Alice is eating brightly colored cotton candy, lollipops, kettle corn and other nostalgic foods. Her arms are overflowing with stuffed animals and she wears 1960s housewife dresses, ballet flats, and bows in her hair. She has her own radio show on an alternative station in Los Angeles.

JENNIFER SCHECHTER

Jennifer Schechter is a newcomer to the neighborhood, fresh out of graduate school from the Iowa Writer's Workshop. She will later write a novel and a movie about their clique. The audience is first introduced to Jenny in the series pilot through her boyfriend Tim, who is busy assembling her writing studio table, and preparing for her move from Iowa to be with him. His brute displays of masculinity (his brawny body—he is a swim coach) make possible her transgressions in her writing and her sexual life on that same table, in that same studio, later in the series. Jenny herself is almost impossible to "peg" either way. This blurring of the lines in reference to Jenny and her sexuality seems to be the point. She is made the "queerest" character by her illusiveness and her ability to break boundaries, dismantle and become dismantled herself.

MARINA FERRER

Marina is both a part of, and at the same time set apart from, the rest of the group. She interacts with them primarily because she is the owner of "The Planet," a coffee shop that they frequent. She is presented to the world as charming, powerful, mysterious, erotic and exotic. This is partly because she is from another country, and viewers are never privy to her true origins. As the series progresses Marina becomes more central to the story as Jenny's first lesbian lover. Tina is also secondary to the plot being the long time partner of Bette Porter (Jennifer Beals). She and Bette are Jenny and Tim's next-door neighbors. Tina is a successful development executive who recently quit her job to have a baby.

Since Alice and Jenny are the show's principal protagonists and as they are also the ones dictating the lives and loves of the group for the audience, they will be the primary foci of the analysis. As the narrators, Alice and Jenny weave the intersecting tales together for their respective creative endeavors. Alice on her radio show, "The Chart"; a series focused on connections of love and friendship and Jenny on her movie and book *Les Girls*. These are also the character's the creators imbued with the most mythical significance.

The characters in *The L Word*, particularly Jenny and Alice will serve to help link mythological metaphors to a more involved and interpretational understanding of power, gender, and performances thereof. Ideological criticism, feminist criticism, and related structural theories will help connect the various elements of *The L Word* to a discussion of archetypes and mythology central to the way we read and decode pop cultural texts. Through this examination we will be able to better understand what they disclose about our society at large, what we value, and what we view as not only the norm but as desirable.

Theoretical and Methodological Frameworks

Theories and methods help us make sense of the myths latent in various pop cultural texts and serve as a lens to interpret the larger world around us. Ideological criticism, and feminist theories help us to see society in different ways, through different "terministic screens" (Burke, 1966). Using these methodologies and mythologies in order to create an interpretive framework for the analysis brings forth new understandings of ideas regarding feminine sexuality.

IDEOLOGICAL CRITICISM

Ideological criticism explores the ways in which texts communicate about power. Some critical definitions of ideology include those by Jacques Ellul (2011) and John Thompson (1991). Ellul (2011) describes ideology as "any set of ideas accepted by individuals or peoples, without attention to their origins or values" (p. 1). While Thompson (1991) explains that ideological criticism is "the study of the ways in which meaning serves to sustain or alter relations of domination" (p. 1). In sum, ideological criticism seeks to uncover the myths about power in a text. The myths about power that are explicit in *The L Word* can be seen through a feminist psychoanalytic ideological lens.

Antonio Gramsci (1999), an Italian Marxist, coined a term called "hegemony" in order to discuss the myriad ways in which subordinate classes or groups of people subscribe to a sort of "hidden domination" or "domination by consent." The danger in hegemony is that it is insidious; people do not often realize that they are being dominated, controlled or marginalized and that keeps those in power in power and those at the bottom of the hierarchy at the bottom of it. Gramsci was referring to workers in a Capitalist system of economics, but Dr. Philip Wander (1984) and other rhetorical scholars have applied Gramsci's work in order to examine ways in which *texts* (media artifacts such as speeches, plays, poems, novels, movies, TV shows, etc.) reproduce these power dynamics through the use of carefully controlled images, deployment of dialogue, reference to certain unquestioned cultural myths, and through the underlying subtext and metanarrative-which might often be hidden under the surface of a television show or movie. Hence, we use ideological criticism to explore these hidden myths and meanings further and we seek to uncover what taken-for-granted assumptions or "truths" they reveal about our world.

Feminist Criticism: The F Word on The L Word

Within an ideological framework, critics often explore myths about power in relation to gender and sexuality. These critics are often called feminist critics. They typically look at the ways in which a text communicates about gender and sexuality specifically, and about disempowered and underrepresented groups more broadly (Krolokke and Sorensen, 2006). *The L Word* serves as an excellent example of third-wave feminism and post-structuralism in its ambiguity and contradictions, its reliance on technology, its access to power and its focus on the individual and consumer markets.

Third-wave feminist and queer contradictions can function to make viewers comfortable (if they are a part of the queer or third wave feminist in-group on which the stories focus) but also uncomfortable to unfamiliar viewers because the subtext and metanarrative (story with-in the story) of the show function to make viewers question many heteronormative myths that we, as a "civilized society" hold as sacred. At the same time, these contradictions keep viewers watching and tuned in, cued up. In this way, the show is referencing itself and other texts in its genre. Each time viewers started to sit-back, relax and enjoy the show, without deconstructing the story, they were bumped up against another barrier and were forced into self-reflexivity. The creators of the show made sure that viewers could not get away with easy voyeurism, without questioning why they were watching.

If audiences view roles performatively, then a new critical light is shed on the subject of queer representation and the myths in which our culture so relies. If we continue to see the characters' roles as purely performative, as queer feminist theorist Judith Butler (1999) explains, "the origin can be said to be as performative as the copy" (p. 209). These multiple femininities function as a springboard to question the social systems that hold the normative structure in place (e.g., Joan Riviere's notion of "the masquerade[2]). What keeps a myth mythical is its mystery. Once we can unveil these myths, they can have less power over us, and how we operate in the world.

Introduction to the Myths: Mythical Women

Why are myths so important to storytelling as well as the subtext on a show like *The L Word*? On the surface *The L Word*, like any myth, seems to serve a social function—in this case, making female homosexuality palatable to a mainstream audience. Prior to *The L Word*, lesbians were said to exist in a "representational desert" having little to no visibility in primetime, but what are the costs of this visibility? Whose visibility is being represented? These vexing questions will be further discussed in the following analysis through a mythic lens incorporating well-known archetypes like Amazon, Medusa, Sorceress/Temptress, and Vampire, with implications relating to space and place, self-construal, power, sex, identity, and language. These will be described in relation to the characters.

AMAZONS

Amazons themselves, in common cultural depictions, were said to live in and around the Black Sea. In these myths, they mated with the vanquished men they battled and emerged victorious from, keeping only their female children. The first historical mythical mention of Amazon women is credited to Homer's infamous account of the Trojan War, *The Iliad*. His Amazon women were fighting women who although mentioned only in passing, were able to defeat men in previous wars. According to Doane and Hodges (1992), "Amazons were frequently imaged as fiercely autonomous mothers" (p. 127). The independent nature of these clannish women functioned to make the rest of society wary of them to say the least.

Medusa

Medusa—another implied myth within *The L Word*—was often imaged in mythology as "a powerful, serpent-like woman who is said to be a symbol for woman's power" (Doane and Hodges, 1992, p. 126). In most myths, the Medusa is ugly, with snakes and serpents as hair tendrils/locks curling round a hideous face which never saw the sun. She had the power to turn whoever looked at her into stone. That is, she had power over the "gaze," specifically the "male gaze" which is a motif in feminist and ideological film criticism. It is important to note here, that the Medusa had control over this gaze whereas in contrast to feminist criticism, modern women do not. Instead, they are praised in a patriarchal society for their "to-be-looked-at-ness" (Mulvey, 1989).

Medusa herself was not always an ugly and ferocious creature. She was the only mortal sister of a marriage between Keto and Phorky, and a granddaughter of Gaia (the Earth) and Okeanos (the Ocean). Medusa and her sisters were known as "the Gorgans" a sort of trilogy of young women. Medusa is said to have asked the goddess Athena to see the sun in the south. She was very pale and never saw the sun as she only lived in the north. Naturally, Medusa was extremely curious as to what the sun would look and feel like—again, the theme of the gaze, and the power of seeing comes into play here. Athena refused Medusa's request to travel south to see the sun. Therefore, she controlled Medusa's gaze. This exercise of power and limitation of Medusa's rights angered Medusa who accused Athena of being jealous of her beauty (Walker, 1983).

In terms of modernity and post modernity, women are often accused of being jealous of one another for the attention of others, especially over appearances—and the Medusa myth makes reference to that when Athena retaliates and transforms Medusa into a terrifying creature with snakes for hair and the powers of petrification. In the case of both the Amazon and Medusa, myth serves the function of explication—illuminating the construct of strong femininity as exotic, strange, foreign, and even monstrous. These powerful female characters of ancient mythology reinforce the notion that strong women are often ostracized and isolated from traditional forms or representations of femininity.

Sorceress/Temptress

Lesbian women in contemporary popular culture are often depicted as ravenous women who attempt to "convert" the innocent heterosexual natives to come to their "dark side." They tempt them, they console them, and they do whatever they need to do to get them "in" or get them to "cross-over." They are shown as exclusive and cliquey. They are described as gathering in covens.

All of these stereotypical depictions of lesbian identity are seen on the show. However, the show also examines these myths, these archetypes, in order to implode them from within—in order to get us to question why we hold these myths to be true. When we hold them up to the light, do they disappear? Or re-appear as something darker? Different? Deviant?

Mythologically speaking, we can see the women on the show as tempting not only other women and men, but also the viewer or *voyeur*. Drawing the one who watches in but always at a certain expense, one that is either damaging to the viewer or the woman who lures and allures. To continue, in terms of literature and myth, the women on the show are not only shown as serpent like figures but also as sirens. Specifically, the lore of the Lorelai and Hawthorne's "Rappaccini's Daughter" come to mind. In the later story, we are told of a beautiful girl, Beatrice, being brought up on poisons (her father used her as a variable in his cruel experiments), and therefore anyone that comes into contact with her is doomed to perish due to her toxicity. A young scholar by the name of Giovanni Guasconti cannot tear his eyes away from her when he sees her tending to a lush green garden full of exotic plants and flowers in Padua. In the former, a beautiful and captivating sorceress, Lorelei, has a gaze that prompts men to fall in love with her immediately upon the sight of her. A bishop summons her to be judged and even he falls prey to her temptress-like powers. He sends her away with three knights after denying her the right to end her life that she begs of him. He thinks he is sparing her by sending her to a convent (a symbol of a place where women's sexuality is to be pent up, contained, confined). She pleads to be allowed to be escorted up atop a steep stone precipice to view the river Rhine for the last time before she enters the nunnery and once she reaches the plateau and the viewing is complete there she plunges herself into the waters below and commits suicide. In different versions of the story, she is depicted as either a virgin with spun golden hair, a mermaid/siren or a witch (Wilson, 2013).

In both stories the women as well as her loves are tortured and suffer due to a gift/curse of their ability to transfix, to draw people in. To "make people fall in love" with them. Jenny specifically, resembles Circe, with the power to turn people into beasts as she does in several Technicolor dreamscape scenes, particularly at a carnival and in a forest. She too, is often in a garden, muttering spells over herbs, robbing the heavens of the moon and therefore darkening it, poisoning her enemies with juices and potions and calling the spirits of the crossroads, Gods like Hecate and Chaos. Circe too, though, is a victim of the spells she conjures up and the incantations she sings. The message of both the myth and the show's depiction of Jenny: "witchcraft is dangerous young ladies, don't try this at home."

Vampires

In literature, vampires (both in Eastern in Europe and in Great Britain) have been associated with polyphonous sources of desire and fear. They have been associated with freer, more liberal attitudes surrounding sexuality, which automatically makes them a site of socio-cultural anxiety. They are often said to have unknown origins and not to age. They are rarely seen in daylight (Karlsen, 1989). The hypersexuality of lesbian vampirism projected through media often highlights the mix of both eroticism and the macabre. According to Grosz and Probyn (1995) "Like an animal, the lesbian vampire [is] prey to her own sexual lusts and primitive desires" (p. 98). Moreover, comparisons to the mythical vampires can create dissonance because of this binary. Grosz and Probyn add, "The image of the lesbian as part of the natural world-as distinct from the civilized- might repel some, but it is also immensely appealing" (p. 98). Horror films and themed erotica have furthered these associations (lesbians/bisexuals as vampiric).

Before we can fully explore how myth is deployed in this rhetorical artifact, it is essential to understand how the story is presented. In terms of vampire lore, it may be helpful to note that most cultures have some version of the vampire myth within their respective myths. This is an anomaly of sorts, especially since most of the cross-cultural descriptions of the vampire (as opposed to some other mythological beings) tend to be very similar. Vampires are often seen as the scapegoat in terms of mythical creature. Whenever tragedy befalls a village, someone must get the blame: vampires. Could we draw a connection between vampires as scapegoats and characters in the L word? Parallel to Jenny specifically and the L Word women more generally, someone, the Medusa and the siren specifically must die and suffer (Dana—transposed as the Medusa, and Jenny as the vampire/siren).

Analysis

Venus (and Penis Envy)

Alice's storytelling also includes a disfigurement and a radical reimagining of cultural myths that narrate and dictate a search for the lost signifier, the missing phallus. In its place we can discover a legitimate wholeness, a unification of our own bodies, minds, desires and those other bodies, minds and desires that we derive our pleasure(s) from. Most of all, the phallus foretells entry or grants access into the structure of language, which is extremely important because language and myth structure our reality. In many more current myths (especially myths of old that get reiterated and retold) the protagonist is a hero and not a heroine: a boy/man and not a girl/woman. In *The L Word*, the opposite effect of this myth can be seen and this helps to challenge the heteronormative order through a mythical reading of the show's story arcs. Feminist critics and the show's creators refute this argument about penis envy and they call for a radical re-reading of mythology to include the feminine side of the story for its own sake, because it is valued; to revise and repurpose her to more progressive ends.

Alice's Reading

In Alice's reading of the story, the insatiable hunger (for the missing phallus, which is the destructible form of "penis envy" described above) is not eternally postponed or displaced, but achievable, eventually. While Alice is writing in the first season, she mentions that just as some women may have penis envy (not necessarily a lust for the actual organ, but for the power that is heaped upon it by society), some men may have "Venus envy," and become jealous of the life-giving force of the female; as embodied (both literally and metaphorically) by her breasts and vagina. That statement, made by Alice in the first season of the series, later became the slogan for the advertisements of the show's second season run.

In the show's advertisements proclaiming nothing but (no text but) "Venus Envy" each woman in the group is posed naked, draped over one another. They cover each other's most intimate parts and it is difficult to distinguish which body part belongs to which woman. Unlike other popularized series posters/advertisements, all the men in the series are left out. This again incites the notion of the missing phallus, allure by lack of penis, or rather allure by the portrayal of "Venus envy" by alluding to lesbian orgy. The orgy itself, although not essentially freeing just by the mere power of the sex act alone with its frantic, hands and limbs everywhere in a disembodied state and with the entire group participating in it, is a way to throw away the constraints and shed the myths of old.

There are many myths we have about female athletes in particular, and it is interesting that the show shines a spotlight on lesbian tennis player Dana Fairbanks who has recently come out in the public about her relationship to her publicist/agent Tonya. One can see issues of power already at play here. While the publicist is no doubt fierce (as publicists must be in the sporting industry), she is also the most physically large character on the show (the heaviest and the tallest). She has naturally untamed curls of red hair, which adds to the physical likeness of her to her Amazon mythological representation. She has a domineering personality and a loud, booming voice. She is referred to many times as a "ball buster," a "castrator," etc. She is depicted as an ominous individual, somebody who will eat men (and women) for breakfast. She has a domineering personality and a loud, booming voice. Much like Amazons used and discarded men for their needs, the transposed Dana/Tonya persona reflects aspects of both domination and desire for temporality in partnerships.

In physical appearance alone, it is easy to draw the connection between Tonya and the mythical character of Medusa. The untamed hair for instance can be construed as a visual metaphor comparing the mythical and the modern. The strength and forcefulness that Tonya displays is likened to that of the Amazon. Amazons were described to be larger in physical size and stature, which matches Tonya's character. Dana is thin and muscular and seems to pale in size in comparison to Tonya, her partner. Her mythical counterpart and namesake, Danu is the Celtic fertility goddess—a fecund creature who is known for her size and shape. Likewise, in Arabic, Dana means "the most perfectly sized, valuable and beautiful pearl" (Bell, 1991). The name is used for both female and male sexes and is conflated with "knowledge."

The relationship between Dana and Tonya is one of Dana's first relationships, essentially about power and ways of knowing. It is certainly the first open relationship that Dana has had under the spotlight. Dana, in this scenario, seems tightly controlled by Tonya. Dana is often referred to as Tonya's "puppet," her keepsake, her doll, her toy; something Tonya can put in her pocket or play with, take off her shelf, and put back when she is finished with her. Their relationship correlates with the conflict and control of the Amazon in contrast to traditional forms of femininity. Tonya represents the ostracized forceful female while Dana represents more traditional notions. Dana, however, eventually dies of breast cancer and the limits of the body (even a healthy, athletic body) are called into question.

In Alice and Jenny's world in particular, and in the L-world more generally, the conundrum is the trials we have to go through to get there (to this magical state of liberation, in whatever form it may take)—and the fact that there are multiple endings and not merely one fictive end. This sometimes makes Western readers/viewers uncomfortable because we often seek narrative closure. These myths are not mono-causal nor are they predetermined. They do not have to be rigidly adhered to in order to make sense of the world. Even the fear (of the woman-making-myth) is consumed.

By writing, dreaming and desiring, Alice is presenting a critique of a cultural myth that women's writing, especially lesbian women's writing, is outside of the accepted culture/order/canon for story telling or myth depiction. It is *the thing that cannot be said* (or thought to exist) given our language and the binaries our language has set up for us. Alice invites the viewers to pay particular attention to the subtle, the subtext and the metanarratives within the dominant story arc. This reveals the multiple ways that we can both collude and consume the symbolic representation of ourselves and of others.

Jenny's Reading

A cursory review of the literature reveals that other authors have picked up on Jenny's character as temptress and Marina as vampire. As literary and performance critic Mark Bundy (2006) describes Marina, he calls her a "sirenic/vampiric lesbian, *qui est de la maison tire-bouchon*," French slang for "who is of the lesbian world" (p. 73). Marina is vampire-esque (of unknown origins, mysterious, appearing at night and in dreamy sequences) and she is certainly unabashedly "of the lesbian world." She gives the L.A. lesbians a world, a "planet," of their own. They are lost without her. Marina is also the lesbian who manages to "turn" Jenny. She "shows her" "the way," and the way into their little lesbian world. The audience is made to believe that Jenny always had these feelings inside of her, but with her demon-like powers of possession and persuasion, Marina merely brought them out in her. At this point in the storyline, the audience is led to believe that Jenny is bisexual, or "in transition." The desire is again rhizomatic, always becoming, always doing and never "being." It is never static and in Jenny's case it is particularly transformative. In Ken Gelder's (2002) *Reading the Vampire* he explains the ambivalent and ambiguous nature of vampires and how they function as foreign scapegoats for a close inner circle or community. Where in this literature, it is Eastern Europe which is described as "a polyphonous source of fear and desire, in the case of Marina in *The L Word*, it is Western Europe (we see Marina speaking flawless French and Italian) with its associations with freer attitudes towards sexuality that is the site of cultural anxiety" (Beirne, 2006, p. 11).

Bundy (2006) goes on to explain Jenny's so-called "phase of bisexuality" as *marcher voile et a vapeur,* which is again, French slang for "to work by sail and stream." Jenny's infatuation with Marina is suggested as being caused by demon possession (p. 73). She is constantly shown in a state of flux, in a stage of liminality. Winterson (1987) explains this phase as in betwixt and in between two worlds. She states, "Somewhere between the swamp and the mountains. Somewhere between fear and sex. Somewhere between God and the Devil passion is and the way there is sudden and the way back is worse" (Winterson, 1987, p. 68). This supposed area of sexuality links the show metaphorically to the myths of the vampire and other temptresses of the sea.

Marina births Jenny into a new lesbian world, as they arrive together on a boat (at sea) wearing matching (or merging) tan tops and black leather bottoms (Jenny's is a miniskirt, Marina's are hot pants). The women are shown as complimentary figures to one another. They look alike in their skin color, hair color, hair length, body type, etc. Both have pale features and dark hair. Viewers are thus reminded of images of the female double as well as images of vampiric lesbians.

In mythological terms, it is interesting to note that two of the episodes (1.3; 1.7) where the most transgressions occur are at sea. It is also difficult to ignore the connection between the sea and the name "Marina" whose root "Mar" in fact means "sea." This is a mythological trend in which many of the myths we are familiar with contain characters whose namesakes are indeed their mythical stories. The sea is reminiscent, not only of the primordial sea, the womb (in the Lacanian mythological reading), but also of Foucault's (1986) notion of the heterotopia as ship. Michel Foucault (1986) a postmodern theorist explains the heterotopia as "a floating part of space, a placeless place, that lives by itself and at the same time [is] poised in the infinite ocean" (p. 61). The women on the show are constantly at sea or in pools, illustrating the water trope and the fluidity of space and infiltration in uncharted, demon infested, waters.

Once Marina "opens up [Jenny's] world" (1.7) a death must also occur. It is a symbolic death as Jenny finally kills off her heterosexual alter ego Sarah Schuster in her story "Thus Spoke Sara Schuster" (a literary allusion to famous philosopher's Frederick Nietzsche's "Thus Spake Zarathustra") which only Marina picks up on. In her writing, Jenny has Sarah drown at sea. The sea in this case can be seen as representative of Marina, who drowned Jenny, yet birthed her. Marina kills off not only the heterosexual Jenny, but also the Jenny that buys into convention. She gives birth to a freer more unconstrained Jenny. Here, viewers can see psychoanalytic underpinnings occurring since (as Lacan theorizes) homosexuality is a "*desire* to return to the moment of primary identification, and lesbianism in particular" (p. 20). It is a longing to return to the original mother-child dyad, and what that "primordial signifier of mirroring" represents (Walker, 1983, p. 203). Once Jenny comes back from being "lost" she is "found" again in Marina's bathtub, dirty and curled up in the fetal position. Once again returning to the original signifier in the psychoanalytic myth of being born.

In more ways than one, Marina functions to dismantle Jenny. In Season One, Episode Three entitled "Longing," Jenny walks in on Marina and Tim "flirting" at "The Planet." Through cinematic techniques what Jenny sees becomes blurred, and the viewers see Marina and Tim only through a haze. The audience is forced to see the world through Jenny's point of view: through strategic shots of the camera's meta-eye. There is no jib arm camera; there are no long shots where the spectator is able to see what is going on in the "real" world of "The Planet." As spectators we are forced to see through Jenny's eyes. Her vision becomes blurred and she passes out (not merely because Jenny suffers from a bit of malnutrition) because the blurring of sexual identity categories is "all too much" for Jenny. Nothing is clear anymore; all sexuality and sexual subjectivities become blurred. Once Jenny regains consciousness she goes back to "The Planet" to find Marina, in her office looking over some paperwork. Jenny tells Marina, "Every time I look at you I feel so completely dismantled" (1.3).

Dismantling means undressing (which Jenny does) and "to take to pieces" (Heller, 2006, p. 63) which is what happens to Jenny when her sexuality is blurred. By looking through Jenny's eyes, and identifying with her narratively, the spectators' sexual subjectivity is also blurred and taken to pieces. Marina goes down on Jenny and Jenny covers her eyes and cries. Again, the blurring of sexualities is all too powerful, for both Jenny and the new queer spectator. This challenges heteronormativity because spectators are forced (or at least asked) to take on a queer subjectivity (where sexualities become blurred and fluid) in order to view and fully make sense of the scenes they are asked to convert as well, with their eyes and minds they cross over, symbolically into the coven.

Jenny's character as a temptress here is crucial to the development of a "queer" recruitment plot and a spectral entanglement—specifically the myth of the lesbian conversion that is so commonly associated with witches and sorcery (Karlsen, 1991). In order to understand how this myth functions we must examine Jenny's relationships, specifically the communication between Jenny and her neighbors, long-term couple, Bette Porter and Tina Kennard. Jenny spies on her neighbors, and becomes interested in their lives for the "creative experience." The narrative of her voyeuristic encounter in neighboring backyards magnetizes Jenny to Tina, and later Bette, Alice, Shane, Dana and the rest of the gang, especially Marina Ferrar (Karina Lombard), the owner and operator of the "The Planet."

When Jenny first officially meets Tina, Tina is gardening. Tina asks Jenny if she would like some Rosemary, because it is "taking over" her garden. The theme of invasion and takeover is made manifest in relation to this pungent herb. Rosemary was used by witches to cast spells of memory, so one was forever remembered (Nicholson, 2002). Tina may also be an allusion to the Roman mythological figure Pomona—a nymph dedicated to the garden who rejected men (Walker, 1983). It is not difficult to draw a connection back to Circe here in conjunction with Pomona. Circe, as mentioned prior, was also famous for mixing herbs for potions. Circe is clearly mentioned in The *Illiad* as also associated with the sea. She fell in love with a brother of the Nereids, called Glaucus, who was once a mortal seaman, but then became a sea–God after chewing on a magical herb. Circe was distressed that he was not in love with her but instead with Scylla and so she poisoned his waters (Walker, 1983).

Either way, after this instance, Jenny can never get Tina, their conversation and all of her newfound lesbians friends out of her head. She seems spellbound with them. Her thoughts are swimming in her head and viewers are made privy through them as we are to Alice's—through her own stream-of-conscious writing. When Jenny crosses the fence (literally and figuratively) over to Tina's home and away from her own, she submits herself over to Tina, and into the queer inner circle (and their domestic space). Jenny will later do the same and convert her own natives when she becomes the director of a movie based on her story *Les Girls*. These meta-level stories continue, as "bonds" theoretical and familial lines between witches and sorceresses (Karlsen, 1991).

It is interesting that Jenny's writing studio is where Jenny's transgressions of both types (in her writing and her sexuality) occur. Marina (1.12) even explains to Robin (Jenny's new girlfriend, whom Marina tries to seduce) "the Greek word, *eros,* denotes want, lack. The desire for that which is missing. The lover wants what it does not have. It is by definition impossible for him to have what he wants, if, as soon as it is had, it is no longer wanted." Marina is quoting Anne Carson here; author of *Eros the Bittersweet* (1998) *and Jenny is meanwhile, writing in her studio. They are both spinning their love scenes through the act of transference.*

In Season One, Episode Four the theme is the "demonized lesbian/bisexual." The episode's title is "Lies, Lies, Lies" (Dickerson, 2004). The word lies is repeated thrice, which is interesting because the number three is often associated with witches (Farrar & Farrar, 1987) and with the notion of The Holy Trinity. Marina, Jenny and the rest of the Los Angeles lesbians are shown to be "unholy" since they are fundamentally sinners by sleeping with "their own kind." Here, the deviance to the norm (and the challenge to heteronormativity) is embraced. The reader should keep in mind the beautiful Greek sorceress Circe, mentioned prior, who was the daughter of Helios and who transformed Odysseus's men into pigs in Homer's infamous epic *The Illiad*. (Bell, 1991). In a wild carnival scene fairly evocative of Mikhail Bakhtin's notion of the carnivalesque—a world turned upside down after the Lenten season, Jenny stares at carnival goers and passersby, paralyzing them and turning them into swine. This scene clearly illustrates the power of looking, the gaze and transformation, which again is related to the myth of Medusa.

The above episode opens with cheating, "wild" women. One of the women is shown to own a statuette of "a minor demon. Forcas or Abraxas or something." Abraxas makes another appearance later in the episode, as he manifests himself in Jenny's story about demon possession, lesbian demon possession at that. She is sitting at her computer and she has an internal dialogue with her demon and/as herself. He is the demon of lies and deceit and he materializes through one of Jenny's old professors/mentors, whom she once had an affair with.

In this particular scene (1.7) Jenny's cheating takes center stage and her lies and deceit set her up to be likened as demonic. Viewers see that lying for Jenny here is twofold, and that she really is leading a secret, or double life. She is lying to her boyfriend Tim, by cheating on him with Marina, whom Jenny is hypnotized by (again, the witches theme), and she is lying to herself and her lover by not confronting her issues about her sexuality. As for the other women in and around Bette and Tina's pool, viewers see them as sort of a cabal, although they are not really planning anything that affects anything outside of their own little world. Perhaps that is where the threat to the outside world lies, in the fact that they do not need or care about the outside world. They are witches and sorceresses but they are contained within their own coven, their own safe haven. They dismiss the world around them, and the only world that matters to them is their own. However, even in their own little private world, they lie to each other. They are "too intimate," as only women who love women can possibly be, they touch each other and themselves far too much. Tina plays with Bette's hair, and Dana hops into Lara's waiting arms in the pool. These women may be considered "too intimate" with one another in heterosexual terms, but in their own lesbian temptress microcosm anything in relation to intimacy knows no bounds. Whether or not these are healthy relationships or "bonds" in the world of witchery/sorcery is another question altogether.

As for the viewers, they are not sure if these women are the liars, if the liar is Jenny, or Marina, or Tim, or if the whole heterosexual paradigm is a lie. Maybe, just maybe these women have it right. Or are they too, doomed to fail? This is where the real threat to the heteronormative social order is said to lie. Witches always had to be burned at the stake, sacrificed, and drowned, which is the way in which Jenny dies in the series finale. When she dies the serialized drama dies with her, since she is the one telling us the entire story. It is through Jenny as a dramatis persona that we are able to see the myths and what they elucidate about how we view our relations to one another.

Discussion

For our discussion, the reader should keep in mind that a myth can only stay a myth if it is constantly deployed and re-deployed in various discursive formations. We thus, even in our self-reflexivity, are contributing to these cultural myths, participating in its systems. The characters in *The L Word* take apart and contribute to tasks, scripts, narratives, and most of all, myths, which define and re-define their relations to the world and to one another given their multiple markers of identity. If they can hold up these categories to the light (the vanity mirror), they can show their constructedness, their transparency, and their facetiousness. Perhaps, instead of being left with a rigid identity category, they are left with a mutable social and discursive construction.

LANGUAGE, DISCOURSE AND MYTH

Desire is not merely manifested as a "lack" in this show, especially if we examine the setting. We see multiple sites of desire made visible in: the bodies of the three women (Dana, Alice and Tonya), the allure and repulsion of the sorceress and the vampire in Jenny and Marina's affair, the *mis-en-scene* of Alice's bedroom and Jenny's writing studio (where they each awake alarmed and aroused), the jungle, the writing chair, the writing table, the patio furniture, and the laptop. All of these places figure as multiple sites and spaces of desire. The "becoming" power of desire, looking and seeing continue. Alice is both terrified and turned on. The sites and spaces are ambivalent and powerful. The search is no longer surrounding the postcolonial anxiety about the lost phallus. That is made laughable by the civilization/barbarian trope.

The women are not hunting/searching for some lost phallus, some floating signifier that they cannot get their hands on or wrap their "pretty little heads around." The women have what they want even if it is fleeting, messy, complicated and ambivalent, truly third wave. There is no need for the phallus in representational forms. The fear is not necessarily that of the phallic woman (in this case Tonya). The desire, the sexuality, it is all ambivalent and purposefully ambiguous in this scene, where both the phallus and the lack can circulate more freely in this hypercommodified lifeworld. It all becomes parodic, and laughable. The scene then also becomes about Tonya's "animal appetite," (acting as the Medusa/Amazonian woman here) but the women are not easily consumed or consumable sex objects, or mere objects of desire. They are more than that, different from that. The search for the lost (floating, free to circulate, easily consumed) phallus, the floating signifier continues into the next scene in the same episode. The first/primal scene is shattered, and the viewers, along with Dana and Tonya transposed as one figure, end up laughing, literally "The Laugh of the Medusa" (Cixous, 1974).

Freud himself reads the symbol of the Medusa as both evoking male anxiety and reassuring the structuring of men's fear, which is where the issue of spectatorship of *The L Word* once again comes into play (Doane and Hodges, 1992). If anyone who, insomuch as glances at it turns to stone, then why are the women excluded from this story? In their exclusion, lack or negation, it can be argued that they are empowered and developed, both as characters and as viewers.

A traditional reading of Freud's Medusa, and one that Doane and Hodges (1992) give their readers, offers the penis as given "multiple replacements," which can be seen as represented in the serpent like hair of the Medusa. Her powers of petrification, although grim, allude to the hardening of an erection (Doane and Hodges, 1992, p. 26). However, it would be a true "impossibility" for this allusion to be transposed on Alice who cannot be said to have an erection. This fact, therefore, displaces the notion of penis envy or impotence. This is especially true since Alice is indeed shown to be on the verge of female orgasm. Viewers cannot tell if she ever really gets there because the scene is purposefully disrupted. This calls into question the ability to pin down female sexuality. In this scene, the viewers cannot tell if Alice is about to go "hysterical" (which is what traditional psychoanalytic theories would lead viewers to believe), instead the image threatens representation—and therefore the ubiquitous mirror cracks. The image is never so cut and dry or black and white. Instead, it manages to break the binaries and it ends up being all too much and so the scene is shattered, the scene annihilates itself ending in a cackle. Thus the viewers, along with Dana and Tonya transposed as one figure, end up laughing, literally "The Laugh of the Medusa" (Cixous, 1994). If spectators are laughing at the phallus it means it no longer has control over them, its mythical powers are made laughable and trivialized. Female sexuality, on the other hand, is seen as multiple, malleable and fluid and unable to be pinned down so easily.

To continue, as post-structualist ideological critics we can see that in Jacques Lacan's (1977) "graph of desire" we find "the unconscious and the other" on one hand and "the barred subject" on the other hand. For Alice and for viewers, these two concepts manifest themselves in representational forms as Tonya (the unconscious and the Other) and Dana (the barred subject). These two figures are then transposed as one when the episode begins. Prior to the beginning of the traditional episode, utilizing the customary narrative structure (as described above), Alice literally freezes before the vignette is shattered visually. The scene is stopped, and then the image of the screenshot shatters as a broken mirror would. This petrification can be read as purposeful as it can function to remind familiar viewers of Freud's analysis of the Medusa as a symbol of petrifying power. One of the three Gorgon sisters in Greek mythology, Medusa had a glance so terrible that she could turn any living thing into stone. Medusa's power was one that was an embodiment; a terrible release of a terrible force that the ancient Greeks believed was active in nature. Perhaps this is why the setting where Alice comes face to face with the Medusa figure is in a jungle dream sequence.

Jacques Lacan, one of Freud's predecessors, outlined a way to discuss various myths as they pertain to language and discourse. *The L Word* creators seem to follow Lacan's reading by asking the viewer to identify with one of two subject positions and thus transporting viewers into the realm of the male viewer or voyeur, who is made invisible, invalid, infertile and paralyzed by this scene involving Alice's confrontation with the Medusa/Amazon figure. Here, all of the women portrayed (both viewers and the characters on screen) ultimately end up laughing [at the phallus], literally and figuratively having the "last laugh" before the "real" episode even begins. The mirror is being held up and shattered. The viewers then hear Tonya's laugh, artificially reproduced, transposed and mixed with Dana's (literally, "the laugh of the Medusa") echoing in their heads as the opening credits begin to roll. If the Medusa functions as the vagina, as it does in Freud's analysis, then it is a "place of hideous lack" that turns the man who even so much as glances at it into stone (Doane and Hodges, 1992). Once Medusa laughs, she breaks through the cracks in the patriarchal foundation. With her laugh she is dismissive of the whole system.

If the conventional "worst-case scenario" in the traditional psychoanalytic narrative is castration, Alice is disrupting that narrative and challenging it by having the viewer, especially the male viewer, identify with her subject position. The love that the women have for one another is mythological, archetypically feminine. It is a spiritual connection of nurturance, love and support as well as a physical, sexual one. In the Lacanian sense (rather than the Freudian one), castration relates to a subject's subjectivity. The debt is symbolic and not "absolutely realist," as it was for Freud. Alice can be seen as subverting the

Lacanian narrative since the notion and the fear of castration (moving beyond Freud's theory of object relations as tangible and castration as real rather than phantasmic/fantasmic) is no longer pertaining to lacking and giving.

In the scene described above, a sort of fantasy sequence of a romantic encounter between Alice and Tonya, instead of the penis being bitten or cut off, the vagina is being consumed, something that is difficult to do if viewers are traditionally told to imagine the vagina as a lack. Tonya claims to be hungry when she is moving down on Alice and then when she comes back up the audience sees Tonya's face as transformed into Dana's, Alice's lover, and Dana exclaims that she is now "starving." What does this combination of the two figures suggest? A post-structuralist ideological way of reading this scene is that the battles with Amazons are often control over discourse, as Doane and Hodges (1992) explain. The battle is control over "the ability to give order, meaning and shape to our lives" (Doane and Hodges, 1992, p. 26). Discourse is not always assumed to be phallic here, so the issue cannot be who is going to have control over it. Instead, female sexuality is seen as something radically different, one that cannot be compared to the phallus or talked about through traditional means of storytelling. The whole incident between Alice, Dana and Tonya cannot be explained otherwise and therefore ends as a dream, and then the "traditional" episode begins. Alice, herself, seems to have multiple or fractured identities here, illustrating post-structuralisms postulate that not only does the individual have the ability to bring the structure (in this case— the heterological, Western structure of Cartesian dualism) into crisis, but in this fractured state of split (mind, body, heart), Alice's dissonance becomes not only cognitive but emotive. It is essentially a feminine form of writing (Kristeva, 1980; Cixous, 1976). If the struggle is indeed over discourse (what is said conversationally but also societally), as Doane and Hodges (1992) posit, then such "unnatural systems" of order and of structure and of shape (as viewers see represented in the undoubtedly "female" triad of Alice, Dana and Tonya) will threaten a "natural legitimate order" with its "supposedly legitimate inequalities," both sexual and political (Doane and Hodges, 1992, p. 26).

While Doane and Hodges (1992) explain that since both Amazon and Medusa function as symbols that simultaneously control and portray male anxiety, it is also interesting to note the civilization/barbarian trope that comes into play in this scene. Alice, the civilized white woman, is the one rendered helpless by Tonya—who represents and is imaged as the exotic other, and who also represents Alice's unconscious desires, if we follow the Lacanian reading, through the perspective of the fierce Amazon woman. Colorful, exotic birds cry in the distance, beautiful butterflies flutter by, and sounds of the rainforest (rain, trees and bushes rustling) can be heard in the background.

Conclusion

The primary goal of the ideological critic is to discover the dominant ideologies both embedded and muted in an artifact. The ultimate aim of an ideological critic is the emancipation of human potential that is thwarted by existing ideologies. Along with utilizing ideological criticism; some light has been shed on the subject by analyzing *the L Word* using post-structuralist feminist psychoanalytic methods.

If we follow the post-structural ideological analysis (both feminist and psychoanalytic) and we assume that women enter language (and its structure differently) because of their sex or their gender, then they would seem to take a more ambivalent and polyvocal (polysemic) understanding of and attitude to symbolic representation. Women then, as *always already* daughters and potentially as mothers, enter the world through Lacan's (1977) "different doors."

Lacan (1977) uses the metaphor of restroom doors (before the invention of unisex bathrooms) to explain that boys and girls have a binary choice, of which world, (like which restroom) to enter, male or female. Every choice they make and every action they take from then on will be made based on their gender. It monitors how they act and how they speak. Women have a unique subject position from which they speak because they are tied to the body, to nature and to mothering, while men are often tied to the rational, the logical, the external and the cultural. Rather than arguing for an exclusion of women into the position of privilege that men have, women (by both their literal sexual/biological difference, and their different symbolic structural position) must then read and write their subjectivities differently. How this is done in *The L Word* is quite unique.

Instead of threatening that literacy, women have multiple choices regarding how to make sense of it. Does it matter that the one who dreams, who writes, is also a woman here—Alice? In this case, it does. Both writing and womanhood here, power and gender continually re-inscribe these meanings, these culturally constructed activities and ways of being in the world (womanhood/gender and writing which Alice combines and inscribes into nature on her laptop in a jungle setting). Those who deviate from culturally or socially prescribed meanings regarding either their authenticity as writers (their legitimacy into that privileged order—which we see Alice constantly struggling against), as women, or as women who desire women (as the L-girls undoubtedly do). Perhaps those who articulate the deviance from that social order (as both Alice and *The L Word* creators are doing), are giving us as viewers, new ways to map, chart, mediate and co-create their collective experiences and unique subject positions.

Jenny, the sole woman writer depicted is resonant as the strident and sirenic rasp of the vampire—a Medea, a Dido or a Phaedra. Jenny's short life ends in a macabre series finale where it is not clear if she is murdered or if she committed suicide. Her stories are immortalized in the narration of the whole series; it is only after her death that her storytelling powers are fully realized. Relating back to the concept of the gaze, viewers become quizzical as to whose tale is being told and who is watching. The audience becomes privy to the series' plot through a video that Jenny made for the group, weaving together all of their intersecting stories. As each woman in the group is questioned about Jenny's death we see very little but hear the interrogation tapes over static where we get the feeling that our minds or our senses might be playing tricks on us and we might not be getting the whole truth.

Suggestions for Future Research

The *L-Word* can be read both literally and figuratively as the lesbian-figures in this sense can channel widespread concern over how the image is being reproduced in the postmodern, postindustrial city (in this case L.A.). The series makes room for others to interrogate these critical questions and as scholars and viewers we should look for opportunities to discuss both practical (televisual and cinematic) and theoretical/mythical suggestions for future research in the field. It would be interesting to explore which mythological archetype each character can be seen embodying on *The L Word*. Because of the limitations of time and space, the scope of this research had to be contained to a reading of the primary characters.

Other readings can explore the ways in which the mythical muses (they were nine in number) are deployed in various discursive formations in popular literature and culture. We should keep exploring the archetypical, the mythological. As Virginia Woolf (1942) challenges us, "How can we combine the old words [ways of knowing, of depicting, of representing] in new orders [structures, series] so that they tell a truth? How can we deconstruct myths further to examine what they illustrate about us?" (p. 29) [my brackets].

Based on Woolf's (1942) challenge, it may also benefit us to inspect the various metamorphoses of myth into modern and postmodern literature. This study may help us determine the point at which recycled myth and mythological figures become completely reborn and held in the minds of generations completely anew. Alice's character for instance, holds a strong resemblance to Lewis Carroll's infamous Alice who encounters adventures in "wonderland" and later continues her journey in *Through the Looking Glass*. One cannot help recognizing the resemblance of a creature like the "Jabberwock" to mythological monsters of the past. In turn, by having *The L Word*'s Alice enact such a vehement scene which clearly draws connections to renewed and distorted visions through a mirror or "looking glass," that is later shattered, should not go unmarked. It begs the question of whether or not the literature and narratives we produce are simply recycled and remodeled versions of ancient mythology. Have we continued to tell similar stories that are simply revamped to fit each generation? Further, are the stories of the characters presented in *The L Word* acceptable only because we recognize, on a semiconscious level, that they are stories we are comfortable with?

It may also be beneficial to examine how mythological views of women move cross-culturally, for instance the likening of the Amazons to that of the Valkyries of Norse mythology. It would be prudent to question why there is such a commonality drawn between so many mythological representations of feminine figures worldwide and how they are made manifest in our pop cultural forms today. What purpose does myth truly serve in our understanding and "meaning-making" of the world around us and of each other?

This chapter, and this collection more generally, suggests looking backward and examining how stories have functioned in the past (both mythological and archetypical) and how they function as a springboard to envision the future. By exploring how myths of the past become rearticulated and reproduced in media portrayals of marginalized groups we are likely to reveal aspects about our sense-making that perhaps we have never seen before, or had just taken for granted. Hopefully, when we know better, we do better, as we think so we speak, and as we speak so we act. Perhaps, with these thoughts in mind, we can become more open to differences in society.

Notes

1. Heteronormativity is the impulse and desire to perform heterosexually because it is the taken for granted, the norm that our culture (tacitly or overtly) agrees upon. When examining how myths of power are deployed and re-deployed in various "discursive formations" (in language and in society) it is important in our discussion and understanding to define a few terms. "Discursive formation" is Foucault's (1972) term for a social dialogue that is larger than a conversation. It is a system of "thoughts composed of ideas, attitudes, courses of action, beliefs and practices that systemically construct the subjects and the worlds in which they speak" (p. 24).

2. Joan Riviere's (1929) notion of "the masquerade" helps to further emphasize the point that the women on *The L Word* hold femininity at a distance while also embracing certain aspects of this gendered performance. Most of the characters on the show look like mirror images of "feminine" women (mostly white, mostly skinny, mostly pretty), but by "looking like" traditional notions of the feminine, they are able to both critique and challenge the very notion of what it means to be "feminine" through its most sacred means, myths and rituals, and through the means of appropriation and subversion. Appropriation

is the use of familiar objects and images, in the arts, to create a new meaning. Subversion is similar—it is a way to change or challenge the system from within the system's own means. Riviere (1929) argues that the masquerade, by flaunting femininity, is able to hold femininity away from itself (like a woman holding a make-up/vanity mirror in her hand) in order to examine the social construction of femininity more critically.

REFERENCES

Baudrillard, J. (2001). Simulacra and simulations. In M. Poster (ed.), *Selected writings* (pp. 166–184). Palo Alto: Stanford University Press.
Beirne, R. (2006). Fashioning the l word. *Nebula* 3(4), 1–37.
Bell, R. E. (1991). *Women of classical mythology: A biographical dictionary*. New York: Oxford University Press.
Blundell, S. (1995). *Women in ancient Greece*. Cambridge: Harvard University Press.
Bundy, M. W. (2006). Lipstick leviathans: Demonologies of the lesbian body in *The L Word*. In K. Akass and J. McCabe (eds.), *Reading* The L Word*: Outing. contemporary television* (pp. 69–78). London: I.B. Tauris.
Burke, K. (1966). *Language as symbolic action: Essays on life, literature, and method*. Berkley: University of California Press.
Butler, J. (1999). *Gender trouble: Feminism and the subversion of identity* (2d ed.). New York: Routledge.
Butler, J. (2004). *Undoing gender*. New York: Routledge.
Carson, A. (1998). *Eros the bittersweet*. Princeton: Princeton University Press.
Cixous, H. (1976). The laugh of the medusa. *Signs* 1(4), 875–888.
Creed, B. (1995). Animalistic lesbian body. In E. Grosz and E. Probyn (eds.), *Sexy bodies: The strange carnalities of feminism* (pp. 96–101). New York: Routledge.
Dickerson, E. (Director). (2004). *The L Word*. [Television series]. Los Angeles: Showtime.
Doane, J. L., and Hodges, D. L. (1992). *From Klein to Kristeva: Psychoanalytic feminism and the search for the "good enough" mother*. Ann Arbor: University of Michigan Press.
Downing, C. (1984). *The goddess: Mythological images of the feminine*. New York: The Crossroad Publishing Company.
Ellul, J. (2011). *The subversion of christianity*. Grand Rapids: Eerdmans.
Farrar, S., and Farrar, J. (1987). *A witches' bible-compleat*. Carlsbad, CA: Phoenix.
Foucault, M. (1972). *The archeology of knowledge and the discourse on language*. New York: Pantheon Books.
Foucault, M. (1990). *The history of sexuality, an introduction: Volume 1*. New York: Vintage.
Freud, S. (1962). *Three essays on sexuality*. New York: HarperCollins.
Gelder, K. (2002). *Reading the vampire*. New York: Routledge.
Glock, A. (2005). "She Likes to Watch." *New York Times*. Retrieved on March 16, 2009.
Gramsci, A. (1999). *Selections from the prison notebooks*. London: Cambridge University Press.
Grosz, E., and Probyn, E. (1995). Animal Sex: Libido as Desire and Death. In E. Grosz and E. Probyn (eds.), *Sexy bodies: The strange carnalities of feminism* (pp. 278–300). New York: Routledge.
Haraway, D. (1991). *Simians, cyborgs and women: The reinvention of nature*. New York: Routledge.
Hawthorne, N. (2007). "Rappaccini's daughter." *The Cambridge introduction to Nathaniel Hawthorne*. Cambridge: Cambridge University Press.
Heller, D. (2006). How does a lesbian look? Stendhal's syndrome and *The L Word*. In K. Akass and J. McCabe (eds.), *Reading* The L Word (pp. 55–69). London: I.B. Tauris.
Homer. (2004). The Iliad: Book 10. *Poetry X*, Jough Dempsey, ed. Retrieved 8 June 2013 from http://poetry.poetryx.com/poems/4758/.
Irigaray, L. (1985). *This sex which is not one*. Ithaca: Cornell University Press.

Jung, C.G. (1916 [1912]). *Psychology of the unconscious: A study of the transformations and symbolisms of the libido, a contribution to the history of the evolution of thought*. Charleston, SC: Forgotten Books.
Karlsen, C. (1989). *The devil in the shape of a woman*. New York: Vintage.
Kristeva, J. (1980). *Desire in language: A semiotic approach to literature and art*. New York: Columbia University Press.
Krolokke, C., and Sorensen, A.S. (2006). *Gender communication theories and analyses: From silence to performance*. Thousand Oaks, CA: Sage.
Lacan, J. (1977). The agency of the letter in the unconscious, or reason since Freud. *Écrits: A Selection*. London: Tavistock.
Lacan, J. (1998). The seminar xx encore. In J. Miller (ed.), *On feminine sexuality: The limits of love and knowledge*. New York: W.W. Norton.
Mulvey, L. (1989). *Visual and other pleasures*. Basingstoke, UK: Macmillan.
Nicholson, V. (2002). *Among the bohemians: Experiments in living, 1900–1939*. New York: Viking Press.
Nielsen Company. (2009). *The L Word* season premiere in the U.S., 18 January 2004. [Table].
Nietzsche, F. W. (1977). Thus spake zarathustra. *The Portable Nietzsche*. New York: Penguin.
Pearson, E., and Simpson, P. (2001). *Critical dictionary of film and television theory*. London: Routledge.
Riviere, J. (1929). Womanliness as a masquerade. *International Journal of Psychoanalysis* 10(1), 303–313.
Robohm, J. S., Litzenberger, B.W., and Pearlman, L.A. (2003). Sexual abuse in lesbian and bisexual young women: Associations with emotional/behavioral difficulties, feelings about sexuality and "the coming out" process. *Journal of Lesbian Studies* 7(4), 31–47.
Studlar, G. (1984). Masochism and the perverse pleasures of the cinema. *Quarterly Review of Film and Video Studies* 9(4), 267–282.
Thompson, J. (1991). *Ideology and modern culture: Critical social theory in the era of mass communication*. Cambridge: Polity Press.
Walker, B. (1983). *The Woman's encyclopedia of myths and secrets*. San Francisco: Harper & Row.
Wander, P. (1984). The third persona: An ideological turn in rhetorical theory. *Central States Speech Journal* 35(1), 209–301.
Wilson, A. (2013). *Mad girl's love song: Sylvia Plath and life before Ted*. New York: Simon & Schuster.
Winterson, J. (1987). *The passion*. New York: Grove Press.
Woolf, V. (1942). *The death of the moth and other essays*. London: Harcourt Brace Jovanovich.

The Day Environmentalism Stood Still
Film, Myth and the Ecological Jeremiad

RICHARD D. BESEL

The 1951 film *The Day the Earth Stood Still,* directed by Robert Wise and starring Michael Rennie and Patricia Neal, has long been recognized by movie critics as a science fiction classic. The motion picture tells the tale of an alien visitor, Klaatu, who warns humankind that their recent space explorations and appetite for violence has their galactic neighbors concerned. Historically situated during the Cold War, *The Day the Earth Stood Still (DESS)* can be read as a commentary against nuclear weapons and a source of pacifist ideology. By the end of the film, inhabitants of Earth are faced with a grave choice—humans either need to correct their moral failings or face extermination.

In 2008, *DESS* was remade under the direction of Scott Derrickson. Starring Keanu Reeves and Jennifer Connelly, the re-imagining replaced the Cold War narrative with an environmental message. It is no longer humanity's predisposition for violence that is of concern to our galactic peers, but the irresponsible stewardship of our planet. In Derrickson's rendering, humanity is once again given a choice—stop traumatizing the Earth or confront extinction.

Although the two *DESS* films were created and released nearly sixty years apart, Michael Shermer observes in his comparison of the two movies that the 2008 version "closely parallels Robert Wise's 1951 science fiction film classic that was a Cold War warning shrouded in a Christ allegory" (Shermer, 2008, p. 68). Despite their numerous similarities to one another, each film received dramatically different responses from their respective audiences. According to film scholar M. Keith Booker, the original *DESS* is "a courageous film that can rightly claim to be the first truly important work of American science fiction cinema" (Booker, 2006, p. 27). As the first of its kind, Booker also notes that the movie "paved the way for future developments in the genre, setting the stage for the explosion in SF films that marked the decade of the 1950s" (Booker, 2006, p. 27). *Village Voice* critic James L. Hoberman observes that the 1951 *DESS* "would become the best-loved science fiction film of the Cold War era" and the eventual "precursor to, if not inspiration for, Steven Spielberg's 'Close Encounters of the Third Kind' and 'E.T.: The Extraterrestrial'" (Hoberman, 2008, p. 4). Without a doubt, the original version of *DESS* is "a landmark of American science fiction cinema" (Booker, 2006, p. 31). In contrast to its predecessor, the 2008 remake of *DESS* was the target of much harsh criticism. For example, the *New York Times* film critic Anthony Scott blasted the film because he felt the movie's "scenario and many of its scenes feel ripped off rather than freshly imagined ... we can surely do better" (Scott, 2008, p. C7). Viewing the film from a different perspective, theologian Ted Peters concurs with Scott when he writes the film "could have hit a home run. Instead, it struck out" (Peters, 2009, p. 121).

Given the obvious similarities between the films, how does one make scholarly sense of their drastically different audience reactions? I argue the *DESS* films are understood best from a mythic perspective that recognizes minute differences in the films' rhetorical forms. More specifically, I contend both films expose audiences to what media studies scholar A. Susan Owen calls a "cinematic jeremiad," or a list of lamentations in which the possibility of salvation from a spiritual, material, or moral downfall is still possible (Owen, 2002, p. 250). Working within a broadly mythic framework and following two recent strands in jeremiad scholarship, this essay illustrates that films can accomplish the mythic work of the jeremiad and that there is additional evidence for the existence of a unique subset of the jeremiad known as the ecological jeremiad. In addition, this essay advances scholarly understanding of the jeremiad by arguing the *DESS* films underscore the rhetorical and mythic limits of the ecological jeremiad. The films provided audience members with different types of empowerment; the first gave a sense of mythic hope and the second left audiences enlightened, but impotent. Before analyzing the films, a consideration of myth in film and an explication of the rhetorical form known as the jeremiad are in order.

Myth in/and Science Fiction Film

In an interview with Bill Moyers, Joseph Campbell noted that if one were to look up a dictionary definition of "myth," one would most likely find references to "stories about gods" (Campbell and Moyers, 1988, p. 22). Of course, this definition is too simplistic for Campbell. He expands: "myths are metaphorical of spiritual potentiality in the human being, and the same powers that animate our life animate the life of the world" (Campbell and Moyers, 1988, p. 22). Like Campbell, and many others who have studied myth in a variety of cultures and contexts, this essay begins with a broad understanding of what constitutes a myth. Myths

> are productions of the human imagination. Their images, consequently, though derived from the material world and its supposed history, are, like dreams, revelations of the deepest hopes, desires and fears, potentialities and conflicts, of the human will [Campbell, 1985, p. 55].

Myths thus serve a variety of practical, spiritual, and cultural needs. Myths often help us to "address important questions which a culture is asking about itself" (McGuire, 1977, p. 3).

While folk tales and stories have been the traditional artifacts of mythic study, such as in Campbell's work, in recent years scholars have turned their attention to mediated myths, especially science fiction and fantasy movies. For Stuart Voytilla (1999), in his book *Myth and the Movies*, "Whether rooted in scientific speculation or inspired by imagination's fancy, Science Fiction and Fantasy allow us to go where we've never been, see what we could never see, and behold what we dare to imagine" (p. 260). In other words, movies serve many of the same functions that traditional oral and written myths have served in the past. Some have even gone so far as to suggest that today "science fiction is our mythology" (Shermer, 2008, p. 70). In *Millennial Mythmaking*, the editors of this book have pointed out that "contemporary myths, particularly science fiction and fantasy texts, can provide socio-cultural commentary on who we are, what we have created, and where we may be going" (Perlich & Whitt, 2010, p. 3; also see Whitt & Perlich, 2008). That movies and science fiction texts, such as *Star Wars* or *Planet of the Apes,* can be studied from a mythic perspective seems justified given these recent observations.

While movies generally may be studied for their mythic components, this approach seems especially appropriate for the two *DESS* movies. According to Shermer, "Both touch on timeless mythic themes: destruction and redemption, death and resurrection, mortality and immortality, individual liberty and group unity, national sovereignty and global community, and, of course, scientists playing God and technology run amok" (Shermer, 2008, p. 70). While I agree with Shermer's observation about the movies' content, the mythic themes he mentions do not help scholars understand the rhetorical form that is used to bring these themes to the audiences' attention. This is where a consideration of the jeremiad is particularly relevant.

The Dynamic Jeremiad

The American jeremiad is a rhetorical form that finds its origins in the Puritan discourses of the late 1600s. Perry Miller suggests that this "political sermon" may actually be America's first distinct literary genre (Bercovitch, 1978, pp. xiv). This rhetorical form was used often during "ritual-communal occasions and it intertwined practical spiritual guidance on matters of religion and public affairs" (Johannesen, 1985, p. 158). Foundational to this form of expression was the Puritans' mythic belief that they were "a company of Christians not only called but chosen, and chosen not only for heaven but as instruments of a sacred historical design" (Bercovitch, 1978, p. 6). Turning to scriptures about the Old Testament prophet Jeremiah, who explained divine reasons for impending disasters, the Puritans understood God's covenant to bless Israel to extend to the new world, the new Israel (Stoda and Dionisopoulos, 2000, p. 32). However, the promise of prosperity via divine blessing was bound to conditions of pious living. The Puritans' covenant with God "had to do not with eternal salvation of the elect of God but with a pledge to perform a mission within the world" (Minter, 1974, p. 48). The jeremiad was thus part of the mythic ritual of a "culture on an errand" (Bercovitch, 1978, p. 23; Browne, 1992), an errand to carryout God's will in the new world.

As religious-political leaders confronted drought, perceptions of moral decay, and the harsh realities of their new environment, the jeremiad was eventually appropriated as a "state of the covenant address" (Bercovitch, 1978, p. 4). Societal ills were viewed as the consequences of breaking the community's covenant with God. Early speakers were often cast in the roles of prophet, "acting as a kind of intermediary between the god-like authoritative message source and the intended audience" (Stoda and Dionisopoulos, 2000, pp. 31–32). However, the traditional jeremiad was not a purely apocalyptic rhetoric designed to foretell the coming destruction of the community; it was simultaneously a mythic rhetoric of hope and redemption.

Although there are some minor disagreements between jeremiad scholars about the elements that constitute this rhetorical form (Johannesen, 1985, p. 157), there is enough agreement to offer a general overview. First, to borrow a phrase from Minter (1974), the traditional jeremiad includes a "cataloging of calamity" (p. 49). In other words, a rhetor confronts audience members with a detailed review of current afflictions. Second, the rhetor blames the current crisis on the community's refusal to keep its covenant with God. In a traditional jeremiad, this primarily involves the citation of biblical excerpts and spiritual leaders as a means of highlighting what constitutes sin. Societal ills are viewed as God's punishment for those who refuse to live a pious life while carrying on with His work in the New World. However, the jeremiad is not exclusively a divinely inspired disciplinary form. The rhetor, finally, suggests that by repenting and reaffirming the sacred covenant the community can overcome its ills. By following the advice of the Jeremiah, audience members can halt God's wrath and once again bask in the glory of God's grace.

As American culture changed over time, so too did the jeremiad. According to rhetoric scholar Richard Johannesen, "as this rhetorical form evolved into the 1700s, this faith in the errand or mission to fulfill God's plan increasingly was expanded from all Puritans to include all Protestants and eventually all American citizens" (Johannesen, 1985, p. 158). However, soon after the errand included those of different faith traditions, a secular version of the American jeremiad emerged. Politicians soon adopted the new form to "give meaning and significance to the present by contending that today's public policies must measure up to past ideals" (Johannesen, 1985, p. 160). The review of current afflictions, the determination of blame, and a return to better times are all present in the secular mythic form, but biblical scripture and the principles of religious leaders are replaced by our nation's documents of origin and the principles of our founding fathers. This is not to say that the traditional form is no longer used; spiritual leaders still employ this form on a regular basis (Mitchell and Phipps, 1985). To this day, both the traditional and secular forms of the jeremiad remain rhetorically and mythically potent in the hands of skilled orators and storytellers such as Jerry Falwell and Ronald Reagan.

Despite its widespread use and popular appeal, the secular jeremiad has been heavily criticized. In his study of Robert F. Kennedy's use of the form in response to the assassination of Martin Luther King, Jr., public address scholar John Murphy claims that "while rhetors employing the jeremiad may call for political change to end discord, the jeremiad limits the scope of reform and the depth of social criticism" (Murphy, 1990, p. 402). Indeed, how does one advocate for social change when one simultaneously calls for a return to our founding principles? Murphy explains, "The form of the jeremiad directs what might otherwise be a search for social and political alternatives into a celebration of the values of the culture and of change within the status quo" (Murphy, 1990, p. 404). This "oxymoronic potential" of the jeremiad leads many scholars to question the form's effectiveness (Owen, 2002, p. 253). In addition to noting the form's limitations, scholars have also begun to develop two new strands of jeremiad research relevant for this chapter, one visual and one environmental.

For communication scholar A. Susan Owen, the jeremiad's presence in texts is not limited to traditional public addresses. In her study of the movie

Saving Private Ryan (1998), Owen encourages jeremiad scholars to take seriously the visual turn in rhetorical and cultural studies. Owen successfully argues that *Saving Private Ryan* is a "fully developed cinematic jeremiad" (Owen, 2002, p. 250). Illustrating how director Steven Spielberg skillfully responds to America's post–Vietnam national identity crisis with a World War II movie that maintains and perpetuates American mythic structures by arguing war is sometimes necessary, she clearly places the movie within the jeremiad genre. For example, the killing of the Jewish American soldier by a German officer is especially powerful. The slow stabbing of Mellish, while another American soldier stands paralyzed, reminds us that inaction has serious consequences. In their study of Al Gore's 2006 documentary *An Inconvenient Truth,* Thomas Rosteck and Thomas S. Frentz (2009) argue Gore takes on the heroic role of Jeremiah. In the opening scene of the film, they note how Gore takes us from "the sublime peace of the riverbank" to "the frightening vision of impending global disaster" if we do not stop our immoral and polluting actions (p. 6). Although this movie appears to be about Gore's journey, it is the audience who are asked to act. Rosteck and Frentz concur with Owen's assessment about the presence of the jeremiad in contemporary cinema.

In addition to a visual strand, recent jeremiad scholarship suggests we are witnessing the emergence of a new form called the "environmental jeremiad." Dan Buehler (1998) has noticed the use of the jeremiad in Theodore Roosevelt's calls for additional conservation efforts, and John Opie and Norbert Elliot (1996) have noted the importance of the form in American environmental discourse. Opie and Elliot even go so far as to argue that the jeremiad is "the best rhetorical device for handling a most difficult subject— the representation of the American people in their environment" (Opie & Elliot, 1996, p. 35). Like the traditional and secular jeremiads, the environmental jeremiad follows the same three-part division. However, the covenant is now what Dylan Wolfe (2008) has called an "ecological covenant" (p. 11). Rather than breaking a covenant with God or straying from the principles of our founding fathers, the environmental jeremiad suggests that ecological principles of balance have been upset. Evidence of what these principles are is often found in quotations from heroes of the environmental movement (i.e., Aldo Leopold, John Muir, and Rachel Carson). Humans suffer nature's wrath, not God's, should they no longer live in harmony with the world around them. The environmental Jeremiah is thus one who catalogues environmental calamities, highlights how we are "out of balance" with nature, and suggests a restoration of harmony through changes in lifestyle. With this understanding of the dynamic form known as the jeremiad, it is appropriate to examine the *DESS* movies in turn.

The Day the Earth Stood Still *(1951)*

Based on the 1940 Harry Bates short story "Farewell to the Master," the first *DESS* film opens with ominous music characteristic of 1950s science fiction movies as the credits are displayed in front of stars and space. As the black and white picture moves to Earth, the viewer is immediately made aware that something is not right when a soldier stationed at a radar monitor exclaims to one of his peers, "Call headquarters! Get the Lieutenant!" The news that the United States military is tracking an unidentified flying object (UFO) moving at a blistering 4,000 miles per hour quickly spreads throughout the world as scenes of people listening to radio reports in a variety of languages fill the screen. Shortly thereafter, images of monuments disclose the alien's choice for a landing location: The spaceship makes its approach amid panicking onlookers as it descends on a park in Washington, D.C.

The film wastes little time before moving into its first important action scene. Scrambling to make first contact, local police rush to the landing site and are soon joined by Army troops from nearby Fort Meyers. The alien Klaatu (Michael Rennie) finally emerges from the metallic spacecraft that has had "every eye, every weapon" trained on the ship for nearly two hours. His humanoid form seems similar to that of the earthlings, but he dons an unusual headdress and carries an unknown handheld device. Despite his first words, "We have come to visit you in peace and with goodwill," Klaatu's attempts to give the object to a representative of Earth are nervously mistaken as a sign of aggression. Klaatu is shot by a young soldier and falls to the ground as screams are heard in the background. While soldiers attempt to make sense of what has transpired, the eight feet tall robot Gort (Lock Martin) emerges from the ship. The soldiers pull back and the crowd retreats as additional screams fill the air. Viewers see Gort's face shield rise, revealing what appears to be a light or energy source where one would expect to see its eyes. Without saying a word, beams of energy shoot from the light source and destroy all of the earthlings' weapons surrounding the alien ship until the wounded Klaatu calls him off. Rising slowly, Klaatu divulges that with the unknown object, intended as a gift for the U.S. President, humans could have studied life on other planets. A soldier in command arrives in a jeep and orders that Klaatu be taken to Walter Reed Hospital for treatment.

More than simply an opening scene, the interactions between Klaatu and the human soldiers underscore the first of many mythic themes in the movie and provide the viewers with the first components of the jeremiad form. If the jeremiad provides audience members with a "cataloging of calamity" (Minter, 1974, p. 49), the first calamity in the movie's register is society's overly paranoid and militaristic culture. Indeed, the film teaches us lessons about how humans are supposed to (re)act when faced with questions about weapons, war, and other beings. In this sense, the movie speaks rather directly to Campbell's contention that myth addresses humanity's "deepest hopes, desires and fears, potentialities and conflicts" (Campbell, 1985, p. 55). How many myths exist where listeners are told to "do unto others," or "follow the golden rule" in some form or another? The opening scene suggests that the peaceful and reciprocal covenant with one another that has been passed down for so many generations in a variety of traditions has been forgotten; our new social contract with one another is not founded on faith, connection, and love of life, but on distrust, destruction, and death to others.

The opening scene also sets the stage for an additional element of the jeremiad, that of a superior power capable of threatening humanity's very existence if people do not restore the covenant. The observation that violence (the shooting of Klaatu) begets loss of knowledge and understanding (destruction of the technology to study life on other planets) is not sufficient to consider the movie a jeremiad. The introduction of Gort, after Klaatu's shooting, reminds audience members that a refusal to live by a peaceful covenant does not just allow you to analogically fall out of God's good graces, but it entails suffering God's wrath. Klaatu takes on the role of Jeremiah, speaking on behalf of alien civilizations "out there" while Gort is the first of many technological advancements audience members will encounter that give Klaatu's threats an added dimension of credibility.

While at Walter Reed Hospital, Klaatu meets Mr. Harley (Frank Conroy), a member of the President's cabinet. Klaatu reveals to Mr. Harley that he has a message that must be shared with leaders from all of the world's nations, further evidence of his role as a Jeremiah. Mr. Harley, in wishing to keep any information the alien has to offer restricted to the U.S. government, attempts to persuade Klaatu that the logistics of such a request would be too difficult and that the world is one "full of tensions and suspicions." Klaatu refuses to deliver his message to one person only and proceeds to tell Mr. Harley, "I am not concerned with the internal affairs of your planet. My mission here is not to solve your petty squabbles. It concerns the existence of every last creature on Earth." Once again, the jeremiad is present heavily in this scene of the movie. Klaatu's speedy recovery acts as another sign of alien superiority, while his ability to transcend "petty" politics reminds viewers of the kinds of "sins" humanity should avoid. He even goes so far as to suggest he is only impatient with "stupidity" when Mr. Harley insists gathering the nation's leaders together would be impossible. Mr. Harley's interest in looking out for one nation's concerns instead of the concerns of the world at large speaks to Shermer's observation about of the mythic binary of "national sovereignty" versus "global community" (Shermer, 2008, p. 70). Mr. Harley represents all that is wrong with the way humans interact with one another: characterizing others as "evil," manipulating others with only self interest in mind, and disregarding any sense of the communal good.

Upon Klaatu's miraculous recovery from his wound with the application of a foreign salve, he escapes from the hospital to be amongst Earth's people. After stealing a suit, Klaatu decides to assume the identity of the suit's owner, a Mr. Carpenter. Of course, numerous observers have argued for a strong Christian allusion within the movie seeing that Jesus was a carpenter. While the analysis in this essay does not dispute those observations, the Christian influence does not simply function to deliver mythic content, but it also strengthens the function of the jeremiad, a form that was closely related to Christian religious traditions in early America. As it will soon become apparent, the parallels between the resurrection stories related to Jesus and the encounters Klaatu experiences in the film are unmistakable.

Seeking refuge in a boarding house with his new identity, Klaatu meets the caring widow Helen Benson (Patricia Neal), her son Bobby (Billy Gray), and Helen's beau Tom Stephens (Hugh Marlowe). In his attempts to reserve judgment, Klaatu decides it wise to discover why humans behave the way they do. During his first breakfast at the boarding house, Klaatu listens to a host of arguments about the "space man," fear mongering, and international politics. Befriending Bobby, Klaatu learns about American culture by visiting Arlington National Cemetery, the place where Bobby's father is buried. Disappointed to discover the cemetery is populated by those who have died in wars past, Klaatu and Bobby then visit the Lincoln memorial, where Klaatu comments on the wisdom the sixteenth president must have had. Much like the use of founding fathers in a secular jeremiad, audience members are offered lessons about peace and war, right and wrong, and life and death. Realizing he needs to speak to a "great man," Klaatu asks Bobby who he believes is the "greatest philosopher" and "smartest man" in America. Bobby answers, "Professor Barnhardt, I guess."

After solving an equation the Einstein-like Professor Barnhardt (Sam Jaffe) had been struggling to address for some time, the professor realizes immediately Mr. Carpenter's real identity. Klaatu reveals the purpose of his mission to Barnhardt—that Earth's galactic neighbors are concerned about humanity's aggressive disposition combined with their recent acquisition of atomic energy and wish to bring Earth back into peaceful alignment—and asks for his assistance. His warning is delivered in a jeremiad form: "By threatening danger, your planet faces danger. I am prepared, however, to offer a solution." Barnhardt reluctantly agrees to gather the world's scientists together to receive Klaatu's message, but also asks for a peaceful demonstration of the alien's power to "dramatize" for the Earth's people the situation's seriousness. Klaatu agrees to give Barnhardt, and the world, the demonstration.

Unknown to Klaatu, Bobby has followed him and discovered his true identity as Klaatu returns to his ship to set in motion the necessary preparations for the demonstration of force requested by Professor Barnhardt. Tom Stephens eventually discovers Mr. Carpenter's true identity as well, via Bobby, and reveals it to the authorities despite Helen's pleas not to do so. When Helen attempts to explain that the rest of the world is involved in his decision to reveal Klaatu's identity and location, Tom responds, "I don't care about the rest of the world." Helen is dismayed by what Tom has done and leaves him. Before the implementation of his demonstration, Klaatu informs Helen that should anything happen to him she is to tell Gort "Klaatu barado nikto"— one of the most well-known lines in science fiction movie history. During Klaatu's demonstration, for thirty minutes every mechanical device on the planet is disabled or frozen because the "electricity has been neutralized," with the exception of those that would lead to loss of life. In other words, it is "the day the earth stood still." Tom's self-centered actions represent society's moral failings and the demonstration once again illustrates the alien culture's far superior technology when compared to Earth's advancements, giving added legitimacy to Klaatu's extinction threat.

After Klaatu's demonstration, the military steps up their efforts to track him down, quarantining Washington, D.C. With Tom's help, the military finds Klaatu and shoots him in the back before he can attend the scheduled meeting of the world's scientists. Helen successfully escapes apprehension and flees the scene, now desperate to get Klaatu's message to Gort. Somehow aware of the shooting, Gort kills the two soldiers guarding it as the robot considers its next step. Helen fearfully delivers the message "Klaatu barado nikto" to the towering robot; soon after, Gort forces Helen into the ship while it retrieves Klaatu's body. Upon the robot's return, Helen watches and is amazed by what appears to be the robot's ability to resurrect the fallen divine-like hero. Much like Christ, Klaatu appears to be raised from the dead despite his insistence that even his species does not have the power that belongs to the "Almighty Spirit." The mythic resurrection narrative is present nonetheless.

In the final scene of the movie, the newly resurrected Klaatu emerges from his vehicle before the gathered scientists. He delivers his message as planned, telling the representatives, "There must be security for all, or no one is secure. This does not mean giving up any freedom except the freedom to act irresponsibly." Klaatu goes on to say:

> I came here to give you the facts. It is no concern of ours how you run your own planet—but if you threaten to extend your violence, this Earth of yours will be reduced to a burned-out cinder. Your choice is simple: Join us and live in peace, or pursue your present course and face obliteration. We shall be waiting for your answer. The decision rests with you.

Klaatu then returns to his ship, and leaves just as he came. The final scene of the movie acts as a synecdoche (a part representing the whole) for how the entire film functions as a mythically themed cinematic jeremiad. Klaatu, acting as the warning bearer, tells the earthlings what they are doing wrong: acting out of self-interest instead of for the communal good, participating in acts of violence against one another, and developing technologies that could irreversibly damage all that exists. As the alien Jeremiah, Klaatu's threat appears to be made in self-defense when he notes certain destruction is to follow, "*if* you threaten to extend your violence." In other words, it is not yet too late for humanity to redeem itself in the eyes of superior beings much like the early Puritans believe they needed to remain in God's good grace. No judgment has yet been made about humanity's fate; Earth has been given one final chance at redemption. By returning to a peaceful covenant, and extending that covenant to our behavior with other earthlings and our galactic neighbors, humans can once again live in harmony and without fear.

The Day the Earth Stood Still *(2008)*

Unlike the first *DESS*, the 2008 rendition begins in 1928 atop the snowy, Karakoram Mountains of India, where an unidentified climber (Keanu Reeves) stumbles upon a mystical, glowing sphere. Adventurously, the bearded human uses his pickaxe to chip away the ice that has encased the alien shape, only to be knocked out by a blinding light. After regaining consciousness, the mountaineer discovers the sphere is now gone and that he has a circular scar on his right hand. The movie then fades to "present day" Princeton University, where a lecture about extreme organisms is being given by astrobiologist Dr. Helen Benson (Jennifer Connelly). Viewers do not yet know the purpose of the alien sphere, nor do they yet know the reason for the scar on the mountaineer's hand. The early introduction of Dr. Benson is also a deviation from the original screenplay. Whereas the introductions of the modest Helen Benson and her son Bobby come late in the first film, the introductions of the highly educated Helen and her rebellious step-son Jacob (Jaden Smith) surface almost immediately in the second. It is not until first contact that the similarities between the two movies become apparent.

After discovering Earth is on a collision course with an unknown object moving through space, U.S. government officials retrieve Dr. Benson from her home and urgently caravan her to an airport where she joins a number of other scientific experts. Dr. Benson is briefed that the object is expected to hit New York, and that the U.S. government has gathered the scientists as part of an "aftermath" response team. However, rather than having to deal with the destructive impact of an asteroid, the luminescent object slows down and lands in New York's Central Park.

Once the dust from the landing clears, rather than facing a saucer as in the first movie, the alien craft is a giant sphere similar to the one encountered by the mountaineer in the opening scene of the movie. As in the initial *DESS*, local police and the military surround the vessel. An alien humanoid emerges from the craft through what appears to be a glowing passage. Accompanied by slower, tension-building music, the alien reaches out to Dr. Benson, but is immediately shot by an unidentified, nervous soldier. As in the first film, the robot Gort emerges from the light of the craft and disables all weapons and mechanical devices, but this time with some kind of electromagnetic pulse rather than energy beams. The humans and police dogs are also sonically debilitated until the wounded alien calls off the robot. Although it would be tempting to suggest the second *DESS* develops the same mythic lessons about weapons, militarism, and how we are to treat one another that are observed in the first movie, the message is not as clear. Noticeably absent are the alien's lines about arriving in peace and with goodwill. Without the stark discursive contrast between peace and violence, it is possible to read this early scene as a realistic depiction of how a first encounter with an alien species could go wrong because of nerves rather that a paranoid and overly militaristic culture. As it will soon be made clear in the film, the kind of violence the alien is concerned with is not violence directed toward other humanoid forms of life in the galaxy, but other forms of life already on the planet. But audience members are still left with an uncertain list of lamentations for the jeremiad form. However, as with the 1951 film, the demonstration of superior force is still made clear with the presence of Gort, now a computer-enhanced, twelve feet tall behemoth of a robot.

Paralleling the original *DESS* storyline, the wounded visitor is rushed to a nearby hospital. Unlike the first film, the alien does not yet appear in human form. Doctors discover that the alien has actually been encased in some kind of biological, gray flesh-like material that functions simultaneously as a bio-engineered spacesuit and incubator. After removing the bullet, a surgeon notices the outer layer has begun to fall away. He accelerates the process, only to find what appears to be a forming human within the cocoon. They isolate the alien, and it quickly grows into who appears to be the mountaineer from the opening scene. The audience is thus made aware that the scar on the mountaineer's hand was a DNA sample, and the alien who has emerged from the gray material has taken on his human form. Unlike the first film, the second offers a scientifically up-to-date and biologically informed explanation for why the alien appears as he does.

Once the alien fully matures and (re)gains consciousness, he appears miraculously to have a grasp of the English language already. As the world markets react to the news of the alien visitor, a member of the President's cabinet, Secretary of Defense Regina Jackson (Kathy Bates), becomes the "eyes and ears" of the administration. As additional, smaller spheres begin to land in various locations scattered around the globe, their purposes unknown, Jackson meets with the alien visitor. He tells Dr. Benson his name is Klaatu. The scientific superiority of the alien culture is made apparent through their knowledge of biological, rather than purely mechanical, engineering. As in the first film, Klaatu tells Secretary Jackson that his purpose will be explained to a gathering of world leaders, but she refuses to allow this. She encourages him to tell her alone why he has come to "our planet." He turns to her and asks, somewhat offended, "Your planet?" It is here that the environmental message of the movie becomes visible for the first time. The mythic themes of individual property and free market capitalism are pitted against communal ownership and the symbiotic relationships of all beings. When she replies, "Yes, this is our planet," Klaatu clearly responds, "No, it is not."

Paranoid about Klaatu's intentions, Secretary Jackson orders that the alien be placed in a drug-induced state and interrogated. Believing the actions to hold Klaatu against his will are unnecessary and, perhaps, even unjustified, Dr. Benson helps Klaatu escape from the interrogation facility. Again, Helen's role as an important character in the storyline is developed in a way it is not in the first version. With every resource at the government's disposal attempting to track him down, and with the reopening of his gunshot wound, Klaatu contacts Helen to retrieve the medicinal cocoon sample she obtained from his bioengineered spacesuit. With her help, his wound is healed. When she asks him if he is a friend to "us," he responds, "I'm a friend to the Earth."

The use of the jeremiad in both films is clear. However, the second develops an ecological jeremiad. In much the same way Dylan Wolfe (2008) has observed the development of an "ecological covenant" in environmental jeremiads, Klaatu's poignant reminder that we are in a state of balance with other beings, a kind of symbiosis, teaches viewers that any activity that upsets that balance could be met with harsh consequences, including extinction. Although Wolfe is the only scholar to date who has argued for the existence of an explicit environmental jeremiad, the second *DESS* film suggests its use is ubiquitous in our society and in a variety of media. However, in the following scene there are variations in the form that hinder its reception significantly.

Unlike the first *DESS*, the recent version contains a scene where Klaatu meets other alien visitors who have been living among the humans. In a meeting with Mr. Wu (James Hong) at a McDonald's, arranged with Helen's help and with Jacob in tow, the audience learns that Klaatu wishes to reason with the humans. However, Mr. Wu points out humans are "not a reasonable race"; instead, with his seventy years of firsthand knowledge, Mr. Wu has concluded humans are "destructive" and "won't change." Klaatu responds, "It's decided then." It is in this scene where audiences encounter a change in the jeremiad form. Rather than offering hope of survival and the possibility of redemption for the sins humans have committed against nature, the superior beings have passed judgment, thereby emphasizing the apocalyptic elements of the film. However, doing so limits the effectiveness of the jeremiad. Stoda and Dionisopoulos (2000), for example, have argued, "even when an audience is willing to acknowledge the speaker's claim to enact the role of the prophet, there may be limits concerning how threatening the message can be to the audience's self-image, or how readily they will accept the prescribed act of expiation" (p. 47). In this scene, judgment in favor of humanity's extermination is passed over fast-food tea served in a paper cup, thereby limiting the redemptive aspects of the form because humans are never given a chance to correct their wrong actions.

With the decision to exterminate humans now made, the small spheres scattered around the globe begin to capture various forms of life so that Earth's biodiversity can be restored after the extermination. Like the first movie, the Christian allusions to powerful god-like beings are clear, further adding legitimacy to the jeremiad threat. The extermination is analogous to the flood myth, with the small spheres functioning like a giant Noah's "Ark," as Secretary Jackson noted; in a scene where Klaatu makes contact with one of the spheres, he walks on water; and yet in another scene, Klaatu raises from the dead a police officer he has killed in self defense. Confronted by Helen, Klaatu reveals humanity's sin, that the covenant of balance and harmony has been broken: "This planet is dying. The human race is killing it." When asked if Klaatu is there to help the humans, Klaatu simply answers, "no." In a startling follow-up, Klaatu reveals the logic of extermination to Helen: "If the Earth dies, you die. If you die, the Earth survives." In her attempts to convince Klaatu that humans should be extended a second chance, that "we can change," she takes Klaatu to meet with Professor Barnhardt (John Cleese).

That the second *DESS* film uses the jeremiad form is clear in Klaatu's encounter with professor Barnhardt. After helping the professor with an equation and hearing Bach playing in the background, Klaatu states he finds the music, "beautiful." Professor Barnhardt observes, "so we're not so different after all." Despite having already passed judgment on the human race, Klaatu begins to change his mind about exterminating the species. Professor Barnhardt pleads with the alien, "every civilization reaches a crisis point eventually" and begs Klaatu to help humanity. After discovering that Klaatu's race only evolved after being threatened with destruction, the professor points out, "that's where we are. You say we're on the brink of destruction and you're right. But it's only on the brink that people find the will to change. Only at the precipice do we evolve." These lines echo the logic of the jeremiad. Just when it appears that Klaatu is about to change his mind, authorities interrupt the conversation. Similar to the first film, the young boy, Jacob, has revealed the alien's location. It is only after witnessing Helen's connection with Jacob that Klaatu finally changes his mind. However, the extermination process has already begun.

Although the first *DESS* film does not reveal how humans were to be exterminated, the second makes the process explicit. Audiences discover that the giant robot Gort is actually made up of nano-insects that multiply by consuming all matter around them. By the time Klaatu decides humans deserve a second chance, the robot has already disintegrated into an exponentially expanding swarm. To stop the nano-insects, Klaatu must electronically disable them, forcing humans to "pay a price to your way of life." This act requires that all electricity on the planet be forever halted, thus revealing the "day the earth stood still." Although humans are given a second chance at redemption, they are left technologically crippled.

Conclusion

In this essay, I have analyzed two *DESS* films from a broadly mythic perspective while recognizing minute differences in the films' rhetorical forms. From this analysis, I draw a number of conclusions. First, this essay provides additional arguments and support for two additional strands of jeremiad scholarship. Similar to A. Susan Owen's (2002) observations, this essay illustrates the presence of the jeremiad form in film, a cinematic jeremiad. Extending the observations made by scholars such as Dylan Wolfe (2008), this essay also demonstrates how the jeremiad form is now used as an ecological jeremiad in texts other than books, thereby providing an additional rhetorical resource for the advancement of mythic understandings and lessons to movie- going audiences. However, this analysis also reveals how the *DESS* films underscore the rhetorical and mythic limits of the ecological jeremiad.

How do we account for the different reactions to the two films given the similarities in forms? I argue the key distinction between the films has to with how far the second takes the threat found within the jeremiad form, thereby alienating part of its audience. According to Mark Jendrysik (2008), the jeremiad can only function within a delicate balance: "In effect, modern Americans want to be told things are bad. But, as I will demonstrate, they also want to be only lightly chastised before being let off the hook" (p. 4). The analysis in this essay concurs with Jendrysik's observations. In the first *DESS*, audiences were not left crippled at the hands of the more technologically advanced beings. In the second, the aliens appear less like gods and more like beings who made a mistake and left humanity to suffer the consequences of their bad decision-making. Audience members were faced with different levels of empowerment in each of the films, giving the original mythical and rhetorical traction the second could never attain. In other words, the possibility of humans engaging in redemptive action was left intact in the first film, but severely limited in the second. Humans were to be led by a group of their best and brightest as they tackled the challenges of peace. In the second, humanity is left in an uncertain state with no one to lead them. Evidence for this interpretation is also found in some of the reviews of the more recent film. According to Peters (2009), "the 2008 version leaves us without the equivalent of a church—that is, without a prophetic fraternity of scientists within terrestrial society to carry on the mission of advocating ecological health, let alone global peace" (p. 124). It was this difference in the jeremiad form that limits the audiences perceived ability to engage in right action. In terms of environmental communication, practitioners and scholars should observe where use of the jeremiad may go too far in its level of threat. Mythic lessons about the environment delivered in rhetorical forms such as the jeremiad should spur audience feelings of an optimistic future (*DESS* 1951) and not leave audiences wondering what they are supposed to do next (*DESS* 2008). The last thing those using an environmental jeremiad want is to discover they have gone so far with their threat that they have actually created conditions for the day that environmentalism stands still.

REFERENCES

Bercovitch, S. (1978). *The American jeremiad*. Madison: University of Wisconsin Press.
Blaustein, J. (producer), and Wise, R. (director). (1951). *The day the Earth stood still* [Motion Picture]. United States: 20th Century–Fox.
Booker, M.K. (2006). *Alternative Americas: Science fiction film and American culture*. Westport, CT: Praeger.

Browne, S.H. (1992). Samuel Danforth's "Errand into the wilderness" and the discourse of arrival in early American culture. *Communication Quarterly 40*, 91–101.
Buehler, D.O. (1998). Permanence and change in Theodore Roosevelt's conservation jeremiad. *Western Journal of Communication 62*, 439–458.
Campbell, J. (1985). *The inner reaches of outer space.* New York: Alfred Van Der Marck.
Campbell, J., and Moyers, B. (1988). *The power of myth.* New York: Doubleday.
Hoberman, J. (2008, November 2). The Cold War sci-fi parable that fell to Earth. *New York Times,* p. 4.
Jendrysik, M.S. (2008). *Modern Jeremiahs: Contemporary visions of American decline.* New York: Lexington.
Johannesen, R.L. (1985). The jeremiad and Jenkin Lloyd Jones. *Communication Monographs 52*, 156–172.
Jones, J.M., and Rowland, R.C. (2005). A covenant-affirming jeremiad: The post-presidential ideological appeals of Ronald Wilson Reagan. *Communication Studies 56*, 157–174.
Minter, D. (1974). The Puritan jeremiad as a literary form. In S. Bercovitch (ed.), *The American Puritan imagination: Essays in revaluation* (pp. 45–55). New York: Cambridge University Press.
Mitchell, M.E., and Phipps, K.S. (1985). The jeremiad in contemporary fundamentalism: Jerry Falwell's "Listen America." *Religious Communication Today,* 54–62.
Murphy, J.M. (1990). "A time of shame and sorrow": Robert F. Kennedy and the American jeremiad. *Quarterly Journal of Speech 76*, 401–414.
Opie, J., and Elliot, N. (1996). Tracking the elusive jeremiad: The rhetorical character of American environmental discourse. In J.G. Cantrill and C.L. Oravec (eds.), *The symbolic Earth: Discourse and our creation of the environment* (pp. 9–37). Lexington: University of Kentucky Press.
Owen, A.S. (2002). Memory, war and American identity: "Saving Private Ryan" as cinematic jeremiad. *Critical Studies in Media Communication 19*, 249–282.
Perlich, J., and Whitt, D. (2010). *Millennial mythmaking: Essays on the power of science fiction and fantasy literature, films and games.* Jefferson, NC: McFarland.
Peters, T. (2009). Klaatu barada nikto: Reviewing "The Day the Earth Stood Still." *Dialog: A Journal of Theology 48*, 121–125.
Scott, A.O. (2008, December 12). It's all over, earthlings. *New York Times,* p. C7.
Shermer, M. (2008). Klaatu Gort redux. *Skeptic 14,* 68–70.
Singer, R. (2010). Neoliberal style, the American re-generation, and ecological jeremiad in Thomas Friedman's "Code Gree." *Environmental Communication 4,* 35–151.
Stoda, M., and Dionisopoulos, G.N. (2000). Jeremiad at Harvard: Solzhenitsyn and "The world split apart." *Western Journal of Communication 64,* 28–52.
Stoff, E., Boardman, P.H., Goodman, G. (producers), and Derrickson, S.(director). (2008). *The day the Earth stood still* [Motion Picture]. United States: 20th Century–Fox.
Voytilla, S. (1999). *Myth and the movies: Discovering the mythic structure of 50 unforgettable films.* Studio City, CA: Michael Wiese Productions.
Whitt, D., and Perlich, J. (2008). *Sith, slayers, stargates, & cyborgs: Modern mythology in the new millennium.* New York: Peter Lang.
Wolfe, D. (2008). The ecological jeremiad, the American myth, and the vivid force of color in Dr. Seuss's "The Lorax." *Environmental Communication 2,* 3–24.

PART 3
REALITY BITES

Fields of Dreams and Gods of the Gridiron
The Trinity of Myth, Sport and the Hero

KAREN L. HARTMAN

Myths hold a long and complex grasp on how humankind makes sense of the world. Like a hand stretched out that alternately clutches and loosens its grip, myths work themselves into our society where they grope along the spectrum of obvious untruths and clear reality. Myths, however, serve a fundamental part of cultures providing early humans ways to understand life, death, and the creation of the universe. Today humans still rely on them to guide their actions and offer explanations for chaos. The necessity of myths and their ability to create reality quickly reveals the power myths hold.

At the heart of myth, and this essay, lies the role of language to create symbolically and socially constructed meaning. This rhetorical viewpoint of myth emphasizes the struggle over symbols to create meaning as well as the ability for the meanings of the symbols to evolve. Custodians of myths impose a rhetorical frame on events and constantly reinscribe the major components of the relevant myth. For example, American agriculture was long sustained by the myth of the yeoman farmer as the ideal citizen. Jefferson and other founders of the Republic taught that the farmer had a stronger sense of responsibility and morality than city dwellers or wage workers and that the Republic could only be sustained by a large mass of small family farmers. This myth could not survive massive urbanization and industrialization, and though it survives as an aesthetic bit of nostalgia, it is dead as a living force. Myths can become highly coherent and powerful forces, but they can also lose power or evolve over time depending on the rhetoric that surrounds them.

For this essay I have chosen a very robust and pervasive human practice for study: sport and myth. Recognized as "the most important and quite possibly the sole repository for myth in American society today" (Oriard, 1982, p. 212), sport's institutional form and guiding myths have shaped perceptions of sport and athletes such as Jack Johnson, Babe Ruth, Mickey Mantle, Michael Jordan, Peyton Manning, and Venus and Serena Williams. Shuart (2007) argues that sport hero worship is still prevalent, and in survey research he found that over three-quarters of college students admitted to having at least one famous sports hero whom they admired, looked up to, and sometimes modeled their behavior after. The fixture of the sports hero has and will remain strong in American society.

Specifically, this essay examines the interplay of myth, sport, and the hero by exploring the myth of the athlete as a moral hero. This myth has existed in sport since the 5th century B.C. when the poet Pindar first compared athletes to Gods in his poetry for winners of Olympic games. Over thousands of years as people participated in sport, various myths developed out of the value placed on athletes and sport itself. The myth of the athlete as a moral hero exists today through sports discourse that valorizes athletes and keeps the myth alive.

Analysis of this myth, however, comes at a time when American sport is struggling to withstand the threats of the steroid era in baseball and cycling, sexual abuse at Pennsylvania State University, and larger conversations about the role of the National Collegiate Athletic Association (NCAA) and the culture of sport. Transgressions by athletes threaten to weaken the myth of the athlete as a moral hero. I argue that even though there are rips in the myth, the myth is so strong and constantly reinscribed, that the myth will maintain power and continue to shape how we view athletes and sport.

This essay is divided into five parts. The first section discusses the rhetorical nature of myth by analyzing how myths function through communication and power. The second section analyzes the interplay of sport, morality, and myth. The third section examines the myth of the athlete as a moral hero in literature emphasizing the monomyth (Campbell, 2004; Jewett & Lawrence, 1988; Westbrook, 1996) and the combat myth (Burke, 1968; Carter, 1996; Fontenrose, 1959). The fourth section views sport through athlete transgressions that threaten the myth of the athlete as a moral hero and the resulting dialectic between the myth and the reality of sport. Finally, the chapter considers how the myth of the athlete as a moral hero is still perpetuated even though the myth has been tarnished. This fifth section focuses on how sports broadcasters, writers, advertising, movies, books and novels keep fans enamored and maintain the myth as a powerful message. Even though there are damaged and immoral heroes, the myth of the athlete as a moral hero encourages and permits the sporting public's desire to consistently return to that ideal.

Ultimately, this essay hopes to address the lack of researchers who apply myth to modern societies and popular culture. Mythology often is considered to be the study of narratives from ancient societies, thereby becoming relegated to issues and concepts that seem very distant from contemporary times. Campbell (2004) echoes this argument by emphasizing the need for the application of mythic systems specifically to modern societies in order to appreciate and grasp the cultural value traditional mythic orientations convey. Looking at myth through sport offers an opportunity to address this gap in research.

The Rhetorical Nature of Myth

Myth has been studied for hundreds of years by academics and out of that has spurred numerous definitions. Burke (2001) defines mythos as the name for some particular action or the choosing of one story over another and views myth as a part of cultural coherence and a force for identifica-tion. Barthes (1957/1972) offers a concise definition when he relates that myths are stories we tell ourselves about ourselves. Puhvel (1987) argues that through myth the sacred past impacts the present, and both sacred and secular myths are some of the most powerful myths in society today. Regardless of the particular definition one uses, many academic definitions of myths are based on the power that myths hold and their narrative or rhetorical underpinnings.

The role of rhetoric is fundamental to myth and Cassirer (1953) asserts that language and myth are so intertwined they are like related family members. Myths that rise above the others or those that have more power are dependent on how myths function as acts of speech. Myths as forms of speech derive from specific sites and power relations but can be articulated and experienced as natural and eternal truths. For example, Hitler manipulated language about Jews to empower the National Socialist party and to justify concentration camps. Rape myths abound as justification for nonconsensual sex. Myths of how marriages and families are supposed to work often result in divorce and dysfunction. Conversely, we do not have myths about things we do not talk about. It is harder, if not impossible, to find myths about leaves or hairdryers because they do not have mythical power. Myths, therefore, are dependent on language and the myths that become stronger than others are due to their rhetorical effectiveness.

Myths give groups notions of identity and existence that can become so ingrained in the societal fabric that they are virtually indistinguishable from reality. In sport, the infiltration of myths form a society that gets lost within the realities of sport and the rhetorical portrayal of sport heroes as moral and altruistic. Fans might know that athletes on and off the field participate in all kinds of illegal and immoral behavior, but the overall perception of athletes representing goodness reigns as a supreme myth. This myth brings fans to the games, sports pages are filled with tributes to athletes who demonstrate the myth, and movies exemplify the underdog who wins through hard work and perseverance.

From a rhetorical perspective, however, the research on athletes that demonstrates if athletes are moral or not is not necessarily important, as the only thing that has value is the myth. It does not matter if sport produces moral or immoral athletes or some of both. What matters is the larger myth that holds power to shape perceptions of what people perceive athletes to be, and today there are several powerful owners of the discourse that keep the myth alive and powerful. The myth is perpetuated through the discourse that surrounds and creates the athletes as heroes.

The role of communication is inherent to the hero and heroes are constructed in an interactive process that is based on communication. According to Strate (1994):

> [A]s a general rule, members of a society are separated from their heroes by time, space, and social class and therefore know their heroes only through stories, images, and other forms of information. In this sense, there are no such things as heroes, only communication about heroes. Without communication, there would be no hero [p. 16].

Klapp (1962, 1964) argues that heroes and heroic narratives serve various social functions such as offering role models that embody values and ideals, unifying social forces that permit audiences to escape their everyday roles and social structures, as well as serving as symbols to console people for falling short of the ideal that they think they should achieve. For example, when LeBron James, nicknamed "The Chosen One," was drafted by the National Basketball Association's (NBA) Cleveland Cavaliers in 2003, he was seen as a savior for a franchise and a city that experienced years of sporting disappointments. James was perceived as a hero who could redeem a city's losing tradition by making them winners again. This perception of James changed, of course, when he went to the Miami Heat in 2010. Although Cleveland fans vilified James (the myth of James as Cleveland's hero lost its rhetorical power and transformed), he was immediately loved by Miami fans who then started to view James as *their* savior. The myths of sport and the constructions of the hero have the potential to paint athletes as individuals to pin a community's hopes and struggles on.

Sport, Morality, and Myth

In sporting cultures, there seems to be a clear utopian vision of how sport and morality work together. Sport myths in the West include an idealization of sport as positive, humanistic, progressive, and "civilizing." Sport also builds friendships, promotes social mobility, develops liberal viewpoints, and can serve as a deterrent to war. These myths serve as positive and healthy ways to view the role of sport for individuals and society. The positive nature of the myth of sport, however, goes much deeper than superficial notions of making its participants good or happy people in society. Instead, the myth of sport becomes conflated with notions of hero worship and morality. Kyle (1990) describes this myth, and the subsequent conflation of athletes and morality, in the following manner:

> Sport is seen as heroic and its stars as worthy of hero worship. Sport is morally didactic, teaching teamwork, initiative, and self-reliance. Sport is healthy, building body and character as well as moral well-being. Sport is refreshing—a temporary reversion to noble savagery with cathartic and enduring benefits and lasting moral elevation [p. 9].

Barthes (1957/1972) argues that morality is inherent to sport as sport is a public display of Suffering, Defeat, and Justice; this also explains the public excitement of seeing an athlete struggle and then succeed. When an athlete succeeds, there is a sort of moral concept associated with the justice of "good" beating "evil." The mundane success is transformed or made sacred through the lens of the myth. The sudden developments in games through changes in scores, players getting hurt, teams losing, or teams winning, all present a sort of moral beauty. According to Barthes (1957/1972): "The greater the contrast between the success of a move and the reversal of fortune, the nearer the good luck of a contestant to his [sic] downfall, the more satisfying the dramatic mime is felt to be" (p. 22). Fan participation can demonstrate that the public is looking for the construction of a highly moral image and holds a desire for justice and a moral image within the sport world. While Barthes's observations analyze the cultural meaning of wrestling in terms of French culture, they can provide a frame through which to observe the desire for a moral and just athlete in any culture that views athletes as heroes: "In the ring [...] wrestlers remain gods because they are, for a few moments, the key which opens Nature, the pure gestures which separates Good from Evil, and unveils the form of a Justice which is at last intelligible" (p. 25).

The myth of the morality in sport offers a realm where positive life enhancing skills can be taught and learned. It serves as a battle between good and evil through which fans desire the "good" side to overcome "evil" and for justice to prevail. This theme has been recycled over and over, and one area where this is demonstrated and has flourished rhetorically is in literature.

The Circulation of the Myth

The link between myth and sport that is understood today originated and is often circulated through various literary texts. In literature, the combat myth is known as the monomyth and is described in classic stories that illustrate the account of someone going on a perilous journey. Campbell (2004) describes the monomyth in the following manner:

> A hero ventures forth from the world of common day into a region of supernatural wonder: fabulous forces are there encountered and a decisive victory is won: the hero comes back from this mysterious adventure with the power to bestow boon on his fellow man [p. 30].

Jewett and Lawrence (1988) argue that the classic monomyth revolves around the concept that a young hunter-warrior-hero departs on a solitary journey to kill a wild animal, confront an enemy, or experience a wonder vision, upon returning to his community with full service.

Westbrook (1996) explicates the creation and circulation of the monomyth in literature through her analysis of *The Epic of Gilgamesh* and *The Odyssey*. The story of Gilgamesh describes his journey to a distant land in search of the secret of immortality. After finding and then losing the plant of life, Gilgamesh returns home with wisdom and knowledge to enrich his community and is received and reintegrated into society. Similarly, Odysseus goes on a long journey to the underworld, but returns home after rejecting Kalypso's offer of static and childlike immortality. Both stories illustrate the romantic return of a traveler to his home who is renewed after a long and heroic journey. Westbrook argues that this ancient archetypal plot is incorporated into the rules of baseball as the purpose of the game is to travel out and then return home. Westbrook's (1996) insight into the journey and home as illustrated through Gilgamesh's and Odysseus's travels establishes a link between the understanding of myth, how it is circulated through literary texts, and how the myth transposes onto sport.

For Burke (1968) the most perfect story is "heroic" in scale and he provides a more layered perspective of the monomyth through the combat myth. Burke was interested in what constituted the perfect combat myth and compared the combat myth to a warrior culture or one that heavily reflects warrior values. The perfect combat situation must have at least two combatants and the champion needs to fight someone his own size or "like the figure he opposes." Both situations must have origins, habitations, and characteristics proper to their opposite missions according to the imperatives of "artistic consistency" (p. 385) as the combatants copy each other, reach for similar weapons, and strike similar blows (Carter, 1996). The drama of the event is heightened as the outcome of the event will be in doubt. Burke states: "Obviously, a story about someone who simply goes out and wins is much less effective (hence less perfect) than a story about someone who nearly loses, then wins at the last moment as the result of a new development" (p. 386).

Burke's description of a perfect combat myth is a strong illustration of what happens in sport. The players are participants in a "warrior" culture through the reliance on physical strength in order to accomplish a mission. Burke even acknowledges the relation between athletics and warrior culture when discussing the need of at least two combatants to be present: "Meanwhile, any athletic contest or war is sufficient evidence, that so far as drama and narrative are concerned, a combat to be 'perfect' in form needs at least two combatants" (p. 385). Baseball provides an excellent example of just how inherent the combat myth is to a sport.

In baseball, the perfect combat myth is encountered several times throughout a player's time at bat: the batter versus the pitcher, the batter leaving home base to encounter an "enemy" at each of the three bases, and then a final combat as the batter returns home. Not only does the player have to encounter one combat myth, but there are multiple combats throughout the journey around the bases, thus illustrating how central the myth is to the basic formulation of the game.

The tension between the achievement and the challenge presents the perfect combat story since the hero always wins, but the outcome is always tested at some point. The literary constructions of the hero and the monomyth explicate ideal notions of sport and its participants, but what happens to that ideal when players break the moral and heroic mold?

Rips in the Myth

The perception of athletes as moral individuals is a powerful myth, but obviously not all athletes are that way. Cheating often goes hand in hand with sport, and athletes have found ingenious ways to justify their actions in the name of winning. Various incidents in sport introduce important concepts about sport, morals, and myth, yet moral characteristics of athletes (especially successful athletes) and the reality of the sport realm lie in stark contrast to the mythical notions they hold. Research indicates that athletes may have to be selfish and self- absorbed in order to succeed in sport (e.g., Goodman, 1993) and sport maintains a paradox of violence and nonviolence (Gorsevski and Butterworth, 2011). Simply opening a newspaper reveals stories of athletes who cheat, rape, lie, murder, or commit any number of indiscretions.

Negative stories about athletes have existed for years. The Baltimore Orioles in 1890 are thought to be the dirtiest team in the history of the league. Players John McGraw, Wilbert Robinson, Hughie Jennings, and manager Ned Hanlon comprised a team that purposefully tripped opposing players, threw equipment in the middle of running paths, and filed the spikes on their cleats until they were as sharp as razor blades (Gutman, 1990). The National Football League's (NFL) Denver Broncos gave monetary rewards to players who hit their opponents the hardest, and in 1997, a Kansas City Chiefs player related on a radio show that his coach, Marty Schottenheimer, offered to pay off any fines received by breaking the jaws or knocking down any Denver Broncos player (Schefter, 1997). In 2010, professional football player and former University of Southern California star, Reggie Bush, lost his 2005 Heisman Trophy winner recognition after the NCAA ruled that he received improper cash and benefits. In 2012, the New Orleans Saints were penalized and the head coach suspended without pay for a year for participating in a bounty program that paid athletes for violent tackles.

The reality of sport and the state of modern commercialized sport, therefore, introduce layered conceptions of the traditional hero who is understood to display high morals, consummate sporting behavior, courage, loyalty, and bravery (e.g., Chidester, 2009; Horne et al., 1999; Lines, 2001; Mangan, 1981; Radford, 2005; Trujillo, 1994; Vande Berg, 1998; Walton, 2004; Whannel, 1995). One type of hero is the modern day celebrity hero (Boorstin, 1978; Strate, 1994; Vande Berg, 1998). This hero differentiates him/herself from traditional notions of a hero as this hero is constructed by the media as an image, a trademark, or as a name only. These heroes become known superficially by their physical appearance and strength. According to Boorstin (1978), contemporary mediated heroes perform acts far less significant and have characteristics far less idealized than mythological heroes of ancient times. Furthermore, Vande Berg's (1998) research explicates the changing role of the hero in contemporary sports media. She emphasizes the role of mass media as primary vehicles through which society learns of accomplishments, courage, and the deeds of cultural heroes, and the faults and shameful deeds of the villain. Another type of hero is the sport heroine who is marginalized, trivialized, and objectified rendering them invisible and questionable role models (Lines, 2001). Finally, there is the hero that is the "damaged hero." Lines defines this hero as: "the male sports celebrity exemplifying contemporary laddishness, drunken exploits, wife and girlfriend beatings and gay relationships [...]" (p. 285). Models of the damaged hero are prevalent in today's sporting news. For example, former professional football player Terrell Owens publicly feuded with teammates and coaches, demanded to be traded to different teams, and allegedly threatened to commit suicide. The NBA's Kobe Bryant was accused of raping a 19-year-old girl in 2003, but just several years later was in the adoring eye of the public as the league's 2008 MVP, and Tiger Woods has spent years trying to repair his reputation after the 2009 sex scandal. The damaged hero serves as a standard fixture in today's sporting arena.

These examples of heroes that stand in contrast to the myth of the athlete as a moral hero presents what Eitzen (2006) discusses as the paradox of sport. He states: "[S]port [...] fosters the admirable traits of courage, determination, hard work, fairness, respect, sacrifice, and loyalty. But sport also promotes rule breaking, selfishness, greed, contempt for opponents, and violence on the field as well as deviant behaviors off the field" (p. 54). The conflicting stories and perceptions of sport and athletes create an interesting dichotomy that cannot be easily assessed or sorted.

Owners of the Discourse

As myths gain power from discourse, the myth of the athlete as a moral hero is created by the language surrounding sport. Not everyone acts as a moral ambassador on and off the field, but there is a constant drumbeat of discourse promulgating the perception that sport holds a positive role in society and people who participate in it acquire positive life enhancing traits. Today there are four major purveyors of the myth that keep it powerful: sports broadcasters and writers; advertisements; the movie industry, and books and popular novels.

SPORTS BROADCASTERS AND WRITERS

The first major owner of discourse and enforcer of the myth the athlete as a moral hero is the world of sports broadcasters and writers. Since the beginning of organized sport in America, newspaper writers made athletes household names and glorified the actions and accomplishments of athletes. Writers such as Red Smith, George Plimpton, Rick Telander, Grantland Rice, Rick Reilly, Paul Gallico, Roger Angell, Robert Creamer, Ring Lardner, and Stanley Cohen are a few who wrote about sport and created narratives of winning, justice, teamwork, and purity. Similarly, sports commentators such as Vin Scully, Chick Hearn, Howard Cosell, Marv Albert, Tony Kornheiser, Mike Wilbon, Jim Rome, and Bob Costas are a few examples of prominent sports commentators that present sport as an arena for similar narratives of sport and hope, family, love, unity, and American values. One of the most prolific sports writers of the 20th century, Red Smith (1983), acknowledges the role of the sports reporter in supporting the mythological notion of sport and the athlete: "I won't deny that the heavy majority of sportswriters, myself included, have been and still are guilty of puffing up the people they write about" (p. 15).

Continuing the myth of sport through discourse occurs in daily newspapers, weekly and monthly magazines, nightly football and basketball games, the Olympics, the World Cup, and other news programs and sports shows. The rise of 24-hour sports coverage such as ESPN, ESPN2, and Fox Sports serves to repeat the narrative of sport as a moral arena. National tragedies, however, demonstrate the manner in which sporting discourse maintains the myth of sport on a very large scale. Discourse post 9/11 and after Hurricane Katrina offer examples of the rhetorical power that moves sport beyond the playing field into various narratives about patriotism, renewal, and the hero.

A major national disaster that used the myth of sport as a way for America to heal and find purpose was 9/11. In widespread post–9/11 discourse, many commentators argued that the attack signaled a return of the traditional hero and "manly men" (Young, 2002). Sport commentating post 9/11 portrayed the area as a repository of heroes and as a way to fulfill one's patriotic duty (Chidester, 2009). An exemplification of this discourse was after the first Super Bowl game post–9/11. The game occurred at the New Orleans Superdome and produced a stage that merged patriotism and sport. Steve Serby (2002), a writer for the *New York Post*, illustrates the rhetorical merging of sport and patriotism:

> Inside a red, white and blue fortress called the Superdome, they let freedom ring last night, and they let freedom sing, and then they played a football game that stands today as tall as the Twin Towers once did, as a defiant statue of liberty. On the night they wrapped a star-spangled banner around the neck of terror and squeezed tight, they played a football game that will be remembered as Patriots' Day [p. 70].

Arguably jingoistic, Serby conflates concepts of patriotism and pride within the frame of a football game. The game, the players, and those who watched served as types of soldiers fighting for America through their participation in the sporting arena. His message painted everyone involved in sport as a type of hero fighting for the moral good of American values.

An additional example of post 9/11 discourse and the myth of the athletic hero was illustrated through the rhetoric promoting Pat Tillman as a hero. The story of Tillman is well known to millions of Americans; he gave up a $3.6 million contract with the NFL's Arizona Cardinals to become an Army Ranger and was portrayed as a man who symbolized a very clear message to the American public. A successful professional athlete who willingly gave up fame and fortune to put his life on the line as an $18,000-a-year Army Ranger, Tillman became a symbol for American ideals and heroism all within the sporting package.

When Tillman was killed, sport discourse again portrayed the athlete as the ultimate hero. His funeral was nationally televised and sports agents grabbed onto the narrative of a war hero and football star who died. Sports writers and commentators reflected the narrative in their writing. For example, sportswriter Joe Concha (2004) wrote: Athletes are called heroes all the time by those in the press box. But in terms of the true definition of the word, Pat Tillman was truly brave, truly noble, and most of all, a true American hero that kids and adults alike should look up to (19–20). Tillman served as the ultimate athletic hero fighting for the moral good of America. Not only was he a sporting hero due to his professional career, but writers and commentators took advantage of the narrative resulting in a nationally visible perpetuation of the athlete as a moral hero.

An additional national disaster that spurred commentators to perpetuate the myth of the athlete as a moral hero was Hurricane Katrina. On August 29, 2005, Hurricane Katrina devastated the Gulf Coast region and in New Orleans 25,000 people were displaced to the Superdome (home of the NFL's Saints). Overnight the superdome was transferred from a recreational venue to a homeless shelter (Zirin, 2007). The destruction and eventual evacuation of an entire city placed New Orleans in the national spotlight with many perceiving the federal government's response as inhumane, racist, and utterly incomplete.

Sports writers and commentators, however, used the Superdome and the Saints as hope for renewal and promise for the city. Discourse surrounding the first game (nationally televised and on Monday Night Football) reified the myth of sport as moral and athletes as heroes. Paul Attner's (2006) article "They're HOME. There's HOPE" illustrated the refurbished Superdome as a place of renewal: Now it's a symbol of a new beginning for the city, its roof shiny white again. 'If they can get the dome ready this fast, it should inspire folks to come back and build their homes and open their businesses,' says [Saint's receiver Joe] Horn. 'And for a lot of people who will be there, it will exorcise the demons of what they endured inside the dome during Katrina'" (10). This writing not only offers sport as a return to normalcy, but it plays on the myth of sport to cover up the tragedy and reality of the city that was still in shambles.

National Public Radio's Chris Rose stated on a September 25, 2006 newscast about the Monday Night Football game and used rhetoric such as "a cause for celebration," "[the Superdome's] durability is our durability," "a triumph," a "community reborn," and regardless of the outcome of the game, we should "chalk up a big W for the city of New Orleans."

Commentator Tony Kornheiser also perpetuated the myth of sport as a way for hope and unity. He stated during the telecast of the game:

> [Y]ou rebuild and recover a little at a time, and before you do it with bricks and wood, you do it with symbols, like a team coming back home and a stadium reopening. This night and this game matter dearly to the people of New Orleans, the ones who are scattered and the ones who remain, and if it matters to them it should matter to all of us as well [as cited in Walker, 2007, 6].

Sports writers and commentators are one example of the manner that discourse perpetuates and substantiates the myth of sport. Their articles and broadcasts are read and heard by millions of people and it is their dialogue that promulgates a specific version of the role and opportunity sport can provide and the athletes that participate. Although the sporting public might hear the narrative during the telecast or they might read about it on the front page, advertising serves as a second area that works to reify the myth as well.

Advertising

The rise of television introduced the growth of advertising in the sporting arena. Burstyn (1999) explicates this rise and argues that the 1960s offered a distinct shift in the role of advertising in sport. By this decade, advertisers selling cars, electronic appliances, insurances, clothes, sports equipment, cigarettes, beer and grooming products inundated the airwaves seeking specific male audiences. The use of advertising grew throughout the late 20th century and today not only does advertising bring in millions of dollars a year, but it serves as a powerful way to construct the athlete and create levels of identification between athletes and the sporting community.

In the early 21st century the use of celebrity-hero athletes increased; Nike spent an estimated $1.4 billion in 2003–2004 on celebrity endorsements (Shuart, 2007). Celebrity endorsements alone, however, are not enough to create a connection with viewers. Viewers need to feel some level of identification with the athlete (Basil, 1996) and fans hold a higher level of identification with athletes that are role models than with celebrities (Brown and

Basil, 1995). Shuart (2007) argues that there is much more identification with a hero than with a celebrity and sports heroes are more effective endorsers of products than non-heroes.

There are numerous advertising campaigns that perpetuate notions of the individual athlete as a moral figure. For example, Michael Jordan was one of the first professional athletes to perfect sponsorship and eventually made millions of dollars more in revenue from advertisers than he did as a basketball player. His image was used in a very specific manner and McDonald and Andrews (2001) argue that Jordan used a media image that capitalized on his "humility, inner drive, personal responsibility and moral righteousness" (p. 26). Furthermore, at the height of his career, Tiger Woods expanded on how Jordan utilized advertisement endorsement deals and became the first athlete to make $1 billion (Badenhausen, 2009). Advertisements before his scandal in 2009 emphasized Woods' golfing ability, credibility, and trustworthiness, and he was viewed as a perfect celebrity endorser due to his golfing abilities and his relatively low profile life.

Professional sports leagues also use advertising campaigns to communicate the role of the hero. For example, the NBA created a 2011–2012 campaign titled "Where Amazing Happens" to highlight marquee players and their unique and extraordinary skills. The campaign included videos of when the players were young to suggest how hard they worked to succeed in the sport. Another example is the 2011 postseason Major League Baseball (MLB) campaign that used the tagline "Legends are born in October" to emphasize the heroic nature of those who made it to the playoffs. In hockey, the National Hockey League (NHL) used an advertising campaign during the 2011–2012 season titled "Because It's the Cup" and "History Will Be Made." The latter campaign shows a video of one of the greatest players in the history of the league, Mario Lemieux, scoring a goal with a tagline that asks: "What if Mario wasn't so super?"

Campaigns such as these not only emphasize the heroic nature of players in various leagues, they also emphasize an athlete's moral worth. In football, the NFL Play 60 campaign launched in 2007 aims to fight childhood obesity through encouraging young people to play at least 60 minutes a day. In basketball, the NBA Cares serves as the league's social responsibility commission that uses players to address social issues in the United States and around the world. With the tagline: "The NBA: Where Caring Happens," the advertising campaign uses various players around the league to offer personal testimony of their actions in the community. For example, in one commercial Derrick Fisher, who played with the Los Angeles Lakers, describes how he and his teammates teach teamwork, reading, and sportsmanship through the program.

Not only do the players stress positive issues, but the advertisement campaign portrays the athletes as moral individuals.

Advertising, therefore, serves as an additional way that narratives and language frame sport and athletes and merges them with notions of morality. These thirty-second spots, however, are buttressed by a much longer purveyor of discourse: the sports film.

THE MOVIE INDUSTRY

The movie industry is a third factor that perpetuates the mythologizing of sport and the athlete as a moral hero. Sport is a popular topic for films. Between 1920 and 1960 there were 119 movies just about football (Oriard, 2001). These movies, such as *So This Is College* (1929) and *Horse Feathers* (1932), reached large audiences and used the monomyth to portray a hero who overcomes an obstacle to win the big game in the final minutes. Today a search of the popular Internet Movie Database (imdb.com) lists over 1,750 sports movies suggesting the repeated use of the narrative to not only sell movie tickets but the amount of times the narrative has been used.

Research elucidates how sport films depict sociocultural American issues and serve as a purveyor of values, morals, and customs. Pearson et al. (2003) examined 590 films between 1930 and 1995 and found a strong relationship between film content and social and cultural relevance. McDorman et al. (2006) argue that even films that attempt to show a realistically negative portrayal of the sport industry still use morality and ethics as ways to validate the characters and their role in sport.

Sporting movies often initiate the myth of sport, and arguably give much more power to the myth by conflating sport with romanticized versions of bigger life issues. For example, Roy Hobbes in the movie *The Natural* (1984) deals with his first love and a son he did not know he had until right before he stepped on deck to hit the home run to win the World Series. *Hoosiers* (1986) is not just about a small Indiana basketball team that wins the state championship, but it includes themes of hard work, discipline, commitment, second chances, and helping others all within the frame of Indiana basketball. *Field of Dreams* (1989), although clearly a baseball movie, is ultimately a movie about the main character's relationship with his father. And *Rudy* (1993) is not just a movie about a boy who works hard enough to achieve his dream of playing football for Notre Dame, but it is entwined with narratives of family, education, and relationships.

Although there is a long historical list of movies framing sport, the use of movies to perpetuate the myth of the athlete as a moral hero continues to thrive. In May 2008, ESPN announced the first film fest for sports movies as a part of New York's Tribeca Film Festival. In conjunction, ESPN Classic ran a sports movie marathon the same weekend. That same year, ESPN started their *30 For 30* series that recruited filmmakers such as Spike Lee and Davis Guggenheim to create documentary films about sports from 1979 to 2009 ("ESPN adds movies," 2008).

The movie industry illustrates the ability of a film to rhetorically frame sport in mythological and moralizing manners. Typically the films take sport and correlate it to narratives of love, hope, unity, family, and success in the standard frame of the hero that struggles and is challenged at some point. The use of films is a giant industry that reaches millions of people and ultimately serves as an additional purveyor of discourse to perpetuate and bolster the myth of sport.

Books and Novels

The growth of mass media and technological advances gave rise to the fourth purveyor of discourse to spread the myth of sport: books and novels. The profusion of books in American society and their role to impact the public suggests their ability to frame sport to a large audience through a powerful medium. The popular internet book buying service Amazon implies their reach to a widespread audience. A search on the website reveals over 325,000 books related to sport.

Books and novels promulgate a specific version of sport and the hero. Children's books are one proponent of the myth of sport that reaches a young audience. Dagavarian (1987) analyzed children's baseball literature between 1880 and 1950 and found five major themes among their content: interpersonal support, individual responsibility, sacrifice, modesty, and fair play. Oriard (1982) researched the role of the athlete hero in American fiction between 1868 and 1980 and argues that the stereotypical character of the athlete hero in American fiction can be traced to the Frank Merriwell stories between 1896 and 1915.

Two widely regarded classics in sport literature are Bernard Malamud's (1952) *The Natural* (later turned into a movie), and W.P. Kinsella's (1982) *Shoeless Joe* (later turned into the movie *Field of Dreams*). Both novels use baseball as the central plot feature and both use sport as the vehicle through which the main protagonists find hope, purpose, and life changing experiences. Oriard (1982) argues that *The Natural* marks a distinct turning point in American sports fiction. He states:

Malamud was our first writer to clearly see that the character of the hero, and the relationship of country and city, youth and age, masculinity and femininity in American sport are explicitly mythic concerns[...] It was not until *The Natural* that any American novelist recognized that the major concerns of sport do, in fact, define the essential myths of the American people and related them to the timeless myths of Western civilization [p. 211].

W.P. Kinsella's *Shoeless Joe* also testifies to the mythological notions of sport. The characters and the plot of the book merge the game of baseball with broader narratives of family, hope, doing the right thing, and love of neighbor. Kinsella describes, and thus rhetorically frames, how baseball is larger than the game itself: "It wasn't just the baseball game. I wanted it to be a metaphor for something else: perhaps trust, or freedom, or ritual, or faithfulness, or joy, or any of the other things that baseball can symbolize" (p. 82). The book, therefore, portrays sport as an opportunity for freedom, faith, and joy and serves to perpetuate the myth of sport as a moral and positive arena adding to the larger ability of books and novels to shape discourse through the development of plots and characters.

Overall, writers and commentators, advertising, movies, and books and novels produce discourse that perpetuates the myth. All of these factors work together to keep us enamored with the athlete and the rhetorical devices frame athletes as moral beings who rise above us. It is not necessarily about the game, but it is about the events and emotions related to the participation in the sport. Sport is not just an important part of American folklore, popular culture, or private pastimes that transformed themselves into highly organized visible public practices in a relatively short period. Instead, sport acts as interpretive vehicles through which Americans enthusiastically avail themselves to ponder the various issues and questions they face as individuals and as a nation (Morgan, 2006).

Conclusion

This research attempts to demonstrate that sport is mythically viewed as a morality building and overall positive event and that discourse perpetuates and reinscribes the myth of the athlete as a moral hero. The myth permits the sporting public to view athletes through a specific lens, as many fans want to view their athletes as the unending celebration of good over evil. Even when there are rips, or even gaping holes in the myth, some fans remain overwhelmingly forgiving.

There is a constant infusion of the myth through owners of sporting discourse such as writers and commentators, advertising, movies, novels, and books. The manufactured and produced versions of the hero are staged through the mass and print media, and fans do not like to see the machinery, the illusions, the script, the body changes, the surgeries, or the drugs that go into making the product. Today, sport is a giant industry in which the original hero has been beauracratized—the hero is produced by a vast system that nurtures, winnows, trains, selects, and scripts. Like actors, fans want an illusion of belief and with the athlete, the machinery (steroids, training, and recruitment) are heavy and obtrusive.

The history and widespread reach of the huge sports industry and athlete transgressions threatens to wear out the myth. The sporting public sees that the athlete is not a free agent like the old fashioned hero—he or she is a created product (in huge numbers) by an industrial process. The media, marketing, and the huge industrialization of sport have given fans headaches that will not go away. This reveals the manufactured and scripted charisma of the so-called sports hero and the noise and exposure is arguably ripping at the edges of the myth, yet the rhetorical construction of athletes as moral heroes remains. Because athletes were rhetorically constructed as moral individuals and through the reification of the myth by sports writers, commentators, advertising, movies, and novels, the myth still drives the way many fans want to see athletes today. This myth is so strong that many fans are often willing to overlook the athlete who uses drugs, gambles, cheats, rapes, steals, or any other moral transgression that can arise.

Sporting discourse not only keeps the myth powerful but it also permits a recycling of the hero. The mythic cycle can constantly reinvigorate itself as a new athlete overtakes the old hero and is then replaced by a new hero. This cycle is suggested by Oriard (1982) who states: "The athlete-hero must age and retire—his skills are clearly diminished at the end of his career[...but t]he game continually renews itself—raises up heroes who temporarily reign and then are replaced" (p. 219). For example in the NBA, the era of Larry Bird and Magic Johnson was replaced with the era of Michael Jordan, which was then replaced with the era of Kobe Bryant and LeBron James. In the 2012 Summer Olympic games Missy Franklin replaced Dana Torres in swimming, and Gabrielle Douglas replaced Shawn Johnson in women's gymnastics as dominant in the sport. The mythic cycle provides new heroes to fill the role of past heroes, allows sport heroes to be constantly reinscribed, and thereby suggests an unending cycle even when the myth is threatened.

This research hopes to act a springboard for future analysis and findings in how sport and rhetoric work together and how that can address larger issues of symbols and myth. One area for future research could be to analyze the continuing threats to the myth through athlete transgressions and the discourse that shapes the crisis. A second area for future research is to analyze the changes and developments with the key symbols of sport. This research looks at how a crisis effects the changes in the symbol of the hero, but there are several archetypal symbols associated with sport: identification with the everyman, an ideal of fair play, as a training ground for business, and as preparation for the military. The depths and perpetual nature that sport scandal can reach offer excellent possibilities for other examples of symbolic change.

References

Attner, P. (2006, September 29). They're home. There's hope. *Sporting News*. Retrieved May 12, 2008, from EBSCOhost/Academic Search Complete database.
Badenhausen, K. (2009, September 29). Sports' first billion-dollar man. Retrieved from http://www.forbes.com/2009/09/29/tiger-woods-billion-business-sports-tiger.html.
Barthes, R. (1957/1972). *Mythologies*. (A. Lavers, trans.). Paris: HarperCollins.
Basil, M.D. (1996). Identification as a mediator of celebrity effects. *Journal of Broadcasting & Electronic Media* 40(4), 478–495.
Boorstin, Daniel J. (1978). *The image: A guide to pseudo-events in America*. New York: Atheneum.
Brown, W.J., and Basil, M.D. (1995). Media celebrities and public health: Responses to "Magic" Johnson's HIV disclosure and its impact on AIDS risk and high-risk behaviors. *Health Communication* 7(4), 345–370.
Burke, K. (1968). *Language as symbolic action*. Berkeley: University of California Press.
Burke, K. (2001). "Watchful of hermetics to be strong in hermeneutics": Selections from "Poetics, dramatistically considered." In G. Henderson and D. C. Williams (eds.), *Unending conversations* (pp. 35–80). Carbondale: Southern Illinois University Press.
Burstyn, V. (1999). *The rites of men: Manhood, politics, and the culture of sport*. Toronto: University of Toronto Press.
Campbell, J. (2004). *The hero with a thousand faces*. Princeton: Princeton University Press.
Carter, C. A. (1996). Kenneth Burke and the bicameral power of myth. *Poetics Today* 18(3), 343–373.
Cassirer, E. (1953). *An essay on man*. Garden City: Doubleday.
Chidester, P.J. (2009). "The toy store of life": Myth, sport and the mediated reconstruction of the American hero in the shadow of the September 11th terrorist attacks. *Southern Communication Journal* 74(4), 352–372.
Concha, J. (2004, May 5). Tillman, an American hero. Retrieved May 13, 2008, from http://nbcsports.msnbc.com/id/4816850/.
Dagavarian, D. (1987). *Saying it ain't so: American values as revealed in children's baseball stories 1880—1950*. New York: Peter Lang.
Eitzen, S. D. (2006). *Fair and foul: Beyond the myths and paradoxes of sport*. (3d ed.). Lanham, MD: Rowman & Littlefield.
ESPN adds movies to empire. (2008, May 2). *USA Today*. Retrieved from EBSCOhost/Academic Search Complete database.
Fontenrose, J. (1959). *Python: A study of Delphic myth and its origins*. Berkeley: University of California Press.
Goodman, M. (1993). Where have you gone, Joe DiMaggio? *Utne Reader* 57, 103.
Gorsevski, E.W., and Butterworth, M.L. (2011). Muhammad Ali's fighting words: The paradox of violence in nonviolent rhetoric. *Quarterly Journal of Speech* 97(1), 50–73.
Gutman, D. (1990). *It ain't cheatin' if you don't get caught*. New York: Penguin.

Horne, J., Tomlinson, A., and Whannel, G. (1999) *Understanding Sport. An introduction to the sociological and cultural analysis of sport.* London: Routledge.
Jewett, R., and Lawrence, J. S. (1988). *The American monomyth.* Washington, D.C.: University Press of America.
Kinsella, W.P. (1982). *Shoeless Joe.* New York: Ballantine.
Klapp, O.E. (1962). *Heroes, villains, and fools.* Englewood Cliffs, NJ: Prentice Hall.
Klapp, O.E. (1964). *Symbolic leaders: Public dramas and public men.* Chicago: Aldine.
Kyle, D. G. (1990). E. Norman Gardiner and the decline of Greek sport. In D. G. Kyle and G. D. Stark (eds.), *Essays on sport history and sport mythology* (pp. 7–44). College Station: Texas A&M University Press.
Lines, G. (2001). Villains, fools, or heroes? Sports stars as role models for young people *Leisure Studies* 20, 285–303.
Malamud, B. (1952). *The natural.* New York: Farrar, Straus and Giroux.
Mangan, J.A. (1981). *Athleticism in the Victorian and Edwardian public school: The emergence and consolidation of an educational ideology.* Cambridge: Cambridge University Press.
McDonald, M. G., and Andrews, D. L. (2001). Michael Jordan: Corporate sport and postmodern celebrityhood. In D. L. Andrews and S. J. Jackson (eds.), *Sports stars: The cultural politics of sporting celebrity* (pp. 20–35). New York: Routledge.
McDorman, T. F., Casper, K., Logan, A., and McGinley, S. (2006). Where have all the heroes gone?: An exploration of cultural therapy in Jerry Maguire, *For Love of the Game,* and *Any Given Sunday. Journal of Sport and Social Issues* 30, 1997–218.
Morgan, W. J. (2006). *Why sports morally matter.* New York: Routledge.
Oriard, M. (1982). *Dreaming of heroes: American sports fiction, 1868–1980.* Chicago: Nelson-Hall.
Oriard, M. (2001). *King football: Sport and spectacle in the golden age of radio and newsreels, movies and magazines, the weekly and the daily press.* Chapel Hill: University of North Carolina Press.
Pearson, D. W., Curtis, R. L., Haney, C. A., and Zhang, J. J. (2003). Sport films: Social dimensions over time, 1930–1995. *Journal of Sport & Social Issues* 27, 145–161.
Puhvel, J. (1987). *Comparative mythology.* Baltimore: Johns Hopkins University Press.
Radford, P. (2005). Lifting the spirits of the nation: British boxers and the emergence of the national sporting hero at the time of the Napoleonic Wars. *Identities: Global Studies in Culture and Power* 12, 249–270.
Rose, C. (Writer). (2006, September 25). Saints in superdome signals New Orleans' Return [Radio broadcast episode]. In E. McDonnell (producer), Morning Edition. Washington, D.C.: National Public Radio.
Schefter, A. (1997, November 22). Chiefs players confirm what the coach won't. *Denver Post*, 7C.
Serby, S. (2002, February 4). Color the Pats red, white and blue—Bill, Brady & co. pull off super stunner. *New York Post*, 70.
Shuart, J. (2007). Heroes in sport: Assessing celebrity endorser effectiveness. *International Journal of Sports Marketing & Sponsorship* 8(2), 126–140.
Smith, R. (1983). I'd like to be called a good reporter. In D. Anderson (ed.), *The Red Smith reader* (pp. 3–16). New York: Vintage.
Strate, L. (1994). Heroes: A communication perspective. In S.J. Drucker and R.S. Cathcart (eds.), *American heroes in a mediated age* (pp. 15–23). Cresol, NJ: Hampton Press.
Trujillo, N. (1994). *The meaning of Nolan Ryan.* College Station: Texas A&M University Press.
Vande Berg, L. R. (1998). The sports hero meets mediated celebrityhood. In L. A. Wenner (ed.), *MediaSport* (pp. 134–153). London: Routledge.
Walker, D. (2007, September 25). Saints-Titans ratings: Strong locally, weak nationally.

The Times-Picayune. Retrieved from http://blog.nola.com/ davewalker/2007/09/saintstitans_ratings_strong_lo.html.

Walton, T.A. (2004). Steve Prefontaine: From rebel with a cause to hero with a swoosh. *Sociology of Sport Journal* 21, 61–83.

Westbrook, D. (1996). *Ground rules: Baseball and myth.* Urbana: University of Illinois Press.

Whannel, G. (1995). Sports stars, youth, and morality in the print media. In G. McFee, W. Murphy, and G. Whannel (eds.), *Leisure: Cultures, values and lifestyles* (pp. 121–136). Brighton: Leisure Studies Association.

Young, C. (2002, September 17). Feminism's slide since September 11. Retrieved July 23, 2006 from http://www.reason.com/cy/cy091702.shtml.

Zirin, D. (2007). *Welcome to the terrordome.* Chicago: Haymarket.

Reclaiming the Wolf Myth in the Shadow of the *Twilight* Films
The Quileute People's Exhibit

LINDSAY R. CALHOUN
AND KEATON MADDOX

There is no such person as Jacob Black. I want to put that on a T-shirt.
—Quileute youth.

In January 2012, a new exhibit opened at the National Museum of the American Indian, Smithsonian Institution, in Washington, D.C., after spending a year at the Seattle Art Museum. It was billed, "Behind the Scenes: The Real Story of Quileute Wolves," an exhibition of rare works from the Pacific Northwest that serve as a counterpoint to the supernatural storyline of the *Twilight* book and film series created by author Stephenie Meyer ("Museums Openings," 2012). The exhibit, while modest, is a focused effort at developing a broader understanding of Quileute cultural identity, consisting of 23 items from the Quileute nation as well as a 12-minute film that plays in a constant loop at the exhibit's end. While the exhibit is designed to help viewers separate what is fiction from what is genuine Quileute culture, the film and arrangement of artifacts comes off as too reliant on *Twilight* to make a clear distinction between the two.

As the Quileute prove, becoming the target of public interest can be both empowering and terrifying for indigenous groups. They are caught between the simultaneous desire to retain control over their stories and histories while also utilizing the economic, political, and cultural opportunities such focused attention provides for the benefit of their people. Tourists have flooded into the tribe's home of La Push, Washington, leaving many Quileute unsure if they should welcome or fight against *Twilight*'s influence. However, it would seem

185

that impact of Stephenie Meyer' books may be inescapable. The tribe is, therefore, left with little choice other than to adapt to life under *Twilight*'s shadow.

Such a dilemma requires a rhetorical strategy that allows the Quileute people to not merely survive the transition, but also benefit from it. By using a dialectic strategy of accommodation and resistance, the Quileute people are able to both welcome the attention of *Twilight* fans, while simultaneously transforming the werewolf myth depicted in the books and films back into the origin myth that has defined them for centuries; a myth that will last long after *Twilight* has left the fickle public imagination.

Twilight introduces the narrative that the Quileute people are shape shifters that can transform into giant wolves at will in order to protect the residents of Forks, Washington from supernatural vampire beings. For the Quileute the challenge of converting the *Twilight* narrative back into their original mythology is no small feat. First, with only 23 items and a short film, the exhibit does not have millions of dollars behind it. Additionally, unlike Stephenie Meyer, the Quileute do not have the same kind of exposure and expensive media infrastructure at their disposal for distributing their own version of the wolf narrative to the public. However, the advantage of *Twilight* is in its ability to attract people to the exhibit. The Quileute are able to indirectly use the popularity of the films and books as inducement to draw people in and then supposedly downplay *Twilight*'s influence.

The critical question is whether the exhibit is able to rhetorically resist the redefined wolf myth established by Stephenie Meyer. Our argument is that ultimately the exhibit is no more than an initial step. Unfortunately, their ethnic identity has ultimately been circumscribed by American popular culture and the exhibit does not change this for the Quileute. We will begin by discussing the *Twilight* phenomenon and how the wolf narrative has been altered in the books and films. Second, we will examine the Quileute people, their history, and the original mythology from which Stephenie Meyer drew her inspiration. Next, we will delve into the noble savage mythology that pervades American popular cultural narratives about American Indian[1] peoples. Finally, we will examine the rhetorical maneuvers in the Quileute people's exhibit meant to reclaim Quileute identity and cultural mythology and their problematic attempts at resistance.

The Twilight *Phenomenon*

Twilight's narrative tells the story of Bella Swan and her eternal love for the vampire Edward Cullen. After Edward leaves her in the second book, *New*

Moon, she finds solace in a young Quileute named Jacob Black. A love triangle ensues, creating the central conflict for the remainder of the series. When Stephenie Meyer began to write *Twilight*, she did a Google search for the rainiest place in America. The result was Forks, Washington. As she furthered her research, she found a small American Indian tribe in nearby La Push—home of the Quileute. Fascinated by their mythical tales, she included them in her first book as a way to expose the vampires to Bella. Even when Bella dreamed of the Quileute boy Jacob Black turning into a wolf, it was only meant to be symbolic. However, by the time she began *New Moon*, the Quileute tales had become more than mere fantasy in Bella's world. Meyer modified the Quileute origin story in which a mystical shaman named K'wati transformed two wolves into the tribe's ancestors, and made the shirtless Quileute boys that ran through her story into shape shifting werewolves, able to protect the innocent people of Forks from the blood-thirsty vampires (StephenieMeyer.com). *Twilight* has had a myriad of effects on the small northwestern tribe of less than 1000 members, half of which do not even live in La Push (Whitehouse, 2011). From a financial and legislative perspective, the sudden interest in this region of Northwest Washington has been largely beneficial. To deal with the influx of tourism, the tribe opened an Oceanside Resort that offers the ultimate experience for fans who want to see where the film's characters lived, including "*Twilight* Tours" and "Wolf Dens" for rooming accommodations ("Quileute Oceanside Resort"). The Quileute have also been negotiating for three decades on a deal that would give them reservation land at higher ground to protect against potential Tsunamis. The tribe's chairwoman, Bonita Cleveland, capitalized on this recent influx, stating that the legislation's passage was crucial, as it would "protect all the tourists" (Hotakainen, 2011). However, many Quileute believe *Twilight*'s growing prominence within La Push to be an outrage. Tribe member Ann Penn-Charles conveyed to the *Seattle Times*:

> A lot of elders are hurt because we were portrayed as werewolves, and they didn't want us portrayed as these wild Indians, they want people to know we are not these crazy Indians that change into werewolves when we get mad. We settle our differences peacefully.... Our council was getting a lot of flak from our elders, saying "Show them the real Quileute, not this Hollywood Quileute." [Tourists visiting the reservation] didn't think real Quileutes actually existed; they just thought somebody made it up [Mapes, 2010].

Many of those living on the reservation still have tourists knocking on their doors, asking where Jacob Black lives (Walker, 2012). In order to establish the difference between the real Quileute and the *Twilight* Quileute Jacob Black represents, we will next discuss the Quileute history and their origin mythology.

The Quileute

The Quileute are one of many American Indian nations scattered along the Pacific Northwest Coast. According to Wilson (1998), the Quileute were one of many nations such as the Chinook and the Makah, greatly influenced by the complex "Northwest Coast" cultures of what is now Western Canada and Southern Alaska, supported by salmon fishing and whaling historically. As a result of a relatively stable economy, these cultures developed complex hierarchical and ceremonial societies. They are best known for their signature longhouses, distinctive woodcarving, and their fascinating potlatches, a ritual feast where property was redistributed amongst the tribal community to formulate social and cultural bonds and to reinforce tribal organization and internal economic relations.

The Quileute belong to a group of first tribal nations clustered along the Olympic Peninsula, which "forms the extreme northwest corner of Washington State and the coterminous United States" (Wray, 2002, p. 3). While the Quileute have always been part of the many nations that make up the Olympic Peninsula and share many traits with them, they are also very unique, speaking a language shared by only one other nation in this region. It is believed indigenous peoples have occupied the Olympic Peninsula since just before the last glaciers retreated about 14,500 years ago. Wray (2002) points out that archaeological research across the peninsula, including the interior and the coast, supports the long term and widespread presence of various indigenous peoples.

The Quileute's history with the U.S. government is typical of other American Indian groups in that it is troubled by extensive government manipulation and deception used in the establishment of treaties and land deals by U.S. federal officials. It was not until the mid–1940s that tribes in the Pacific Northwest began renegotiating rights to fishing and land use as well as compensation for lost land (Wray, 2002). Additionally, in the past 60 years, tribes across the country have been legally reestablishing the right to self-governance after Congress stopped negotiating treaties with tribes as sovereigns in 1871.

As is the case with nearly all native peoples, Quileute history goes back much further than merely their interactions with the "white man." They have a deep and rich history built from a series of myths that have defined their civilization for centuries. According to Brunvand (1998), myths are "traditional prose narratives, ... considered to be truthful accounts of what happened in the remote past. Typically, they deal with the activities of gods and demigods, the creation of the world and its inhabitants, and the origins of religious rituals" (p. 170). In the case of American Indian myths, they

> often freely mix human and animal characters, and the animals may have both human and godlike qualities (both physical and mental). The stories often tend to combine believable and fantastic elements, and even when they seem to be explanatory in purpose, the specific facts of life "explained" may not be as apparent to the non–Indian reader of published stories as they were to the original audiences for their oral performances [Brunvand, 1998, pp. 171–172].

So while the myths of the Americas' indigenous peoples may provide creative inspiration for popular fiction and fantasy novelists, their purpose and longevity has much more depth and complexity in terms of articulating native history and identities. In addition to expressing values, beliefs, and rituals, tribal mythologies also often detail "the creation of a landscape and people's relationship to it" (Wray, 2002, p. 5). In the case of the Olympic Peninsula, Wray explains, "these legends depict a reliance on waterways, forests, and valleys for the acquisition of vital resources and give detailed descriptions of travel into the mountains for pleasure, social interchange such as marriage, and spiritual pursuits" (p. 5).

In Quileute territory, the land and water are inextricably interconnected. Mountains create rivers that flow into the ocean and it is between these waterways that the Quileute territory resides. Their mythological conception of the world reveals the interconnectedness, movement, and frequent dynamic transformation of land and water. In Quileute narratives, land and water animals often change into each other and are equally valued in Quileute mythology, regardless of form. Additionally fishing, whaling, and canoeing are just as historically important as land gathering, hunting, and foraging methods to the Quileute economy, although, whaling was phased out in the early 1900s (Wray, 2002).

In the *Twilight* books/films, author Stephenie Meyer alters the wolf origin myth of the Quileute people to depict the tribe as shape shifters. Although other indigenous communities may have incorporated shape shifter myths involving humans into their history, the Quileute have not. Ritual animal transformations in Quileute cultural dances do not represent humans transforming into wolves, but do represent humans embodying the magical spirit and identity of animals who do have transformative power.

Originally, the wolf myth Meyer appropriated came from the Quileute origin story, in which "a Changer known as K'wati went around transforming features of the landscape and living things into the forms they have today" (Morganroth III, 2002, p. 136). K'wati is not a singular creator God but he is an important deity because of his power to alter and influence nature. K'wati was being chased by wolves while transforming the landscape of the Olympic peninsula because he had killed a wolf (Farrand and Meyer, 1919). He escaped by altering the landscape into rivers and lakes so that the wolves could not catch him. Later, after he had escaped, K'wati returned and changed two wolves into the ancestors of the Quileute (Farrand and Meyer, 1919; Morganroth III, 2002; Powell and Jensen, 1976).

What is distinctive about this myth in its original form is that the power to transform is not one that the Quileute people ever possessed. It was a deity that transformed them from wolves into humans, a feat which only happened "in the time of the beginnings" (Morganroth III, 2002). Additionally, other animals have as much cultural significance to Northwest coast tribes. Many tribes, including the Quileute, view the Thunderbird and the Orca (killer whale) to be as important as the wolf in their cultural mythology. Morganroth III (2002) states,

> Quileute ancestors felt that most living things had souls and fell into the beings-with-souls category; animals great and small, birds and fish, the great trees (but not the small ones), Fog and the great rocks that are transformed creatures, Rainbow, some mountains, and, of course, the people.... Some beings-with-souls were thought to be in a special; spiritually, privileged subset because they travel in two natural elements; the powerful frog and otter live on land and in water; the raven lives in the air and on the ground; and the diving kingfisher lives in the air and under the water. Wolf belongs in this group because it was thought that when wolves leap into the ocean, they change into killer whales [pp. 138–139].

These myths revealed the dynamic interconnectedness of life, as well as its interdependency. The orca, wolf and Thunderbird spirits all share similar traits, with the wolf and orca sharing transformative ability at times. Shearer (2000) describes the Thunderbird as "a giant, supernatural bird named for his habit of causing thunder and lightning. Beneath his wings, he carries *Lightning Snakes*, which are his weapons.... He is large enough and strong enough to hunt *Killer Whale*, which he strikes dead with the wolf-headed, serpent-tongued lightning snakes" (p. 104). The Thunderbird is often depicted with a killer whale in Northwest coast art.

The transformative nature of humans and animals "in the time of beginnings" reveals much about the interdependence of people and the environment, a cultural reality that disappears in Stephenie Meyer's *Twilight* novels where the transformative nature of the wolf is reappropriated to serve narratives of heroism, dominance, and "the noble savage." Morganroth III (2002) reasons,

> The old people believed that all of the First Beings had features of both people and animals. It is basic to the Quileute perspective that people are not higher or more special than other living things. It was a matter of concern that the

Quileute were themselves beings-with-souls yet hunted and killed other beings-with-souls. And for that reason hunting was a pursuit that required sensitivity and ritual [p. 139].

Morganroth III's explanation and analysis affirms the notion that the transformative capacity of humans, animals, and nature revealed in the myths demonstrates the spiritual interdependence and compassionate attitude toward all forms of life rather than an imposed ethic of savagery towards and dominance over these forms.

Today the Quileute number just over 700. They now supplement their fishing economy with tourism, an industry that undoubtedly has been bolstered by the introduction of *Twilight*, at least for the short term. They are autonomous with their own police, courts, schooling system, health clinic, and, of course religious and cultural traditions, as the books and films portray. Unlike many other American Indian communities, particularly those of the U.S. East Coast and interior, which have been ravaged by federal government intervention, the Quileute have maintained autonomy without much devastating disruption, population declines, or relocations from outside sources. Additionally, they retain much of their cultural traditions and practices, although few speak the Quileute language fluently (Morganroth III, 2002).

The Noble Savage

The discussion of myth, narrative, and popular culture in relationship to native peoples inevitably leads to discussion of the "noble savage." A powerful trope, "the noble savage" is the primary way in which the American Indian is constructed in American popular culture. Modern commercial and critically acclaimed films that have indigenous people at their core include *Dances with Wolves* (1990), *Pocahontas* (1995) and *Avatar* (2009), all of which evoke the myth of the noble savage. For example in *Dances with Wolves*, while viewers are reminded that native people held the land first, "the mythic noble Indians in the movie—the Lakota—are ultimately tragic characters who in classic noble vein 'vanish' from the west, thereby implicitly and *inevitably* opening the west to Euro-American civilization" (Bayers, 2011, p. 43). In short, native peoples are depicted primarily as docile savages that seek only to aid in achieving the goals of the "white man," rather than dynamic, culturally independent individuals and tribes with unique histories and desires.

The noble savage is an enduring construct that traces its roots back to the founding of the United States, but has modern origins in the 1893 Chicago Columbian Exposition when Buffalo Bill Cody debuted his Wild West Show.

Deloria (2004) explains that "Cody's show engaged American popular culture in ways that helped manage the tensions created as older stories of violent contest gave way to a new understanding that frontiers had closed and Indians had been—and become—pacified" (p. 63). Buffalo Bill's show captivated audiences with highly stylized and powerful dramatic reenactments of the successful conquest of the Western frontier that sometimes involved actual iconic historical participants such as Sitting Bull, even though historical accuracy was not generally the goal of the show.

The noble savage is a persistent and enduring invention of the American Indian that has successfully painted most indigenous people in the United States with broad strokes. Vizenor (2008) submits that the "Indian" is a pose or a simulation in dominant culture, reminding us that the word Indian "has no referent in tribal languages or cultures," enabling whole swaths of people to be invented by the culture that has dominated and exploited them (p. 90). According to Vizenor (2008):

> People are precoded with the simulation of what they desire so that they process their relation to the world through images. The world is thus made in the simulated images of people's desire. For example, the image of simulated *indian* is the product of such consumer culture, and the *indian* simulation gradually stands in for native cultures [p. 93].

Yu (2008) argues, "Simulation is no longer the pure reflection of reality. [Rather], it gradually takes the place of reality" (p. 94). And as the simulation distances itself from the realm of truth, it becomes easier to commodify. Yu expounds, "in late modern consumer capitalism, 'culture' has become a product in its own right.... Subsequently the representation becomes a source for the production of false social and cultural knowledge" (p. 95). The "noble savage" is the most significant simulation key to understanding our mainstream cultural construction of American Indian identity in popular culture. Yu (2008) elucidates:

> When the tribal people no longer posed any kind of military threat, and the mythical American Eden was rapidly becoming civilized, romantic images of the Native American ... began to capture the popular imagination. The fictional noble savage became a means for satisfying the ageless human longing for knowledge of the mythical lost past, for contact with man in his most pristine state [p. 96].

And through such glorified nostalgia, this myth has seeped into popular culture. Green (1993) states most media portrayals of America Indians have limited them to three longstanding characteristics: noble, savage, and blood thirsty (as cited in Whitehouse, 2011). The wolves of *Twilight* extenuate all of these, as "they are regional protectors (noble), run half-naked through the woods as wolves (savage), and attack vampires (blood-thirsty)" (Whitehouse, p. 241). Further, their sole initial purpose in the books was to protect the people of Forks from dangerous vampires, perpetuating the misconception that American Indians are only there to help Euro-centric cultures deal with the harshness of what lies outside of the civilized world.

But why is the noble savage such an enduring and powerful trope in American popular culture? The Indian, as a symbol, is central to understanding the core of American cultural identity. Philip Deloria (1998) articulated in *Playing Indian*, the persistence of the Indian figure in American imagination is an identity that continues to pursue and define itself in terms of ultimate freedom. But freedom, by definition is not easily contained, setting up a difficult paradox for the American Indian to embody, hence the tendency to attempt control over the American Indian as a symbolic identity. As Americans we need the Indian as a continual symbol of freedom, even if we wish to control that symbol as part of our colonizing history and destiny.

American Indians are also implicated in the perpetuation of the "noble savage" imagery, lending credibility to its use. History is littered with various members of American Indian groups who have made this concession to advance their own ends. From 1843 to 1845, artist George Catlin traveled Europe with Iowa Indian performers who were touted by Catlin as "living examples of 'noble savages.'" Herring (2006) explains that

> these Iowas willingly participated in a deception—a commodification of their own culture and tradition-because they saw an opportunity to ensure a place for themselves and their tribe in a rapidly changing, pre–Civil War America. They presented themselves as noble savages, a fictitious image ... to confirm what Europeans already believed to be true about Indians [p. 226].

Because there is often accommodation on the part of some native peoples to "noble savage" imagery, the simulation gains more credibility and thus more footing with non- American Indian audiences, because it both reifies their own sense of cultural identity while also seeming authentic.

The Rhetorical Maneuvers of the Quileute People's Exhibit

At the heart of the Quileute people's exhibit is the question of authentic cultural identity and its rhetorical projection. The concept of identity has changed from stable and fixed to fluid and dynamic. Philips (2006) claims that "these two sides of poststructural subjectivity—its fluidity and its positioning—establish not so much two divergent approaches, but the two poles between which the human subject can be thought to operate" (p. 310). The continuum of identity negotiation presented here, as opposed to a set of fixed categories, suggests that subjects operate both with and against the dominant projections of culture, creating a "productive tension" through which people are simultaneously limited and enabled by the dominant cultural formations that formulate our subject positions.

The "noble savage" is a uniquely American driven construct of identity, a fixed projection of the American Indian that resists modification. The goal of this analysis then is to understand how the Quileute people's exhibit functions both within and against the discursive formations of "the noble savage" within popular culture formulated by the powerful and ubiquitous cultural artifacts of *Twilight*. One of the critical questions we are examining is whether the subjective tensions within the exhibit are truly productive for the Quileute in terms of enabling new discursive formations that challenge the "noble savage" constructs of the Quileute within the *Twilight* narratives. Philips (2006) explains that the tension between the perceived stability of the subject, such as the Quileute, and its dynamic qualities is manifested in what he calls a *rhetorical maneuver*.

> In the simplest terms, a rhetorical maneuver is performed at those moments when we choose to violate the proscriptive limits of our subject position and speak differently by drawing upon the resources of another subject position we have occupied: for example when the corporate CEO speaks as a mother, or when the university professor speaks as a Latino.... This is a rhetorical movement in which one violates the constraints of one subject position by articulating the discourse more appropriate to another subject position [p. 312].

Philips claims that what needs to be explored are "the kinds of procedures through which this construction is performed. In this regard, rhetoricians seem uniquely positioned to explore the kinds of re-formations of subjectivity given that such procedures may entail not only the deployment of discourse but the invention of new positions within discourse" (p. 315). Through our exploration of the Quileute people's exhibit, we are answering this call to better develop our understanding of how these maneuvers both succeed and fail. Philips also suggests that we need precise terminology to utilize as part of our analysis.

Philips explains that in the context of uneven power relations, a rhetorical maneuver happens in 4 steps. He discusses a methodology for analyzing rhetorical maneuvering of this kind, providing a conceptual framework by looking at artistry, agency, and memory. Agency for the subject (the Quileute people) is located within the space between the subject position and the subject form (dominant discursive formation). As Philips explains, "By choosing to speak differently than the form prescribed by the subject position, the subject invokes the agency provided by the position but invokes it as a reaction against the contours of that position" (p. 325). In other words, in a rhetorical maneuver, the Quileute would be able to use the discursive formations of "the noble savage" as the source of their ability to resist and ultimately transcend the identity.

Reconfiguring the self within a pre-articulated subject position involves a kind of turning or twisting against the dominant subject position. Within the subject itself, is memory of alternative forms of being, the more invisible aspects of identity. A rhetorical maneuver involves a revelation of an alternative or hidden facet of identity. The deviation is where the artistry comes in, as the creative turn is what enables the possible transformation of power relations. However, such a maneuver, as Philips states, is related to "the amount of deviation from the prescribed form of that position" (p. 327) and its success is also tied to the eventual acceptance of the alternative subject position as typical. For this to occur the subject position's design of the deviation requires a "deeply artistic ethos" (p. 327). The artistry is the aesthetic dimension of the rhetorical maneuver. Philips explains, "the introduced, inappropriate subject form relies purely on its artistic rendering and not on any prior expectations or assumptions" (p. 327).

Memory is crucial to understanding resistance in the rhetorical maneuver and occupies the second step. For this, Philips invokes Foucault's (1977) counter-memory, the idea that subjects recall multiple subject forms derived from multiple subject positions people have occupied and that this recollection inherently dissolves unified subjectivity. Recollection becomes inherently disruptive and enables alternative discursive formations to emerge by providing more ground on which alternative subjectivities can make a stand. Indigenous people like the Quileute often have histories and collective memories that have never been formally transcribed, but are none-the-less just as real. Occasionally these memories even contradict or differ substantially from the official histories that outsiders have written. Indigenous people like the Quileute utilize these hidden memories and histories as a way for new stories, narratives, and often resistant identities to emerge and challenge dominant discourses surrounding their ethnicity.

In summary, the rhetorical maneuver happens in four stages and requires three rhetorical tactics. The first movement occurs in the subject position and is characterized by a lack of fit between the dominant discursive formation and the subject's sense of identity. The second stage shifts to the actual dominant discursive formation itself where the subject elucidates their recollections of past alternative subject positions to begin imagining contrasting and resistant alternatives to the present situation. The third movement is when the subject strategically expresses these alternative positions artistically so that they become visible and clearly contrast with the dominant discursive formation of the subject. Finally, the fourth movement is when the dominant discursive formation is displaced or significantly altered to suggest a new subjective formation of the subject, one that more accurately reflects both the subject's sense of self and the multiplicity of forms the subject can and does take.

The Quileute People's Exhibit as Rhetorical Maneuver: "Less Fit" with "Twilight"

The Quileute people's exhibit had two major components at the Smithsonian: the exhibit itself and a 12-minute documentary film that played in a continual loop. In the exhibit itself, direct negation of the subject position of "werewolf" was not prominent and was undermined by the inclusion of *Twilight* artifacts and references in panel texts. When a visitor walked into the exhibit at the National Museum of the American Indian, a large panel greeted them at the left that stated, "The Real Story of the Quileute Wolves." Next to it was an image of several youth on a beach pointing towards the water, presumably watching for whales. Additionally, there was another panel with the tag heading, "Not werewolves, but Wolves: *Tłókʷali* Quileute Wolf Society" followed by detailed textual descriptions of the society, as well as a timeline and history of the actual Quileute people in Northwest Washington.

Both of these panels were located along the hallways of the entrance to the exhibit and were two-dimensional representations. Upon entering the corridor, a traditional wolf headdress used in Quileute rituals immediately drew the attention of visitors. It was directly perpendicular to the entrance to the exhibit, the largest artifact in the exhibit, and enclosed in its own glass case. The headdress is a large rectangular carved face of a wolf and is around two feet long, a foot tall and a foot thick at its widest base. The underside of the headdress is hollowed out in the shape of an isosceles triangle and narrows at the apex, representing the narrowed snout of the wolf. It sits atop the head of a Quileute wolf society member who wears robes with the headdress and is painted white, red, and black with a predominant black and white eye and painted jaw and snout. The painting style has the abstract and dramatic colors and symmetrical shapes of the Pacific Northwest. The top of the headdress has jagged carved edges, which may represent the shaggy coat of the wolf. It also has a jagged cut out on the top of the snout, near the apex, which may symbolize the teeth of the wolf. The back of the headdress has a carved tail, which may represent the body or the tail of the wolf. There is also a large fan like structure that sits above the headdress that is a symbol of the sun. At the center of the structure is a face. The headdress was also featured on the Smithsonian website advertising the exhibit, whereas the image of the children on the beach whale watching, were featured in the standing exhibit signs outside the Smithsonian Museum. Clearly the impressive wolf headdress draws the viewer in more than the panels and beckons them to come closer.

At the very end of the exhibit was the 12-minute documentary film. Visitors could hear it playing in a loop at other locations in the exhibit but not in the entrance hallway per say. In the film various Quileute members discuss some of their frustrations with *Twilight* and Meyer's portrayal of their people and myths. Several teenage Quileute youth in the film say the following:

"There's no such person as Jacob Black. I want to put that on a t-shirt."
"Tourists sometimes ask me if I'm 'Bella Swan,' but I tell them 'no, I'm not her. I'm nothing like her.'"
"There is nothing factual in any of the movies whatsoever."
"They think we are mean, rude, but we aren't mean or rude."
"We don't run through the woods like wild people."
"We don't run around shirtless for the girls to get more fans."
"It takes a lot more responsibility to be a Quileute than in the movies."

These comments in the film all evoke the "less fit" moment at the start of a rhetorical maneuver, the identification of the constraining aspects of a given subject position. They identify the constraints and problems with the conception of the Quileute as werewolves, however they remain within the appropriate framework of language established by the discursive formation of the noble savage articulated in *Twilight*.

"More Memory" for the Quileute: Remembering Where and What We Came From

The second tactic in a rhetorical maneuver—the use of memory to recall alternate forms of subjectivity—did appear in the exhibit and film. This was perhaps the strongest and most powerful indicator of resistance in the overall presentation of the artifacts and film. The use of the time line in the exhibit is critical to helping audiences understand the long, complicated history of the Quileute people and provides a richer, more detailed record of Quileute identity rather than being thought of as a recent invention by Stephenie Meyer. Additionally, many of the artifacts invoke a detailed history in the panels that accompany them. And that history is a powerful re-articulation of identity that is important to a successful maneuver.

One of the most powerful recollection strategies is a series of hand drawn images of daily Quileute life drawn in the early 20th century by Quileute youth. The preserved images detail cultural rituals and dances performed in the Quileute community complete with headdresses and regalia, storytelling rituals, canoeing, and other daily cultural practices. Games, initiation ceremonies, and rites of passage are detailed in the drawings. Many of the drawings chosen for display are specific to the Society of the Wolf and the drawings have brief panels describing the activities with Quileute linguistic references, dates, and descriptions of the artist's intent. Some of the tags and descriptions also invoke spiritual and magical powers behind the ceremonies and rituals detailed in the drawings.

In the 12-minute film, Quileute also utilize the second tactic of the rhetorical maneuver, memory, to articulate resistance to *Twilight*. The film begins with the retelling of the Quileute origin myth, the story that inspired Stephenie Meyer's version of their history. A Quileute elder explains in detail the story of how K'wati, the changer, transformed two Timberwolves into the Quileute people. However, he also tells the story of how K'wati transformed into the Thunderbird, hovered over the people staring up at him on the beach and dropped down into the ocean, picked up a whale and dropped it in front of the people, thus providing them food and resources to live on. He explains that this is why people engage in ceremonies to call the whales and why the whales are an important symbol to the Quileute people. One Quileute member explains that when he left the reservation to live in Montana he always thought about the whale and how the whale stayed with him wherever he went.

In addition to articulating important origin myths and accurately portraying them for the audience, the Quileute also emphasize—as the timeline panel does in the exhibit—their long history in the Northwest Washington region. They say, "We've been here for thousands and thousands of years" in an effort to resist being associated with the temporal nature of popular culture phenomena and to avoid the suggestion that they are a recent cultural invention. They also emphasize the reservation's history, labeling it "long-standing" and discussing how they were established as part of the United States along with the state of Washington.

"More Displacement" Displacing the Werewolf and the Noble Savage

For the Quileute, the unified subject position is that of the "noble savage," articulated through the werewolf mythology of *Twilight*. The most visible disruptive/alternative subject position to this is that of the "wolf," as it appears in the artifacts of the exhibit and in the 12-minute film. Additionally, the Quileute people make some effort to identify themselves more with water than with land. In *Twilight*, the Quileute characters spend a majority of time in the forest, and are not generally seen operating on water or in direct relationship to water. The whale and the canoe are just as significant to the history of the Quileute people as the wolf and play an important role in distinguishing the tribe from *Twilight* in the exhibit. For example, the 12-minute film shows Quileute making and painting canoes and paddles, engaging in whale watching rituals, discussing the recent renewal of canoeing culture and the mythology of the whale in relationship to Quileute origins and histories.

It is the wolf, however, that takes on the most significance in the exhibit. The wolf headdress is prominently featured, as are other wolf masks belonging to the tribe. There is a wolf image woven into a basket and the children's drawings feature wolf related ceremonies. There are panels with text that discuss the importance of the wolf society to the Quileute and also reference the wolf origin myth. It seems that there is an attempt to provide a counter-narrative and a counter subject position that is "wolf-centered" rather than "werewolf-centered." Other artifacts native to the Quileute tribe included in the exhibit are woven and carved wooden object representations of spirit beings, such as the guardian spirit *t'abale*. There are whaling tools and carved and painted wooden paddles, as well as bird rattles, which typically depicted an owner's guardian spirit. But the most visually prominent artifacts throughout the exhibit are the wolf artifacts. The title "Behind the Scenes: The Real Story of the Quileute Wolves," suggests that the purpose of the exhibit is to offer an alternative mythology to the "werewolf" of *Twilight* with the "wolf" of the Quileute people.

From Werewolf to Wolf: An Incomplete Rhetorical Maneuver

This is where the problems with articulating a successful rhetorical maneuver occur. The "wolf" narrative is offered as an alternative subject position that displaces the "werewolf." Unfortunately the representation and arrangements of wolf artifacts in the documentary film and exhibit are fragmented and lack a coherent alternative framework of narrative and identity. The original narrative that inspired the werewolf myth of the *Twilight* books is told in the exhibit in an effort to correct the viewers' perceptions of Quileute people as werewolves. However, in comparison to the werewolf, the wolf is not adequately presented as a viable alternative subject position. From the arrangement of the artifacts and wolf subject matter in the exhibit, the distinction between the two is not as clear as it could be for the visitor. Simply retelling the origin story in the film alone cannot validate the truth of the new subject position. The wolf also has to have an alternative identity to the werewolf. Audiences need to understand what the story means, how it functions and its role in Quileute culture and identity.

Further, visitors need a coherent sense of what the wolf and other animals represent as contrasting symbols to the werewolves of *Twilight*. Using the exhibit to articulate a deeper understanding of these animals in Quileute culture and history, as discussed earlier, would be necessary to shift the public's thinking away from seeing animals as sources of magical power to American Indians to seeing animals as sacred symbols of cultural values and teachers of how the natural world functions. Ultimately the representation of the wolf and many other symbolic artifacts in the exhibit are often fragmented and contradictory. They are not connected in any logical framework or to each other. More or less, they are merely an array of items placed in a corridor that are claimed to have significance. Our critique of this layout is not to suggest that the logic of the exhibit should simply be altered so as to be readily meaningful or available to a Western audience. However, a new narrative is necessary. The Quileute are very clear in their stories about the interconnected relationships of these various cultural symbols and myths. Yet these connections are not made clear in the exhibit. The layout of the exhibit at the National Museum of the American Indian leaves the beautiful artistry and novelty of such symbols overly opaque, rendering them mere aesthetics to audiences. Thus the exhibit lacks the coherence necessary to formulate a new narrative.

The wolf alternative is undermined as well by the prominent featuring of *Twilight* artifacts and *Twilight* references in both the exhibit and in the 12-minute film. In the film, photo montages of the *Twilight* actors and *Twilight* merchandise like posters and toys appear. And while there are resistant comments about the films and books, there are also very positive comments about both. Quileute tribal members refer to the fact that many Quileute youth are "fans of the *Twilight* films and books" and others refer to the *Twilight* films as a "golden opportunity" to educate people about their community. The video footage shows a paw painted on the sidewalk in La Push that says "wolf pack" beneath it, which immediately evokes imagery of "the wolf pack" in the *Twilight* films and books.

In the exhibit there is a prominent display case that features replicated artifacts from the *Twilight* films. These artifacts include replicas of a paddle necklace worn by the character Emily portrayed by actor Tinsel Korey, a traditional Quileute hand drum that hangs in Emily's house, a shell necklace of Olivella shells that was on the wall of her house and the dream catcher that Jacob gives to Bella as a gift. There are also full color wall photos of the *Twilight* film actors with descriptions of the artifacts and their meaning both in the films and to the Quileute. This mix of Quileute and *Twilight* film artifacts is almost directly opposite the large wolf headdress and mask. Visitors stand between both cases, which are separated by no more than six feet. So while they are not featured as prominently as the wolf headdress, they are very closely located beside the prominent wolf artifacts.

The intermixing of the *Twilight* references with the genuine historical artifacts, particularly the wolf artifacts, undermines the development and creation of an alternative subject position. The exhibit should ultimately distinguish the werewolf from the wolf, but this is not accomplished. Additionally, the *Twilight* exhibit includes a dreamcatcher, an American Indian artifact that originates from the Great Lakes region of the United States and has never been associated with the Pacific Northwest. The panel next to the dreamcatcher acknowledges this but it is still included because it had an important role in the *Twilight* films. The choice to include the dreamcatcher privileges Hollywood mythology over historical accuracy, a phenomenon in representations of American Indians that is unfortunately not new. As a result, the inclusion of the dreamcatcher, a popular and now rather generic American Indian artifact, makes it even more difficult to escape the "noble savage" subject position that paints all American Indian people with a single brush. It is placed in the same glass case as artifacts that are both native to Quileute people and used in the films. Thus, the dreamcatcher blurs the boundaries between popularized American Indian fantasy elements and actual Quileute artifacts, thus making it difficult for the viewer to internalize a clear distinction between the two cultural realms.

"Less unity": The Impact of the Exhibit on Quileute Identity

While the exhibit does not go so far as to show the Quileute people in werewolf form, it does reify the werewolf mythology by blending the elements of the *Twilight* narrative with that of the Quileute narrative in its arrangement. There are resistant discourses to the *Twilight* mythology in the exhibit film, but they are undermined by the film's dependency on *Twilight* to tell the Quileute story and its praise of the film's impact on the community.

Additionally, the Quileute are unable to articulate multiple alternative subject positions beyond the werewolf. Not because these alternative subject positions are unavailable in the exhibit or their culture, but because the arrangement and featuring of these subject positions are not featured in a manner that presents an alternative narrative. For example, the whale, Thunderbird, guardian spirits, and the true history of the Quileute are all potential territory to mine for deeper more powerful resistant subject positions and should have equal prominence with the wolf. In fact, the wolf should have been featured equally alongside the whale, the canoe, the Thunderbird and other important figures in Quileute history within the exhibit design. Additionally, the exhibit artifacts are somewhat piecemeal in their layout and do not draw together a story that can be easily told and retold once a visitor leaves the exhibit. The naturally close association between the wolf and the werewolf in the minds of viewers make critical distinctions and literal separation between the *Twilight* films and the Quileute native art, all the more important for establishing the wolf as an alternative subject position.

For a disruption of the *Twilight* mythology and subsequent re-articulation of the "noble savage" that has been imposed on the Quileute, they would have to not only offer up the wolf as a viable disruptive/alternative subject position, but perhaps also, feature more prominently their identity as canoers, whale hunters, and modern people, in the exhibit and film. They would also do well to feature their other historical mythological figures more prominently such as the whale and Thunderbird who play significant roles in Quileute identity. Additionally, they would have to tell a more coherent narrative of Quileute identity that could be easily and readily articulated, repeated and spread through word of mouth by visitors to the exhibit, an alternative narrative of the wolf, the Thunderbird and other symbols that is more inclusive of Quileute mythological origins and symbols.

These problems with the exhibit mean that the incomplete rhetorical maneuver could undermine future efforts of the Quileute to define themselves independent of *Twilight*. This completion is necessary for the multiplicity of identity to take root in the minds of the public who visit the exhibit. Yet, if the Quileute are able to successfully distinguish themselves as both apart from and associated with Twilight, then the public will be more capable of seeing a more complex Quileute ethnicity.

Conclusion

After examining the Quileute People's exhibit in Washington, D.C., at the National Museum of the American Indian, Smithsonian Institution, it is our estimation that the rhetorical maneuvers within the exhibit are ultimately not successful at articulating an alternative subject position to displace the "noble savage" so powerfully articulated by the *Twilight* books and films. In fact, the exhibit and documentary film strategy may reveal more about how ethnic groups negotiate power relations within a given discursive moment than how they engage the explicit rhetorical maneuvers for redefining the subject position that Philips articulates. The Quileute are occupying a particular time/space location so as to maximize short-term economic and political opportunities arising out of the current popularity of the *Twilight* series. This strategy suggests that the Quileute are vested in maintaining interest in their tribe vis-à-vis *Twilight* mythology for the time being. The implication of this strategy is that it may be more difficult in the long term to engage in rhetorical maneuvering that would provide them more viable alternative subject positions with which to navigate culturally and politically.

In the case of the Quileute, it is to their immediate benefit to invoke the "noble savage" position in the exhibit, much as it was for the Iowa Indians that commodified their culture traveling Europe with George Catlin (Herring, 2006, p. 226). This does not mean that there is no resistance to the existing subject position. However, the maneuvers exhibited are not entirely consistent with the rhetorical maneuver of Philips due to the crucial element of timing. In this case the Quileute are taking advantage of a particular moment in time to speak about their identity. There are examples of "speaking out of place," artistry, memory, and agency at work, but the Quileute do not fully abandon the subject position of the "noble savage," giving validity to the trope. Nor do they offer a coherent alternative mythological narrative or subject position that could disrupt the *Twilight* narrative.

When the *Twilight* phenomena turned the glaring gaze of Hollywood onto the Quileute, they were thrust from obscurity onto a very imposing national stage. However, the Quileute, like many American Indian communities in similar situations, have shrewdly handled the attention by increasing their local economic potential and extending their political influence and reach. Without the popularity of *Twilight*, they may not have been able to get as much tourist interest in the community, a significant source of income for the tribe. Moreover, they may not have been able to get crucial legislation they needed passed, an often difficult and time consuming task for indigenous communities, many of whom wait for years before tribe specific legislation is even proposed, much less maneuvered through Congress. Because of these critical benefits for the Quileute, the *Twilight* books and films have provided a "golden opportunity," as a Quileute tribal member explained in the exhibit film.

Additionally, the Quileute and the Seattle Art Museum may have felt that visitors would not have been inclined to visit the exhibit without the draw of *Twilight* film props. On the National Museum of the American Indian website advertising the exhibit, they indicated that visitors would get a chance to see *Twilight* film artifacts. The accommodation to the *Twilight* films is part of the draw of the exhibit and, given the comments from some of the Quileute members in the films, they see it as a place to begin asking questions, to begin the conversation about the Quileute. Without the *Twilight* artifacts as a lure, the artistic directors and Quileute involved in the exhibit's design may have feared that people would not come. They may have been willing to sacrifice some long-term cultural autonomy as a people, believing that they could eventually overcome the mythology of *Twilight* once this pop culture phenomenon had left the public's imagination.

Accommodation of the *Twilight* series may empower the Quileute in ways not as obvious to outsiders. While there are certainly economic gains, there is also an indirect benefit to keeping the gaze of outsiders on the *Twilight* narratives rather than looking too closely at the Quileute themselves. The Quileute, like many American Indian groups, have a much longer view of their history and place in time. Quileute people protect their cultural autonomy by keeping outsiders from seeing too much of their culture, aspects of the culture they want to keep to themselves and protect from commodification. They also know that there may be opportunities for resistance, agency and multiplicity through multiple other venues in the future. In fact, the Quileute have a website that, upon initial viewing, is much more forthright in defining their identity as independent from the *Twilight* mythology. At the very least, there is little doubt that *Twilight* has given them economic and political opportunities that may never have arisen without the commercial and cultural success of Stephenie Meyer's fiction.

While utilizing the *Twilight* mythology in the exhibit may not be a form of resistance, as Philips (2006) would define it, it is a form of empowerment and that is important for understanding why groups may utilize accommodation strategies as well as resistance strategies to manage power relations. The "noble savage" subject position persists as a result. However, the "noble savage" does not circumscribe the Quileute, even within the context of the exhibit. There are enough elements of resistance present in the exhibit and documentary film to suggest that there is more to the Quileute than Stephenie Meyer's can invent. Hopefully discerning viewers will see those more authentic elements and be able to distinguish the Quileute of La Push, Washington, from the Quileute of *Twilight*. As the Quileute say, "we have no word for Goodbye," and it seems we will continue to see the Quileute, post-*Twilight*, navigate a new world where they are no longer invisible to outsiders, and will always be remembered as "the people who were descended from wolves."

NOTES

1. There are often questions about what terminology to use when referring collectively to indigenous groups in the United States, whether "Native American" or "American Indian." In my research experience speaking to these groups, their preference is "American Indian" when referring to native peoples of the U.S. generally, and their own tribal names when referring to their own people exclusively. This experience came from my ethnographic work with Cheyenne and Arapaho peoples. The reasoning is not clear, just that to them "Native American" is more of a government invention in the same way that "Hispanic" is to some Latin Americans and they tend to be suspicious of it for that reason.

REFERENCES

Bayers, P. L. (2011). The U.S. mint, the Lewis and Clark bicentennial, and the perpetuation of the frontier myth. *The Journal of Popular Culture*, 37–52.
Brunvand, J. H. (1998). *The study of American folklore: An introduction.* (4th ed). New York: W.W. Norton.
Deloria, P. J. (1998). *Playing Indian.* New Haven: Yale University Press.
Deloria, P. J. (2004). *Indians in unexpected Places.* Lawrence: University Press of Kansas.
Farrand, L., and Mayer, T. (1919) Quileute tales. *Journal of American Folklore* 32(124), 251–279.
Foucault, M. (1977). Nietzsche, genealogy, and history. In *Language, counter-memory, practice.* Ithaca: Cornell University Press.
Green, M. K. (1993). Images of Native Americans in advertising: Some moral issues. *Journal of Business Ethics*, 323–330.
Herring, J.B. (2006). Selling the noble savage myth: George Catlin and the Iowa Indians in Europe, 1843–1845. *Kansas History* 29(4), 226–245.
Herring, J. B. (2006–2007). Selling the "Noble Savage" myth: George Catlin and the Iowa Indians in Europe, 1843–1845. In *Kansas History: A Journal of the Central Plains*, 226–245.
Hotakainen, R., and Dodge, J. (2011, April 23). Seeking higher ground: Indian tribe on ocean's edge wants to move out of harm's way; Quileute band asks Congress to give it three square kilometres of wilderness parkland. *The Vancouver Sun*, E22.
Mapes, L. V. (2010, August 10). "Twilight" leads Quileute tribe to help museum tell its true story. Retrieved from: http://seattletimes.nwsource.com/html/localnews/2012589090_quileute11m.html? prmidD related_stories_section.
Meyer, S. (2012). http://www.stepheniemeyer.com/.
Morganroth III, C. (2002). Quileute. (J. Wray, ed.) In J. Wray (ed.), *Native peoples of the Olympic Peninsula: Who we are.* Norman: University of Oklahoma Press.
Museum Openings. (2012, Jan. 13). *The Washington Post*, T21.
Phillips, K. (2006). Rhetorical maneuvers: Subjectivity, power, and resistance. *Philosophy and Rhetoric*, 310–332.
Powell, J., and Jensen, V. (1976). *Quileute: An introduction to the Indians of La Push.* Seattle: University of Washington Press.
Quileute Oceanside Resort: Accommodations. http://www.quileuteoceanside.com/accommodations-overview.
Shearar, C. (2000). *Understanding northwest coast art: A guide to crests, beings and symbols.* Seattle: University of Washington Press.

Vizenor, G. (2008). Aesthetics of survivance: Literary theory and practice. In G. Vizenor (ed.), *Survivance: Narratives of native presence* (pp. 1–24). Lincoln: University of Nebraska.
Walker, R. (2012, December 3). The truth vs. *Twilight*: Quileute website explores reality and fiction. *Indian Country Today Media Network*. Retrieved August 29, 2012, from http://indiancountrytodaymedianetwork.com/2011/12/03/the-truth-vs-twilight-quileute-website-explores-reality-and-fiction–65814.
Whitehouse, G. (2011). *Twilight* as a cultural force. *Journal of Mass Media Ethics* 26(3), 240–242.
Wilson, J. (1998). *The Earth shall weep: A history of native America*. New York: Grove Press.
Wray, J. (2002) Olympic Peninsula intertribal cultural advisory committee. *Native peoples of the Olympic Peninsula: Who we are*. Norman: University of Oklahoma Press.
Yu, Y.-W. (2008). Playing indian: Manifest manners, simulation and pastiche. In G. Vizenor (ed.), *Survivance: Narratives of native presence* (pp. 89–102). Lincoln: University of Nebraska.

The Ultimate Hunger Games

Adam Richman as Comic Hercules in Man v. Food

DAVID WHITT

Since 1916 the corner of Surf and Stillwell Avenues on New York's Coney Island has been the site for one of the more unusual 4th of July holiday events held in the United States, Nathan's Famous International Hot Dog Eating Contest. The rules are simple; eat as many hot dogs and buns as possible in 10 minutes, without throwing up (a.k.a. disqualification by a "reversal of fortune"). Over the decades participants have used a variety of methods to win this gastrointestinal challenge, from the traditional eating of hot dog and bun together, to the now popular technique of chowing down on two dogs at once and then ingesting buns soaked in water. The male and female winners earn, respectively, the coveted Mustard Belt and Pink Belt, and a cool $10,000 each.

While Nathan's is perhaps the most renowned eating contest in the United States, the sport of competitive eating extends well beyond franks and wieners. The Major League Eating and International Federation of Competitive Eating web page lists dozens of contests all over the world including: ribs, hot wings, grits, 7-Eleven Slurpee's, sweet corn, strawberry shortcake, crawfish, Rocky Mountain oysters, funnel cakes, crab cakes, tamales, toasted ravioli, moon pies, cannoli, French fries, and even peanut butter and banana sandwiches. Some professional eaters like Joey "Jaws" Chestnut, Sonya "The Black Widow" Thomas, Tim "Eater X" Janus, and the controversial Takeru Kobayashi, not only net impressive financial rewards for their eating prowess, but also "C-list" celebrity status. The battle of mind over stomach has even played out in popular culture with films like 1967's *Cool Hand Luke* (50 eggs),

1986's *Stand By Me* (pie), 1988's *The Great Outdoors* (96 oz. steak), 2006's *Beerfest* (drinking games), and even a 1999 episode of *The Simpsons* (16 lb. steak).

Taking competitive eating from a niche interest to a larger cable and satellite audience was the Travel Channel series *Man v. Food* (2008–2010). Host Adam Richman best summarizes the premise of *Man v. Food* during the show's opening:

> I'm Adam Richman, a food fanatic who's held nearly every job in the restaurant biz. And now I'm on a mouth-watering journey to find America's greatest pig out spots and take on the country's most legendary eating challenges. I'm no competitive eater, just a regular guy with a serious appetite. This is my ultimate hunger quest. This is *Man v. Food*.

For three seasons Richman traveled to cities around the United States, and even Ontario, Canada and Puerto Rico, highlighting regional delicacies and then participating in a daunting food challenge toward the end of each episode. However, Richman does more than just stuff himself silly. He discusses the history of the challenge, takes the viewer to the kitchen to learn how the challenge is created, and also solicits comments from restaurant patrons about the challenge. During the closing credits he engages in a mock press conference, taking questions from the audience members who have cheered for him throughout the challenge. In 2011 *Man v. Food* transformed into *Man v. Food Nation* (2011–2012), a 27-episode series where Richman still visited eating establishments around the country, but now served as what mythic scholar Joseph Campbell (2005) would call a "guide" (p. 60) or "teacher" (p. 60), coaching others in the food challenge rather than taking it himself.

The purpose of this essay is to analyze *Man v. Food* from a mythic perspective, specifically that of host Adam Richman as a comic Hercules. Richman's attempt to fulfill his "ultimate hunger quest" is worthy of analysis as he is a unique and entertaining variation of Hercules, the demigod worshipped in ancient Greece and Rome. According to the History Channel program "Clash of the Gods" (2009) Hercules was the "greatest action hero in mythology" and "the most popular hero in history—a half-god half-mortal with superhuman strength." While Hercules' reputation as a mighty being is legendary, there is a surprising lack of detail in mythology texts describing his physical appearance. Indeed, one of the more popular and influential classical mythology books, *Bulfinch's Mythology*, originally published in the mid–1800s, only discusses Hercules in terms of his "prodigious strength" (1970, p. 144), who was "worshipped as the god of physical strength" (1970, p. 936).

According to wiki.answers.com Hercules was 6'7," weighed 500 pounds, and had green eyes, brown hair, and a size 13 shoe, but this site does not provide a source for this information. From the images of Hercules on ancient pottery, statues, coins, and gemstones he was envisioned as tall, toned, and muscular; much like a professional body builder today. In dramatic contrast to the immense and powerful Hercules, Adam Richman is more of an "everyman," average in height, with a stout physique, tousled dark hair, dressed in a t-shirt, jeans, with a hoodie or jacket, conveying a personable, relaxed, and friendly demeanor.

Their physical differences aside, Richman, like Hercules, exhibits courage, discipline, strategy, (intestinal) fortitude, and perhaps most importantly, good humor in his epic battle against formidable mythic-sounding food challenges like the Hellfire, the Manimal, the Sasquatch, and the Four Horsemen. Furthermore, the narrative of each *Man v. Food* episode builds Richman into a heroic Hercules-type figure who must defeat a food labor to be rewarded by the "Gods." In Richman's case, the "Gods" are owners of the eating establishments that the food challenges who provide rewards like t-shirts, photos, certificates and bumper stickers.

With the United States experiencing a health care crisis, and obesity rates continuing to climb, some may view programming like *Man v. Food* as the worst example of reality television, highlighting outrageous portion sizes and foods packed with saturated fat and calories. James Poniewozik in *Time* of April 5, 2010, writes,

> If people are what they eat, then nations are what is eaten in them. For countries, food is a statement of culture and identity.... Judged by its food, then, what is the U.S.? To look at our food TV—a mixed-message buffet of indulgence and shame—it's a binge-and-purger. One batch of shows is saturated with fat: Paula Deen cooking "fried butter balls," Adam Richman downing sandwiches the size of dachshunds on *Man v. Food*, Guy Fieri deep-frying S'mores [p. 17].

While Poniewozik's condemnation of food programming like *Man v. Food* is yet another warning about the dangers of overconsumption, I will leave the debate over the impact of *Man v. Food* on our national fitness to those more qualified such as doctors, nutritionists, and other health officials. My purpose is to analyze *Man v. Food* in terms of its mythic themes, specifically that of host Adam Richman as a comic reflection of the Hercules myth, and what this myth says about contemporary American culture. To understand how Richman reflects a comic Hercules, several episodes of *Man v. Food* will be discussed to illustrate how his exposition, training, and quests incorporate mythic references and visual imagery. However, first it is necessary to discuss the Hercules myth and how Richman can be viewed as a comic version of this ancient hero.

Hercules as (Comic) Hero

The mythic lineage of Hercules can be traced back to the ancient Greeks who first worshipped him as the mighty Heracles. According to W.H.D. Rouse in *Gods, Heroes, and Men of Ancient Greece: Mythology's Great Tales of Valor and Romance* (1957) in Greek mythology Heracles was born to a mortal human Alcmena and the "King of the Gods" Zeus. However, Zeus's wife Hera was jealous of baby Heracles and attempted to murder him by putting two deadly snakes in his bedroom. But in his first feat of strength the infant Heracles managed to kill the creatures. As Heracles matured he trained to become a warrior, learning the bow and arrow, sword, javelin, wrestling, and boxing. Eventually Heracles would marry and have two sons, but Hera, still bitter toward Heracles, instilled a "madness" upon him and he killed his children.

Seeking redemption for slaying his sons Heracles solicits advice from the Oracle at Delphi. The oracle tells Heracles he must live in southern Greece, serving King Eurystheus of Mycenai for twelve years, and performing each year a labor demanded by the king with the promise of "immortality if he accomplished them" (Stoneman, 1991, p. 87). According to Graves (1992) the Twelve Labors of Heracles included: killing the Nemean Lion, killing the Lernaean Hydra, capturing the Ceryneian Hind (deer), capturing the Erymanthian Boar, cleaning the stables of Augeias, destroying the Stymphalian Birds, capturing the Cretan Bull, capturing the Mares of Diomedes, securing Amazon queen Hippolyte's Girdle (belt), herding the Cattle of Geryon, fetching the Golden Apples of Hesperides, and finally, fetching the dog Cerberus from Tartaros. After successfully completing these labors, Hercules would go on to have many other adventures, including joining Jason and the Argonauts on their search for the Golden Fleece. However, Stoneman (1991) states that the Twelve Labors "are the most famous part of the saga of Heracles" (p. 87). Later, upon his death, in recognition of his difficult and tortured life, Heracles is allowed to live with the gods on Mount Olympus, is given a house, a wife (Hebe, the goddess of youth), and ultimately "fame and immortality" (Rouse, 1957, p. 71).

In ancient Greece, Heracles was worshipped as a deity and celebrated in everything from plays to poetry to pottery. According to Galinsky (1972) famous Greek writers such as Sophocles, Euripedes, and Aristophanes made Heracles a popular character in their respective plays, but instead of portraying him as a tragic hero these authors emphasized his comic traits. Galinsky states that "in literature, the Greeks knew him best and loved him most in his comic role" (p. xii), adding, the "number of serious dramas in which he [Heracles] has a part is a small trickle compared to the torrent of satyr plays, farces, and comedies" (p. 81). Plays like Sophocles' *Herakles at Taenarus,* Aristophanes' *Frogs,* and Euripides' *Syleus* highlighted Heracles as a fierce warrior, but also his vices such as wine and women. Galinsky explains, "In the *Syleus,* we find all the characteristics for which Herakles was known on the comic stage: he is a gross monster, a brute, a glutton, and a libertine" (p. 84). In Aristophanes' *Birds,* Heracles is "a monstrous glutton, bully, and nitwit, but it is just because of this exaggeration that he comes off as good-natured rather than terrifying" (p. 88). In his final analysis of Heracles as a comic hero, Galinsky contends he

> overdid everything, and that was exactly the reason for his great success. To the reader several centuries later the constant emphasis on the hero's voracity for food, wine, and women —in that order—may appear tedious. But exaggeration is exactly the stuff that makes popular comedy work [p. 96].

The ancient Romans, who had their own gods but borrowed heavily from the Greeks, would later adopt Heracles into their own mythology, slightly altering his name to the now, more common, Hercules. Throughout the centuries Hercules would continue to be embraced as an iconic hero and celebrated in various cultures and artistic forms even into the twenty-century. For example, influential English playwrights such a Christopher Marlowe (1564–1593), William Shakespeare (1564–1616), George Chapman (1559–1634) and John Dryden (1631–1700) used Hercules as a model for many of their characters. Waith (1962) states that these English authors were "aware of resemblances between their heroes and Hercules, though there is no indication that any one depiction of him served as their model" (p. 13). Waith argues that Hercules was foremost in Marlowe's mind when he wrote *Tamburlaine* (1587), and that Antony in Shakespeare's *Antony and Cleopatra* (1623) reflected many of Hercules's heroic qualities. More contemporary interpretations of this hero include the television series H*ercules: The Legendary Journeys* (1995–1999), films like Disney's animated *Hercules* (1997) and *Immortals* (2011), and even videogames like *Age of Empires: Mythologies* (2008) and *God of War III* (2010). There are also two Hercules feature films in development, both tentatively slated to be released in 2014. The first, directed by Brett Ratner and starring Dwayne "The Rock" Johnson as the Greek demigod, will be based on the 2008 graphic novel *Hercules: The Thracian Wars* (Child, 2012). The second film, *Hercules 3D,* will be directed by Renny Harlin, with *Twilight* star Kellan Lutz in the title role (White, 2013).

According to Stanford (1972) when defined as simply a "muscle man" Hercules is "apt to be dismissed by conventional-minded people who assume that brawn always precludes brain, as stupid and uninteresting. This is clearly wrong ... many great writers and artists have found [Hercules] a fascinating subject for creative interpretation" (p. x). I contend that Adam Richman reflects yet another creative interpretation of the Hercules myth, in the vein of the comic persona first celebrated by the ancient Greeks, whose labors are not the capturing or killing of mighty beasts, but conquering food challenges of epic proportions. However, *Man v. Food*'s use of mythology is not limited to portraying Richman as a humorous Hercules. Several episodes contain allusions to other myths, both ancient and contemporary, creating a multilayered text for analysis.

Adam v. Food

The various challenges on *Man v. Food* (*MvF*) can be divided into three basic "s" categories: size, sum, and spicy. The size category is self-explanatory, larger than normal portions of everything from sandwiches to stuffed omelets, some including additional side dishes like vegetables or dessert. The sum category is an "all you can eat" type challenge where the participant tries to set a record eating as much of a particular food, like oysters or fried catfish, as possible. The spicy category is perhaps the most difficult, often generating excruciating pain from face to stomach. Some of these challenges include hot wings, tuna rolls and bowls of curry with ramen. There is some overlap between categories, especially sum and spicy. For example, during the "Fire Brand Chili Challenge" the participant tries to set a record eating bowls of incredibly spicy chili. The record, at the time, was six bowls, an arguably small number that underscores the difficulty of this particular challenge. Within each of these categories there are unique food labors to be conquered, allowing Richman to play the role of comic Hercules who attempts to slay the beast-that-is-food.

SIZE

The very first episode of *MvF* in Amarillo, Texas, establishes the tone for the entire series with the Big Texan Steak Challenge, set at, not surprisingly, the Big Texan Steak Ranch. In this challenge a participant has one hour to eat a 72-ounce steak, shrimp cocktail, dinner salad, baked potato, and dinner roll. According to Richman, 48,000 people have attempted the challenge, but only 8,000 have succeeded. If Richman wins, the meal is free, and he receives his picture on the wall, a mug, and a white t-shirt that says, "I Ate It All!!! & Survived the 72 oz. Steak." As is typical with each episode, Richman shares his strategy for the challenge which includes cutting the meat, using condiments to help it "all slide down and prevent my jaw from wearing out," and saving the starches for last. With the "beef battlefield" on the table in front of him Richman begins his food fight, needing only 29:30 of the 60 minutes to finish the Big Texan Challenge. However, much like Hercules attempting to capture the Cretan Bull or fetching the Golden Apples of Hesperides, Richman quickly learns that not all food labors are created alike.

During the second episode of *MvF*, in Memphis, Tennessee, Richman takes on the Sasquatch: a 4-pound burger with 1½-pounds of toppings (8 slices of cheese, tomato, onions, pickles with added bacon and mushrooms) on a two-pound homemade bun the size of a barstool that he must eat 60 minutes. If successful, he will be rewarded by having his picture on the Wall of Fame. The Memphis episode marks the first time that there are several diverse mythic allusions in one episode. The name of the burger, Sasquatch (a.k.a. Bigfoot), refers to the alleged ape-like beast of the Pacific Northwest. While the mythology of Sasquatch is never explained in the episode the Big Foot Lodge, where the challenge takes place, has a large wooden statue of the furry beast towering over customers. The next tie to myth is when Richman seeks advice from Jeremy Paine, a customer who finished the burger in 53 minutes. Paine's eating tips are quite simple, "speed" and "don't stop," to which Richman proclaims, "He's my Yoda!" in reference to the diminutive Jedi master from *Star Wars*, arguably one of the most popular mythic narratives in contemporary culture. According to Joseph Campbell in *The Hero with a Thousand Faces* (2005) Yoda would be described as a "supernatural helper" (p. 59), an individual who provides guidance to the hero on their journey. Campbell explains this helper "may be some little fellow of the wood, some wizard, hermit, shepherd, or smith" who appears, to supply the amulets and advice that the hero will require" (p. 59). For Richman, Paine becomes his "helper," offering advice on how to defeat the Sasquatch.

The final image in the episode with a strong link to mythic iconography, one that is also included in future episodes, features Richman being kissed by a woman for encouragement. This moment alludes to the Muses of Greek mythology: Erato (lyric poetry), Euterpe (double pipe), Kalliope (epic poetry), Kleio (history), Melpomene (tragedy), Ourania (astronomy), Poly(hy)mnia (hymns), Terpsichore (choral dance), and Thaleia (comedy), who were "principally associated with various aspects of the charming power of artistic expression" (Buxton, 2004, p. 85). However, despite the Memphis muse's inspirational peck on the cheek and Paine's advice, time runs out for Richman with one quarter of the monstrous burger remaining.

Two other episodes from season one illustrate Richman in the role of a comic Hercules, while also incorporating mythic language into their respective narratives. The first episode is set at Lucky's Sandwich Company in Chicago, Illinois, and spotlights the Overstuffed Sandwich Challenge during which Richman must eat three 1½-pound meat-sandwiches covered with cheese and fried eggs, a side order of fries and a helping of coleslaw within an hour. To prepare for this challenge, Richman boldly runs the stairs at the Sears Tower to work up an appetite. However, of the 110 floors, he only makes it to floor 6 and gives up. After this brief training sequence Richman begins the Overstuffed Sandwich Challenge, completing it in 25 minutes, securing a place on Lucky's Wall of Fame, and more importantly, "eternal glory" and "immortality."

Another example of Richman's comic heroism mixed with mythic themes is in Seattle, Washington, at Beth's Café. Here he takes on the Southwestern Exposure 12 Egg Omelet Challenge that showcases a five-pound combination of eggs, chili, sour cream, salsa and cheddar cheese served with a side of toast and hash browns. The omelet is so large it needs to be served on a pizza tray. Richman refers to this challenge as a "chow-down quest," announces that he will "corral the sheer fury that is the Southwestern Exposure," and asserts that this omelet is the "breakfast of Titans." Unfortunately, during the challenge Richman hits his eating-wall stating, "each bite is a labor." Unable to finish the last two bites of the omelet Richman relents and the-beast-that-is-food wins.

Like Cerberus the three-headed hound at the gates of Hades, a 3-pound, 40-inch bratwurst sausage joined with two side dishes (red cabbage and 3 potato croquettes) known as the Meterwurst Challenge would confront Richman at the Gasthof Zur Gemutlichkeit in Minneapolis, Minnesota. However, before he attempts the challenge Richman takes a walk in a local park and sees several men dressed up as Vikings, a nod to the state's professional football team. Richman is taught to eat, drink and fight like a Viking, thus blending his comic Hercules persona with that of the Nordic explorers and warriors of old who had their own unique mythology. During the challenge Richman even receives a kiss from a woman, yet another muse for inspiration. Ultimately, he slays the Meterwurst Challenge and garners his treasure: a certificate with his name and the date recognizing this accomplishment.

While seasons two and three also have their fair share of size challenges with mythic undertones, two in particular stand out. The first is in Waikiki Beach, Hawaii, at MAC 24–7 and their MAC Daddy Challenge: three 14-inch pancakes with toppings (Richman chooses blueberries and vanilla butter) equaling 4 pounds of food. Richman refers to the pancakes as a "breakfast monolith" and a "breakfast behemoth." Despite adding coffee and a side of bacon for additional flavor, the supersized stack of starch and sugar proves to be too immense for Richman to overcome. The second is at Papa Bob's Bar-B-Que in Kansas City, Kansas, and their Ultimate Destroyer Challenge. Richman also describes this challenge as a "behemoth" because it contains seven different meats (sliced pork, pulled pork, ham, turkey breast, sausage, brisket and hamburgers) on a 12-inch hoagie bun coupled with an additional 1½-pound of fries, totaling a gut-busting 6½-pounds of food. During the challenge Richman compares the meats with "the seven delicious sins," but is unable to finish the sandwich in the allotted 45 minutes, bested by this "meaty monster."

One of the more unique *MvF* size episodes was the *Live Special* set at the Alexander Hotel on Miami Beach, Florida, on February 3, 2010—a few days before Super Bowl XLIV. During this hour-long program Richman attempted to eat a 48-ounce Porterhouse steak from Shula's Steak House, a local restaurant owned by former Miami Dolphins head coach Don Shula. If Richman can eat the steak, or "beast," in less than 20 minutes he will reserve a permanent place in the "48-Oz Club," a signed photograph from Shula, and "bask in the ultimate reward of food glory." However, according to Richman this "monster" has "felled 40,000 brave customers." So, to battle with this "beefy behemoth," Richman has a brief training regimen with Shula and his son Dave, also a former professional football coach. Like Jeremy Paine (a.k.a. Yoda) in the Memphis episode, the elder Shula plays the "wise mentor," putting Richman through various football drills and telling him to "think about the steak" and "make it happen." After this session Richman says he has the "agility, speed, strength and the mental determination to win." Before the challenge begins the younger Shula tells Adam he as the "heart of a lion and the soul of a champion." As live announcers and a throng of fans cheer for him throughout the challenge, Richman makes relatively easy work of the steak, finishing it off with 3:23 remaining on the clock.

Of the 59 episodes of *MvF* approximately half of them feature Richman attempting various size challenges. From a purely visual standpoint, many food concoctions are so massive they seem impossible to finish, reinforcing in dramatic fashion the adage of one's eyes being larger than their stomach. Some of these include: the seven-pound Grande Breakfast Burrito containing 12 eggs, potatoes, one pound of ham, a whole onion, and 10 ounces of green chilies at Denver, Colorado's, Jack-n-Grill (food wins); and the Colossal Challenge, drinking a 6-pound milkshake and eating a 1½-pound deli sandwich at Chick and Ruth's in Annapolis, Maryland (man wins). During the Mount Nachismo (also spelled Nacheesmo) Challenge at Tio's Mexican Café in Ann Arbor, Michigan—where Richman must eat a five pound plate of nachos covered with refried beans, cheese, chicken, pork, beef, and other toppings in 45 minutes—there are brief mythic allusions when two women kiss Richman on the cheek (muses) and one man in the audience cheers for Adam and dubs him a "hero." Inspired by the adoration from the crowd, Richman continues devouring the massive mound of tortilla chips and toppings. With approximately three minutes remaining on the clock Richman finishes the remaining chips, thereby earning a t-shirt that boasts, "I conquered Mt. Nachismo. Many go up. Few return." and his name on Tio's Wall of Fame.

Sum

The second category of food challenges is a numbers game; eating as many of one type of food as is possible or required. Richman's first foray into the sum category is the 15-Dozen Oyster Challenge at the Acme Oyster House in New Orleans, Louisiana. Richman has only an hour to eat 180 oysters on a half-shell, but easily finishes them all off in an impressive 21 minutes. In the following week's episode, Richman attempts a dual sum/spicy challenge in Portland, Oregon, at Salvador Molly's when he contends with their Great Balls of Fire Challenge. Richman has five minutes to eat five habanero fritters plus salsa equaling a total of ten pounds of food. When the habanero spices begin to kick in, Richman bravely proclaims that as "the temperature rises, so does my courage!" His fighting spirit helps him vanquish the five fiery fritters, and he gets his picture on the Wall of Flame.

However, at Richman's next sum challenge at Crown Candy Kitchen in St. Louis, Missouri he is unable to drink five 24-ounce malt milkshakes (two vanilla, coffee, mocha, and egg nog) in 30 minutes to win the 5 Milkshake Challenge. Before this challenge Richman visits the kitchen to see how the homemade ice cream for the milkshakes is made. While watching strawberry ice cream move from machine to container Richman enthusiastically proclaims, "Release the Kraken!" which was an edict from the Greek God Zeus in both film versions of *Clash of the Titans* (1981 and 2010), a call to release this mighty and terrible beast out of the depths of the sea. *The Kraken* was also the title of an 1830 poem by Englishman Lord Alfred Tennyson, who vividly describes a beast lying "far, far beneath the abysmal sea" with "shadowy sides," "huge sponges of millennial growth and height," "unnumbered enormous polypi," and "giant arms" (Buckley and Woods, 1965, pp. 13–14). There is a footnote to the poem explaining that the Kraken "was a fabulous Scandinavian sea-monster" (p. 13). "Release the Kraken!" is also used as a slogan in the 2012 advertising campaign for a new-spiced rum "The Kraken" from Proximo Spirits. According to the Proximo Spirits official website the rum was named for "a sea beast of myth and legend."

A "sugary hardship" is the description Richman gives to another sweet sum challenge at the San Francisco Creamery. Richman is given one hour to finish their Kitchen Sink Challenge which showcased eight scoops of ice cream (he chooses three scoops of orange sherbet, three of vanilla, one cake mix, and one Swiss milk chocolate) with hot fudge, sprinkles, bananas, whipped cream and topped with almonds and chocolate sprinkles served in an actual kitchen sink. As the Creamery crowd cheers Richman on he begins to experience "sweetness overload" and eats some salty French fries to change the flavor. The strategy works and Richman finishes this "San Francisco giant" in 45 minutes proudly stating, "In the immortal struggle of man versus food, man won!" He gets his picture on the Wall of Fame, and perhaps more importantly, free ice cream for a year.

Several challenges provide a spin on the sum category, adding variety to the types and quantity of food to be consumed. One is at Humpy's Great Alaskan Alehouse in Anchorage, Alaska and their Kodiak Arrest Challenge. This challenge allows participants 90 minutes to finish a six-pound, seven-course sampling of local seafood delicacies like crab, reindeer sausage and salmon cakes, with sides of sour cream and chive mashed potatoes, vegetables and mixed berry crisp with ice cream. Although dozens have attempted the Kodiak Arrest, in true Herculean spirit Richman is the first winner of this challenge in only 47 minutes, and presented with a blue t-shirt that says "I Got Crabs at Humpy's," with an image of a fish holding a mug of beer on the front.

The next variety trial is The Davy Jones Locker Challenge at the Port Royal Pub & Grille in Islip, New York. Davy Jones Locker is an old sailor's expression that, according to *Webster's New World Dictionary* (1994), refers to "the bottom of the sea; grave of those drowned at sea or buried there" (p. 352). The challenge itself is seven pounds of crab, shrimp, mussels, clam strips, stuffed flounder, with sides of vegetables and coleslaw that must be eaten in less than an hour. Before the challenge Richman meets owner/chef Anthony Mastrantonio, the "man behind the Leviathan," a reference to a mighty sea monster in the Bible (Job 3:8 "May those who curse days curse that day, those who are ready to rouse Leviathan; Job 41:1 "Can you pull in the leviathan with a fishhook or tie down his tongue with a rope?"; Psalm 74:14 "It was you who crushed the heads of Leviathan"; Isaiah 27:1 "Leviathan the gliding serpent, Leviathan the coiling serpent"). The Leviathan is also a creature in English poet John Milton's 17th century epic poem *Paradise Lost*, described as the

> Hugest of living creatures, on the deep
> Stretched like a promontory sleeps or swims
> And seems a moving land, and at his gills
> Draws in, and at his trunk spouts out a sea [p. 210].

During the Davy Jones Locker Challenge Richman's Leviathan is two-pounds of Alaskan Snow Crab that he is in "full on battle" and "in close combat" with to remove all the meat from its shell. With the crowd cheering him on Richman becomes only the second person to successfully navigate through this sea of food, earning a blue Port Royal t-shirt with the image of a tattered pirate map on the back, and his picture on their Wall of Fame.

One other variety sum challenge is Mick & Angelo's Italian Challenge in Niagara Falls, Ontario. This seven pound, six dish challenge is a pasta overload of lasagna, manicotti, stuffed cannelloni, hot Italian sausage, chicken parmesan, spaghetti and meatballs, all covered in sauce and cheese, plus a loaf of garlic bread, soup, salad and apple crisp dessert. If Richman eats everything in 90 minutes he receives a t-shirt (which is never shown) and his picture on the Wall of Fame. Beginning backwards with dessert Richman manages to finish all the dishes, except the spaghetti, his Italian dreams crushed by one lone plate of complex carbohydrates.

In other sum challenges Richman attempts to eat 16 chili dogs in an hour at The Roast Grill in Raleigh, North Carolina (man wins); a five-pound bucket of 50 jumbo buffalo wings in 30 minutes at the West End Tavern in Boulder, Colorado (man loses); 29 fried catfish and two sides in one hour at the Steak & Catfish Barn in Edmond, Oklahoma (man wins); and a five-pound platter of 12 meat, cheese and potato pancake sliders plus onion rings in 30 minutes at Chompie's in Phoenix, Arizona. Richman loses the slider challenge explaining that "time cut my Herculean effort short."

Spicy

The final challenge category, spicy, is arguably the most ominous of the three as it frequently causes Richman the most physical pain, both internally and externally. His first spicy challenge was in Pittsburgh, Pennsylvania at the Quaker Steak & Lube and their Atomic Wing Challenge. The challenge seems deceptively simple; eat 6 hot wings with no time limit. As Richman eats several wings he quickly begins to feel the heat of the spices and refers to his face as "the 7th circle of Hell," a literary reference to Dante's 14th century poem *The Divine Comedy*. However, despite his discomfort Richman finishes the last wing and wins the challenge.

The combination of ingredients in Richman's next piquant challenge is so dangerous that during its preparation the cook wears a gas mask to not choke on the spices. The Brick Land Curry House in New York City is home to the P'hall Curry Challenge, the self-proclaimed "spiciest curry in America," containing ten chilies that are sixty times hotter than a jalapeno pepper. There is no time limit to eat the curry, and each challenger is given milk and a yogurt smoothie as a cooling agent to help control the fiery flavor. During the challenge Richman mixes in rice to temper the curry in terms of its spiciness, then finishes the chicken, and finally has just the sauce remaining. However, Richman makes the painful mistake of wiping his face with the napkin he has been using to wipe his mouth causing his face to be "on fire." Despite this self-inflicted eating injury Richman manages to "tame the incendiary ingredients and reach my final bite." His prizes are free beer, a Certificate of Completion with his name on it, and the "adoration of the masses."

The Spicy Ramen Challenge at Orochon Ramen in Los Angeles, California, is similar to the P'hall Curry Challenge in that Richman must eat a spicy bowl of food with 10 different chilies, a combination that he says turns "ordinary ramen into a howling spice demon." What makes this challenge different is Richman's preparation, specifically his training sequence. While walking along a southern California beach at night Richman sees "a vision of incomparable beauty," four "fire dancing sirens of Sirena Serpentina," a local professional fire dancing group. The Sirena Serpentina are clearly a variation on the mythological Sirens from Homer's epic poem *The Odyssey*, whose song lured sailors and their ships to wreck on the rocky coast of their island. However, unlike the devious and deadly Sirens from Greek mythology the Sirena Serpentina are helpful and supportive, not only painting Richman's face and arms to teach him "the ways of the fire," but two also join him in the ramen challenge. Encouraged by the cheering crowd, Richman finishes the noodles, and then picks up the bowl to drink the remaining broth, thus becoming the latest champion of the curry challenge, and getting his name on the Wall of Bravery.

Three spicy challenges inspire a level of gut wrenching fear and anxiety with their references to Biblical mythology: the Hot Wings Hellfire Challenge at Smoke Eaters in San Jose, California, the spicy tuna roll Hellfire Challenge at Kobe Sushi in Salt Lake City, Utah, and the Four Horsemen Challenge at Chunky's Burgers & More in San Antonio, Texas. The first Hellfire Challenge is so spicy it is not even listed on the menu at Smoke Eaters. Richman has ten minutes to consume 12 hot wings that are covered in 6 ounces of habanero powder. What makes the challenge even more daunting is that he cannot use napkins or have anything to drink. Additionally, when Richman is finished he has to lick his fingers and wait an excruciating five minutes as the spices simmer on his face and in his stomach. Richman eats all 12 wings, but is in so much pain that neither milk nor beer will soothe his digestive discomfort. He even rubs ice on his face to cool it off.

The second Hellfire Challenge at Kobe Sushi requires Richman to first eat three qualifying levels of spicy tuna rolls before he is allowed to compete in the actual challenge. Each qualifying spicy tuna roll is twice as hot as the last, meaning that by the time he gets to the highest level the heat from the various chilies and peppers will be especially intense. Richman passes the qualifying rounds, and eats all 6 pieces of the hottest tuna rolls, but is in obvious pain as tears roll down his face. By surviving the spicy sushi gauntlet Richman is given a black Kobe logo t-shirt signifying "eternal food glory."

The Four Horsemen Challenge is in reference to the Book of Revelation's Four Horsemen of the Apocalypse: conquest, war, famine and death. The challenge is a half-pound burger challenge that combines four increasingly hotter peppers: jalapeno, serrano, habanero, and the ghost, all combined into a sauté. The burger is then topped with cheese and habanero sauce for additional spiciness. Richman has 25 minutes to eat the burger and, like the Hellfire Challenge, must wait five minutes after he is done without drinking any "cooling remedies." Richman is given a pair of gloves to prevent spice burns and wonders, "Will Four Horsemen be my apocalypse, or will I vanquish the flames and be remembered forever on the Wall of Flame?" After the first bite Richman instantly feels the heat and pounds his fist on the table in front of him. He laments that the challenge is "dragging me to Hell" and that the burger is his "mortal enemy" and a "fiery torment." Richman is allowed to drink water, but it does not help as the "heat is overwhelming." He reaches the final bite, waits five minutes and declares victory. However, Richman's mouth and stomach hurt so much he does not want to talk.

Like the size and sum categories there are additional spicy challenges that test Richman's resolve. The Fire Brand Chili Challenge at Joe Rogers' Chili Parlor in Springfield, Illinois is, according to Richman "pure evil" with the odor from the chili burning the inside of his nostrils (he ties a record at six bowls). The Stupid Wings Challenge at Caliente in Richmond, Virginia, is eight oversized chicken wings made from a hot sauce that contains habanero powder, cayenne pepper and sauce from "The Container of Poor Judgment," holding the remnants from all the sauce ever made (making it more potent), plus five drops of capsaicin abstract, the active ingredient in peppers, added to the mix (man wins). The Shut-Up Juice Challenge at The Mean Pig BBQ in Cabot, Arkansas, is a pulled pork sandwich made with a barbeque sauce made from pure habanero abstract (man wins the "hellishly hot" challenge). At Bushido in Charleston, South Carolina, Richman attempts the 10 Spicy Tuna Hand Roll Challenge, which, like the Kobe Sushi Challenge in Salt Lake City, each tuna roll is spicier than the next. During roll number six Richman begins to feel the heat kick in and "calls upon the warrior spirit," completing the challenge in record time. He is presented with headband and his name is placed on Bushido's Legends of the Roll.

Discussion

After discussing several episodes of *MvF* it is clear that Adam Richman both converges and diverges from the Hercules myth in several different ways. In terms of convergence Richman's participation in various food challenges parallels that of Hercules' quest to complete the Twelve Labors. While Richman attempts 59 food labors versus a dozen for Hercules their goal is similar, to defeat the challenge and be rewarded. Hercules was promised "immortality" by the Oracle at Delphi as his ultimate reward, which, over the millennia he has achieved in literature, art, and popular culture. Richman is rewarded with inexpensive and disposable objects such as bumper stickers, mugs, t-shirts and certificates. "Immortality" for Richman is achieved when he wins a challenge and his name and/or picture is placed on a Wall of Fame (or Flame, Bravery, or, for not completing the challenge, Shame). Additionally, Richman's language also reflects his goal of achieving food glory. As discussed in various episodes Richman uses phrases such as "eternal glory," "all the glory," "immortal struggle," "eternal struggle," and "immortality" to both describe the battle of man versus food and the reward for achieving success. At Sweet P's BBQ in Knoxville, Tennessee, before the El Gigante Burrito Challenge (a five-pound burrito with sides of macaroni and cheese and banana pudding) Richman's pronounces he wants to "secure my spot in the annals of Tennessee lore." Before attempting the Spicy Tuna Roll Challenge at Bushido in Charleston, South Carolina, Richman enthusiastically says he is "ready to become a legend." While Hercules has the overwhelming advantage in terms of longevity and name recognition, Richman will forever have "digital immortality" through reruns on the Travel Channel and DVD sales and rentals.

Another similarity between Hercules and Richman is their strategy and creativity for completing their respective labors. For example, for his fifth labor Hercules had to clean in a single day the stables of Augeias, which held 30,000 cattle. Hercules's inspired solution to this seemingly impossible task was to divert two rivers into the stable, which quickly washed it clean (Rouse, 1957). On his quest for the Golden Apples of Hesperides Hercules convinced the Titan Atlas, who at the time was holding up the sky, to fetch the apples for him. In return Hercules agreed to hold up the sky while Atlas retrieved the apples. Upon completing this task Atlas, who was tired of holding up the sky, told Hercules he would take the apples to King Eurystheus. Hercules agreed to allow Atlas to do so, but first asked him to hold up the sky for just a moment while Hercules shifted to a more comfortable position. Atlas did so, and Hercules grabbed the apples, leaving Atlas to once again hold up the sky (Stoneman, 1991).

While eating a five-pound hamburger or two-foot long burrito may not be on par with cleaning a massive stable or tricking a titan, Richman does employ various creative strategies to help him prepare for a food challenge. In a 2009 interview Richman explains that he works out "like a warrior" before a challenge, and stays hydrated to combat salty foods (Lawrence, 2009). During the challenge Richman does everything from cutting large portions into smaller ones (which, psychologically, seems easier to manage) to, surprisingly, requesting additional foods like bacon, French fries and cole slaw or adding hot sauce and drinking coffee for taste variety. Other times he has stacked or mixed foods together, and once even called his mother to ask if he could eat an apple crisp dessert before attempting a main course of spaghetti. Clearly, Richman's eating strategy is not just about speed, but also changing flavors so his palate is constantly tempted to eat more.

One final point of convergence is the comic nature of both Hercules and Richman. As stated previously, Hercules was celebrated in ancient literature and art not only for his strength and courage, but also his gregariousness and voracious appetite. Galinsky (1972) writes, "Preference for good food and drink rather than his labors was a stock characteristic of the comic Herakles" (p. 82). Similarly, Richman has an affable personality, which allows him to interact genuinely with the locals making him an appealing host for the television viewing audience. Moreover, Richman's obvious appreciation for food is exhibited when he takes viewers to the kitchen to learn how a challenge is created. He talks to each chef about the various ingredients, emphasizing their quality, freshness, and what they add to the overall flavor. Then, during the challenge itself, he frequently comments on everything from the texture to the taste of the food. In between Richman cracks jokes, drops puns, and in general, exudes great joy and enthusiasm for the region, people, and its local fare.

In terms of divergence there are distinct differences between Hercules and Richman. The first is their physical appearance. While Hercules was the original hero archetype described in literature and portrayed in art as having a toned physique, extraordinary strength and endurance, Richman is the antithesis with a John Belushi/Jack Black-esque build who not only gets tired during some of his training regimens, but also during some challenges. For example, while attempting the OMG Burger Challenger (12 quarter-pound burgers with 12 slices of cheese) at Lindy's on 4th in Tucson, Arizona, Richman states that his "jaw is getting tired" (a weakness Hercules would never admit), but still wins the challenge. Certainly Richman's frequent admission during a food challenge that it may be impossible to defeat creates dramatic tension in each episode, and parallels that of another type of entertainment programming, professional wrestling.

Initially, during a pro wrestling match, the "good guy" wrestler performs well against the "bad guy" wrestler, but quickly the tide changes with the "bad guy" looking like he will prevail. However, tapping into a reserve of strength and determination the "good guy" manages to ultimately beat the "bad guy." Similarly, most of Richman's battles with food follow this narrative arc. When the challenge begins Richman quickly eats as much food as he can before hitting his personal food wall, and begins to slow down. With the completion of the challenge now seemingly in doubt, Richman taps into his willpower and resolve and somehow finds room in his stomach for another bite, then another, and another. Richman then finishes the final bite, typically standing up in front of the cheering crowd and proudly proclaiming himself the winner. That is, of course, unless he fails to win a food challenge, which does happen. Over the course of 59 episodes Richman defeated food 37 times, giving him an impressive winning percentage of 62 percent. However, unlike Hercules who successfully completed all twelve of his labors, Richman fails almost one-third of the time, which is another point of divergence with the hero of the ancient world.

A final way that Hercules and Richman are dissimilar is the uniqueness of their respective tests. The Twelve Labors ordered by King Eurystheus were dangerous tasks against mighty creatures and daunting obstacles. While Hercules did receive some help along the way (for example, his nephew Iolaus in killing the Lernaean Hydra) he ultimately received individual recognition and "immortality" for completing the labors. In contrast, the food challenges, while creating severe discomfort at times, do not put Richman in any mortal danger. Perhaps, most importantly, Richman is not the first, nor the last person to attempt a food challenge. In fact, in each episode Richman typically states how many people have attempted the challenge and how many have succeeded. Some challenges, like the Big Texan Steak Challenge had (at the time), over 48,000 individuals tackling this 5-item feast, with only 8,000 finishing. Others, like the Manimal Challenge (eating eight cheeseburgers and a milkshake in 20 minutes) at the Tradewinds Café in Portland, Maine, had "dozens" of participants (again, at the time) with only four champions. However, it does not matter if thousands or only a handful of contestants triumph over a food challenge, winning is not an unparalleled accomplishment. Unlike Hercules whose labors were each different (you can only kill the Nemean Lion once after all) Richman cannot claim to be the only person to win a challenge. Granted, he was the first person to win the Kodiak Arrest Challenge, and set records in the Fried Catfish and Bushido Spicy Tuna Challenges, but the majority of challenges are open to anyone willing to pay for the challenge in terms of both its price tag and potential physical pain. Consequently, when

Richman wins he does not have exclusive rights to "victory" and "immortality," but rather shares it amongst the others who have also defeated a food challenge.

Myth and Culture

According to Galinsky (1972), "Myth is kept alive through the ages by constantly being reinterpreted and this reinterpretation most often takes the form of adaptation to the prevailing sensibilities of a given age" (p. 294). Over the past two thousand years, mythic reinterpretations of Hercules, his abilities and labors, have been expressed in art, literature, television, and film. He is truly a character who has stood the test of time. Adam Richman's modern reinterpretation of Hercules as a comic hero not only channels the mythology of this ancient demigod, but also reflects the values of contemporary American culture.

French literary theorist Roland Barthes discussed the relationship between myth and culture in *Mythologies* (1972). He writes, myth is a "type of speech ... a system of communication, that it is a message" (p. 109). However, Barthes expands his analysis of myth beyond spoken word, explaining "It (speech) can consist of modes of writing or of representations; not only written discourse, but also photography, cinema, reporting, sport, shows, publicity, all these can serve as a support to mythical speech" (p. 110). Using semiotics—the study of signs and symbols—Barthes demonstrates the complexity of various cultural myths, such as professional wrestling and drinking wine that reflect French societal norms and values.

From Barthes' perspective a television show like *Man v. Food* is a mythic artifact since it not only highlights the unique cuisine across the United States, but more importantly, reinforces American cultural values. Campbell, Marin and Fabos (2013) explain that culture "is a process that delivers the values of a society through products or other meaning-making forms ... and the mass media help circulate those values" (p. 6). They provide examples of American values conveyed through the media such as individualism, efficiency, rationalism, and progress. The only value of these four that may even loosely apply to Adam Richman is efficiency—attempting to conquer a food challenge in the quickest way possible. However, I contend that Richman reflects other values like diversity, competition, excess, and immediate gratification, all of which may be viewed as positive or negative, depending on the individual or societal norms. By participating in 59 food challenges over the course of 3 seasons Richman naturally perpetuates and reinforces the American values surrounding food, consumption, and culture.

While some have criticized *Man v. Food* as an example of televised gluttony in an age of poor health and nutrition, in Richman's defense he did not invent, nor was he the first person to participate in, any of the food challenges. So, any condemnation of the food challenges should be directed more at the individual creators of the challenge rather than Richman himself. But regardless of whether the viewer is fascinated and/or repulsed by Adam Richman's attempt to best various food challenges, he has successfully tapped into the Hercules myth, as well as other mythic themes, for entertainment value. In doing so this self-proclaimed "regular guy with a serious appetite" has added yet another unique interpretation of history's most famous hero to the popular culture landscape.

REFERENCES

Buckley, J.H., and Woods. G.B. (1965). *Poetry of the Victorian period* (3d ed.). Glenview, IL: Scott, Foresman.
Bulfinch, T. (1970). *Bulfinch's mythology: The age of fable, the age of chivalry and legends of Charlemagne.* New York: Thomas Y. Crowell.
Buxton, R. (2004). *The complete world of Greek mythology.* London: Thames & Hudson.
Campbell, J. (2008). *The hero with a thousand faces* (3d ed.). Novato, CA: New World Library.
Campbell, R., Martin, C.R., and Fabos, B. (2013). *Media and culture: An introduction to mass communication.* Boston: Bedford/St. Martin's.
Child, B. (2012, March 6). The Rock muscles into Hercules. Retrieved April 8, 2013, from http://www.guardian.co.uk/film/2012/mar/06/the-rock-Hercules.
Fitzpatrick, K. (writer), and Cassel, C., and Conway, J. (directors). (2010). *Clash of the Gods: Hercules.* New York: A & E Home Video.
Galinsky, G.K. (1972). *The Heracles theme: The adaptations of the hero in literature from Homer to the twentieth century.* Totawa, NJ: Rowman & Littlefield.
Graves, R. (1992). *The Greek myths.* London: Penguin.
Holy bible: New international version (2005). Grand Rapids: Zondervan Corporation.
Lawrence, C. (August 9, 2009). Host battles giant burrito as "Man v. Food" visits Las Vegas. *Las Vegas Review-Journal.* Retrieved August 16, 2012. http://www.lvrj.com/living/52828527.html.
Man v. Food: Season 1. (2009). [Television series]. Chatsworth, CA: Image Entertainment.
Man v. Food: Season 2. (2010). [Television series]. Chevy Chase, MD: Travel Channel—Gaim.
Man v. Food: Season 3. (2011). [Television series]. Chevy Chase, MD: Travel Channel—Gaim.
Milton, J. (2005). *Paradise Lost.* New York: Oxford University Press.
Poniewozik, J. (2010). Lunch is a battlefield. *Time, 175*(13), 17.
Rouse, W.H.D. (1957). *Gods, heroes and men of ancient Greece: Mythologies great tales of valor and romance.* New York: Mentor.
Stanford, W.B. (1972). In G.K. Galinsky (Ed.), *The Heracles theme: The adaptations of the hero in literature from Homer to the twentieth century.* Totawa, NJ: Rowman & Littlefield.
Stoneman, R. (1991). *Greek mythology: An encyclopedia of myth and legend.* London: Aquarian Press.

Waith, E.M. (1962). *The Herculean hero in Marlowe, Chapman, Shakespeare and Dryden.* New York: Columbia University Press.
Webster's new world dictionary. (1994). New York: Prentice Hall.
White, J. (2013, April 7). Kellan Lutz is hercules. Retrieved April 8, 2013, from http://www.empireonline.com/news/feed.asp?NID=37063.

About the Contributors

Judy **Battaglia** (M.A. California State University, Northridge) is a clinical assistant professor at Loyola Marymount University in Los Angeles.

Richard D. **Besel** (M.A. University of Illinois at Chicago; Ph.D. University of Illinois at Urbana-Champaign) is an assistant professor at California Polytechnic State University.

Lindsay R. **Calhoun** (M.A. University of Denver; Ph.D. University of Utah) is a visiting assistant professor at Northern Illinois University.

Aaron **Duncan** (M.A. Kansas State University; Ph.D. University of Nebraska–Lincoln) is the director of speech and debate at the University of Nebraska–Lincoln.

Jason A. **Edwards** (M.A. Minnesota State University, Mankato; Ph.D. Georgia State University) is an associate professor of communication studies at Bridgewater State College in Massachusetts.

Sharon Dee **Goertz** (M.A. University of Kentucky; Ph.D. University of Kentucky) is a professor of English at Hanover College in Indiana.

Karen L. **Hartman** (M.A. University of South Carolina; Ph.D. Louisiana State University) is an assistant professor in the department of communication studies at California State University, Stanislaus.

Keaton **Maddox** is a student at George Mason University, Virginia, majoring in communication with minors in English and philosophy.

Michael W. **Marek** (M.A. University of South Dakota; Ed.D. University of South Dakota) is a professor in the department of communication arts at Wayne State College, Nebraska.

John **Perlich** (M.A. Minnesota State University, Mankato; Ph.D. University of Nebraska–Lincoln) is a professor of communication studies at Hastings College in Nebraska.

Lisa **Weckerle** (M.A. University of North Carolina–Chapel Hill; Ph.D. University of Texas at Austin) is an associate professor of communication studies at Kutztown University in Pennsylvania.

David **Whitt** (M.A. University of Nebraska–Lincoln; Ph.D. University of Nebraska–Lincoln) is a professor of communication studies at Nebraska Wesleyan University.

Pin-hsiang Natalie **Wu** (M.A. National Kaohsiung Normal University, Taiwan; Ph.D. National Kaohsiung Normal University, Taiwan) is an associate professor of applied foreign languages at Chienkuo Technology University in Changhua City, Taiwan.

Index

Abraxas 138
Afghanistan 90, 97
Age of Empires: Mythologies (2008) 211
Albert, Marv 174
Alien (1979) 63, 106
Al-Jazeera 91, 93–94
Al-Qaeda 83–84, 87–89, 92, 94–97
Amazons 128, 133, 142, 145
American Indian myths 188–189, 191, 200
Angell, Roger 173
Antony and Cleopatra 211
archetypal feminine 105, 115
Arizona Cardinals 175
Athena 129
attachment parenting 120–121
Avatar (2009) 3, 191

Baltimore Orioles 172
Baring, Ann 103, 104
Barthes, Roland 167, 169, 224
Bates, Harry 154
Bates, Kathy 160
Battle of Kosovo 86
Battlestar Galactica (2004–2009) 3
The Beatles 1, 52
Beerfest (2006) 208
Belushi, John 222
Bin Laden, Osama 84, 86–88, 91, 93, 97
bisexuality 131, 134
Booker, M. Keith 148–149
Bosnia 90, 98
breadwinner 10, 16
Bryant, Kobe 173, 181
Buehler, Dan 153
Bundy, Mark 134
Burke, Kenneth 87–88, 126, 166, 167, 170–171
Bush, Reggie 172

Campbell, Joseph 1, 5, 8, 35, 51, 56, 84, 103, 149, 208; *The Hero with a Thousand Faces*
37, 213; *The Masks of God* 37, 46: *The Power of Myth* 5; *see also* monomyth
Captain America 43, 49
Carroll, Lewis 144–145
Cartesian dualism 142
Cashford, Jules 103
Castro, Fidel 96
Chapman, George 211
Chechnya 90
Chestnut, Joey "Jaws" 207
Circe 109, 130, 137
Clash of the Titans (1981) 216
Clash of the Titans (2010) 216
Cleese, John 161
Cleveland Cavaliers 168
Cohen, Stanley 173
collective memory 95, 195
combat myth 166, 170–171
Connell, R.W. 9
Connelly, Jennifer 148, 158
Conroy, Frank 155
Cool Hand Luke (1967) 207
Cosell, Howard 174
Cossacks 85
Costas, Bob 174
Creamer, Robert 173
Creed, Barbara 105
Crone 104–105, 111, 113
Crusades 89
Cuba 96

Danu 133
Davy Jones Locker 217
The Day the Earth Stood Still (1951) 148, 154–158
The Day the Earth Stood Still (2008) 148, 158–162
Demeter 108
Denver Broncos 172
Derrickson, Scott 148
Dido 144

Die Hard (1988) 10, 12, 43, 54
discursive formation 144, 145, 194–196
The Drifters 52
Dryden, John 211

East Timor 90
Eastern myths 34, 43, 56
Elliot, Norbert 153
The Epic of Gilgamesh 170
Eros the Bittersweet 137
ESPN 174, 179
Ethiopia 90
The Exorcist (1973) 106

Falwell, Jerry 152
feminism 79, 102, 127
feminist criticism 126–127, 129, 143
Field of Dreams (1989) 178, 179
Fight Club (1999) 12
Fisher, Derrick 177
The Flintstones (1960–1966) 10
Forcas 138
Foucault, Michel 54, 124, 125, 195
Four Horsemen of the Apocalypse 220
Frankenstein 3
Frentz, Thomas S. 84, 153
Freud, Sigmund 45, 140–142
Frontier myth 65–67

Gaia 129
Gallico, Paul 173
Game Theory 53–56
Gaza 90
Gimbutas, Marija 103–104, 114–115
Glastonbury Tor 1
Glaucus 137
God of War III (2010) 211
good and evil 23, 26–30
Gore, Al: *An Inconvenient Truth* 153
Gramsci, Antonio 127
Gray, Billy 156
The Great Outdoors (1988) 208

Hanlon, Ned 172
Harpy 118–119
Harry Potter 36, 42, 44
Hawthorne, Nathaniel 130
Hearn, Chick 174
Hecate 130
hegemonic masculinity 9, 19
hegemony 124, 127
Helios 137
Heracles 210–211
Hercules 44, 208–209; as comic hero 210–212; Disney's *Hercules* (1997) 211; *The Legendary Journeys* (1995–1999) 211; Twelve Labors 210, 223

hero 8, 12, 21, 168–70
Hero's Journey 35; *see also* monomyth
heteronormativity 124, 136–137, 145
Hitler, Adolf 167
The Hobbit 44, 49
Hoberman, James L. 149
Home Improvement (1991–1999) 10
Homer: *The Iliad* 128, 137: *The Odyssey* 12, 109, 219
Hong, James 161
Hoosiers (1986) 178
Hurricane Katrina 174–175

ideological criticism 123, 126–127, 143
The Iliad 128, 137
Immortals (2011) 211
An Inconvenient Truth (2006) 153
Indonesia 90, 93
Iraq 88–91, 93
Iron Man (2008) 3
Iron Man (2010) 3
Iron Man (2013) 3
Islam 2, 83, 86, 87–97
Israel 87–89, 151

Jaffe, Sam 156
James, LeBron 168, 181
Janus, Tim "Eater X" 207
Jason and the Argonauts 44, 50, 210
Jason and the Argonauts (film, 1963) 53
Jennings, Hughie 172
jeremiad 151–153; cinematic 149; ecological 149, 160–163
Jihad 94–97
Johnson, Jack 166
Jordan, Michael 166, 177, 181

Kansas City Chiefs 172
Kashmir 90, 93–94
Kennedy, Robert F. 152
King, Martin Luther, Jr. 152
Kinsella, W.P. 179, 180
Kobayashi, Takeru 207
Kornheiser, Tony 174, 176
The Kraken 216
Kristeva, Julia 106
K'wati 187, 189–190, 198

Lacan, Jacques 135, 140–143
Lardner, Ring 173
Lazar, Knez 86
Leave It to Beaver (1957–1963) 10
Lebanon 88–90, 93, 97
Lemieux, Mario 177
Leviathan 217
London Summer Olympic Games (2012) 1
The Lord of the Rings 41, 44

Lorelai 130
Los Angeles Lakers 177

Major League Baseball (MLB) 9, 177
Major League Eating and International Federation of Competitive Eating 207
Malamud, Bernard 179
male gaze 129
manga 47–49
Manning, Peyton 166
Mantle, Mickey 166
Marlowe, Christopher: *Tamburlaine* 211
Marlowe, Hugh 156
Marti, Jose 96
Martin, Lock 154
Marxism (Italian) 127
masquerade 26, 30, 128, 145–146
McGraw, John 172
Medea 144
Miami Heat 168
Michener, James: *The Drifters* 52
Miller, Perry 151
Milosevic, Slobodan 86
Milton, John: *Paradise Lost* 217
Minnesota Vikings 214
monomyth 8, 36–37, 47, 49, 112, 170, 178; see also Campbell, Joseph
Moyers, Bill 5, 42, 149–150
Munafiqeen 9
Murphy, John 152
Muses 144, 213, 216
Musharraf, Pervez 92

Nathan's Famous Hotdog Eating Contest 207
National Basketball Association (NBA) 168, 173, 177, 181
National Football Association (NFL) 166, 172
National Hockey League (NHL) 177
The Natural (1984) 178, 179–180
Neal, Patricia 148
Nereids 137
Neumann, Erich 103, 105
New Orleans Saints 172, 175
New Orleans Superdome 174, 175, 176
Nietzsche, Friedrich 135
Nike 176
9/11 174
Niobe 108

The Odyssey 12, 109, 219
Okeanos 129
Old South 65–69
Olympic Peninsula 188–190
Opie, John 153
Oracle at Delphi 210, 221

Orca (killer whale) 190
Owen, A. Susan 149, 152, 162
Owens, Terrell 173

Pakistan 92–93
Palestine 88, 89, 90
Paradise Lost 217
Peters, Ted 149, 163
Phaedra 144
Pindar 166
Pinter, Harold 54
Planet of the Apes (1968) 150
Plimpton, George 173
post-structuralism 127, 142
Proximo Spirits 216

Quileute 188–191
Quran 95–96

Reagan, Ronald 152
Reeves, Keanu 148, 158
Reilly, Rick 173
Rennie, Michael 148, 154
rhetorical maneuver 194–196
Rice, Grantland 173
Robinson, Wilbert 172
Rome, Jim 174
Roosevelt, Theodore 63, 153
Rosteck, Thomas 153
Rudy (1993) 178
Rushing, Janice Hocker 63–64, 67, 71, 84
Ruth, Babe 166

San Francisco Creamery 217
Saudi Arabia 92–93, 95
Saving Private Ryan (1998) 153
Schottenheimer, Marty 172
Scott, Anthony 149
Scully, Vin 174
Scylla 137
Sept 104, 105, 111
Serbia 86
Shakespeare, William: *Antony and Cleopatra* 211
Sharia law 92, 96, 98
Shelley, Mary: *Frankenstein* 3
The Silmarillion 51
The Simpsons 208
Sirens 50, 130, 219
Smith, Jaden 158
Smith, Red 173
The Social Network (2010) 2
Somalia 90, 97
The Sopranos (1999–2007) 10
Soviet Union 85
Spielberg, Steven 149, 153
Stand By Me (1986) 208

Star Wars: Episode IV: A New Hope (1977)
  36, 44
Star Wars: Episode V: The Empire Strikes Back (1980) 40, 44
Star Wars: Episode VI: Return of the Jedi (1983) 42, 44
subjective camera 21
Sudan 90
Super Bowl 174, 215
Superman 11, 22–24, 26–27, 43

T-Rex 34, 52
Tamburlaine 221
Taoism 43
Tarantino, Quentin 62
Taymiyyah, Ibn 95–96
Telander, Rick 173
Tennyson, Lord Alfred: *The Kraken* 216
The Terminator (1984) 36
Thomas, Sonya "The Black Widow" 207
Thunderbird 190, 198, 202
Tillman, Pat 175
Tolkien, J.R.R.: *The Hobbit* 44, 49; *The Lord of the Rings* 41, 44; *The Silmarillion* 51
Trojan War 10, 43, 128
Trujillo, Nick 9
Truman, Harry 96

Ukraine 85
ummah 87–88, 90–92, 94, 97
United Nations 90
urban cowboy 70–71

vagina dentate 105, 108–109, 117–119
Venus of Willendorf 103
Vietnam War 89, 153
Virgin Mary 102, 105
Voytilla, Stuart 150

Western 7, 10, 12, 26–27
Whedon, Joss 40
Wilbon, Mike 174
Williams, Serena 166
Williams, Venus 166
Wise, Robert 148
wolf origin myth 186–187, 189–190, 198; *see also* K'wati
Wolfe, Dylan 153, 160, 162
Woods, Tiger 173, 177

X-Men 36

Zeus 10, 11, 43, 210, 216
Zionist crusader 87–92

www.ingramcontent.com/pod-product-compliance
Ingram Content Group UK Ltd.
Pitfield, Milton Keynes, MK11 3LW, UK
UKHW041944140426
5217IPUK00014B/642